Tornado

Polk Laffoon IV

Harper & Row, Publishers / New York, Evanston, San Francisco, London

TORNADO

Grateful acknowledgment is made for permission to reprint the following:

Excerpt from an article by Paul Hendrickson. Reprinted by permission of the Detroit *Free Press.*

Excerpt from "The Controversial Red Cross" by Richard Harter. © 1960 The Curtis Publishing Company. Reprinted by permission of *Holiday* magazine.

977.174
LAF

4/76

FIRST EDITION

Library of Congress Cataloging in Publication Data

Laffoon, Polk.
  Tornado.

  1. Xenia, Ohio—Tornado, 1974. I. Title.
F499.X4L34   977.1'74   74-20405
ISBN 0-06-012489-X

---

75 76 77 78 79 10 9 8 7 6 5 4 3 2 1

For Pinky

ILLUSTRATIONS

ACKNOWLEDGMENTS

WITHOUT THE FRIENDLY and willing help of dozens of people in Xenia and Wilberforce, this book could not have been written. To all of them, my gratitude. Several individuals I should like to single out: Robert and Yvonne Stewart, Jack Jordan, David Graham, Ricky Fallis, Grady and Juanita Hall, the Mallow brothers, and Hal and Wink Black. Each gave generously of his time, many, I know, when it was painful to do so. To Jackie Hupman and Cart Hill I am particularly indebted. Their insights into the town, both before and after the storm, as well as their many hospitalities, were invaluable.

I thank all the busy people at HUD, the Red Cross, the Federal Disaster Assistance Administration, and the Mennonites for taking the time to answer my questions, and to walk me through the intricacies of their complex and essential labors. Charlie Betterton, Don Hannah, Norm Steinlauf, and Eli Nissley—should I ever be caught in a disaster, I hope that four people half as capable are somewhere nearby. My appreciation to all the doctors and medical personnel who introduced me to the psychological effects of a natural catastrophe. Their comments gave me a perspective on the community and the people I was working with that I could not have had otherwise.

Finally, special thanks to Stephen Birmingham for helping me to get this project off the ground. His advice on how to approach a book of this nature was unfailingly correct and encouraging. The last word is for Frances Lindley, my editor at Harper & Row, without whose patience and expertise the book might never have achieved final form.

P.L.

April 30, 1975

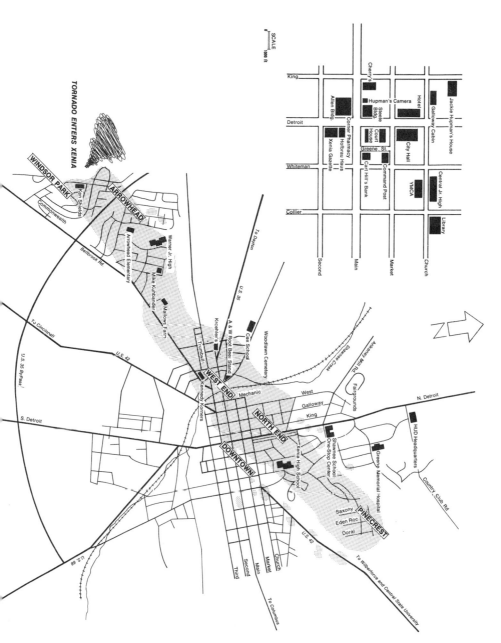

Map of Xenia during the tornado

1

MIDWESTERN WEATHER is seldom kind. It features clammy summers when cowlicks droop and brittle winters with winds that cut. Sandwiched between are long weeks of damp, gray gloom, frustrating farmers with false signs of spring or torturing toddlers waiting for snow.

In southwestern Ohio, where Christmas is rarely white and Easter is usually unsunny, people have learned not to count on the weather, but to cope with it the only way possible: they ignore it. They plan their picnics and plant their corn as though the heavens would not have it otherwise, and if—as frequently happens—the outing fails or the crops falter, they are not surprised. "The weather," they say, "if you don't like it, wait fifteen minutes and it'll change." They know; they've seen it happen too often. And that is why, in the early afternoon of Wednesday, April 3, 1974, people in the little town of Xenia, Ohio, who had heard the weather reports were paying no attention.

They were going about their business as they always did, buying groceries and selling insurance, unconcerned that they were undistinguished. Their town was a county seat, founded in 1803, fed by the railroads, then left casually to confront the jet age. Midway between Cincinnati and Columbus, and still separated from Dayton by a diminishing margin of cornfield, it was connected to all of them by a thousand psychological dependencies and three state

1

highways. The only other major road was a bypass that somehow never got completed—symptomatic, in a way, of Xenia's unsettled personality. Some of its people were farmers, some worked in town, and many commuted to Dayton. It had a City Hall, traffic lights, and tensions of its own, yet residents could not decide whether it was urban, suburban, or rural.

Later that afternoon, before dinnertime in fact, that identity would be resolved by a confusion of hot and cold air that was even now hurtling toward them. It would surface in a combined will to rebuild their city, ravaged by a storm that convulsed most of the Midwest and later proved to have been the worst of its kind on record. These people, the last candidates on earth for national attention, were thrust into the limelight because, of all places, Xenia was hardest hit.

The reports had been emphatic. "Stormy weather is moving into the area from the West at noon today," the Xenia *Gazette* had cautioned. "The National Weather Service at Vandalia has issued a severe storm watch in effect until 3 P.M., forecasting severe thunderstorms with large hailstones and damaging winds." But the *Gazette* never appeared until late morning, for it was an afternoon paper, and garnered most of its readership at night. By then Dan Rather was repeating much of the front page anyway, conditioning Xenians to flip quickly past weather to see what basketball bombshells had rained down upon their town. A forecast of bad weather, like the four o'clock commute from Dayton, was a mild unpleasantness, scarcely noticed.

In the cheery new headquarters of WGIC—Xenia's one radio station—disc jockey Jay Bracken was a little closer to the moment. He knew that a storm was brewing, that it was doing nasty things in Indiana, and that it was heading vaguely northeast. His periodic newscasts charted its progress, but between the singsong security of his voice and the mesmerizing flow of golden oldie/ gooey newie, there seemed little cause for alarm. As he said later, "I've been here seven years and never given a second thought to a tornado."

2

A lot of people who had lived in Xenia a lot longer than Bracken were of the same mind. Tuffy Snider, for instance, the blue-jeaned druggist with the handlebar mustache who ran the Corner Pharmacy downtown. He had a smile as big as his business (which he had inherited from his father), and occasionally would offer free beers to friends with one hand while dispensing birth-control pills with the other (an innovation all his own). "We just like people and they like us," he would say. "We get a lot of competition from the discounters, but if they want to pay my price—and the old ladies get a goose once in a while—they come to us." Clouds were gathering as Tuffy left the store and crossed the street that afternoon, but they weren't threatening him. Any tempest he foresaw would be of his own making, and that a friendly one, in his favorite haunt, the Hofbrau Haus, with Don Hilgeford, proprietor of what most people considered the coziest bar in Xenia. It was Don's fifth or sixth effort—he'd taken it on a what-the-hell basis, and vowed to run it for only a short time before quitting the bar business altogether. But Xenia had been different, with nicer people in a good part of town. He had built up a steady clientele of some of the younger workingmen nearby, men like Tuffy who liked the close-knit camaraderie and the casks in the wall and the certainty that after work on any night they could find two or three of their closest friends sitting at the bar in the Hofbrau Haus, sealed off from the world, from nagging wives and sagging balance sheets and kids who couldn't pass math.

By 1:00 P.M., an Air Force reconnaissance satellite had beamed back a photo of the eastern United States, plainly showing a shadowy mass of clear, cold air moving diagonally across south-central Illinois, and a lighter mass of warm, moist air already over Kentucky and Ohio. When the two collided, some kind of eruption was almost certain. The cold front was moving at 55 mph. At 2:30 a tornado was sighted ten miles southwest of Bradford, Indiana.

Xenia that afternoon was a place most people had never heard of, but almost everybody had visited. You had been there if you had ever read a novel by Sinclair Lewis, or looked at a painting by Norman Rockwell, or planned a pilgrimage to the farm town where your family had its roots. Old brick houses with wrought-iron fences merged indiscernibly with the shops on Main Street, and the County Courthouse added a dollop of distinction. "Xenia's not a pretty town," locals were prone to say, but that afternoon it was. It was a one-horse kind of place, with one Kroger's—"*the* Kroger's," one drive-in—"*the* drive-in," and one hotel—"*the* hotel."

The Xenia Hotel. In a way you had to laugh at it, as City Manager Robert Stewart had when he first came to town two and a half years before to be interviewed for the job. He had taken a room in the hotel, almost directly across from City Hall, and retired early. Finding that the light next to his bed didn't work, he walked downstairs and asked for a new bulb. Wordlessly, the clerk at the front desk, the only man on duty, pulled one from beneath the counter and handed it to him. The hotel was like that. Built in 1843, it had been in the same family for seventy-six years and they liked it the way it was. No liquor license, no new fixtures, no concession to the twentieth century.

So ultimately you had to love the hotel too. Filled with beautiful antiques—fifteen Northern rockers, countless marble-topped dressers, and the bed that William H. McKinley slept in—it was almost a museum itself. It was three stories high, red brick with white arched windows, and the old-fashioned lobby was distinguished by its original mosaic tile floor and seven shimmering stained-glass panels.

Within the past few months the hotel had finally come to Hal and Willa (alias "Wink") Black, heirs to the teetotaling proprietors. They had other ideas, however. They would cut out the sleeping facilities, transform the hotel into a great country restaurant, and keep the antiques and bedrooms for atmosphere. The food had always been good anyway, and the Blacks were now beginning to implement their plan. Three weeks before, all operations had ceased, and the remodelers were already at work.

Xenia had a funny relationship with that hotel, a mixture of benign indifference and love. It was a typically Midwestern atti-

4

tude. The thing had always been there, and yes, when you stopped to think about it, it did add a measure of charm, but why stop and think about it? It wasn't going anywhere. Isolated by their cornfields and impervious to big-city sorrows, Xenians had little time for municipal introspection. They had businesses to run and families to raise. While other cities struggled to fund their orchestras, Xenia opened its Old Soldiers and Sailors Home to the Cincinnati Symphony once a year. When the East Coast couldn't get gas all winter, Xenia could. When other regions of the country ran out of raisins, Xenia didn't.

There is, in all the Midwest, a dedication to the unhassled and a reverence for simplicity. Natives are perplexed at the egocentric East and maddened when outsiders call them provincial. In small towns especially they propel themselves by a hard-charging pragmatism and a distrust of chic. "We've lived well for years without reading the *Wall Street Journal*," they seem to be saying, "now state your business." In Xenia, the hotel, like the historical complex one block up the street, was a point of pride reluctantly recognized. The complex was full of century-old houses, the Snediker Museum for early agricultural implements ("Lest we forget," said the brochure, "our forefathers were mostly farmers here in Ohio"), and the Galloway Log Cabin, said to be the site of young Rebecca Galloway's courtship by the famous Indian Chief Tecumseh. The romance, alas, never worked out, but Xenians continued to get a lot of sentimental mileage out of the memory. And no one understood all this better than G. Carlton Hill, Jr., president of the Citizens' National Bank.

Hill was a runaway. Born to the manor in nearby Cincinnati, he had spent most of his career there in a much larger bank, inching his way to a vice-presidential post, and a lot of travel and some salary increases. By the time he was forty, he began asking why. The future, even if it held the presidency, promised more of the same with few redeeming benefits. He did not want to serve his stint as chairman of the local United Appeal, nor fuss over another Fine Arts Fund, nor submit to any of the thousand and one other pressures that the Queen City exerted upon its executives. He wanted to fish and farm and spend more time with his

5

family. When the job with the Xenia bank became available, Hill was ready. He bought thirty acres south of town (complete with one well-stocked pond), placated his pals with assurances that Xenia wasn't the end of the world, and moved. Now, sitting in his office just above Main Street, he was almost a *Town and Country* face in a *Farmer's Almanac* setting. His Brooks tweed and rep silk tie contrasted sharply with the double knits and cardigans around him. The prints and pictures on his wall were unlike anything in Xenia's other offices.

Hill was blissfully happy. Locals had received him warmly from the start, and he really had been able to create the new life he sought. He was fascinated and gratified by the variety of people he encountered, and echoed their enthusiasms like a native. "It's not as sophisticated as the Cincinnati group," he would say, "but there are a lot of smarts in different ways. A lot of enjoyment in simpler pleasures. Like the whole town goes berserk at mushrooming time. I've learned about spears and spikes and all kinds of things I never heard of." Archly, he would note that good patches were often family secrets, handed down from generation to generation. Hill learned quickly that Xenians were an oddly chauvinistic lot too. The old County Courthouse, built in 1902 to look like a German town hall, was a favorite of no one—old-timers insisted that its predecessor was far handsomer—but it represented security. From virtually any point in town its spire was visible and was the highest structure around. People liked that. They liked, too, the Steele Building directly across the street. Oh, it was ugly, they would say, with its dishwater brick turrets and fortress façade. But woe to the outsider who criticized it. Hill laughed at the memory of one Ohioan's published odyssey through the state's eighty-eight counties, which included an unflattering picture and a description of the Steele Building as "a theatrical heap." Xenians were livid when they read it.

Best of all, Hill was having fun. It was fun to run a bank, fun to build a new base, and very gratifying to become an important part of a new community's life. Already he was doing the kinds of things he had sworn off in coming to Xenia—representing the Montgomery-Greene County United Appeal Board in Dayton, sitting on the Salvation Army Board and a tricounty Boy Scout Council. But it was different here—fun here—because he did it by choice. Now, just back from lunch, Hill thought wistfully of the warm air outside and wondered if he might get in some preseason fishing tonight. But it was hours before quitting time, and he had not an inkling that the air might change, because his office was windowless, like a great vault, and he could not see what the weather was doing outside.

By 2:35, the National Severe Storms Forecast Center in Kansas City—mission control for the nation's major storms—had revised its 3:00 P.M. deadline. All day, as reports of the worsening weather rolled in, it looked for areas of particular unrest. Now it issued tornado watch No. 98, for a strip seventy miles on either side of a line from Jackson, Tennessee, to Covington, Kentucky, and from a point fifty miles south of Jackson to fifty miles north of Covington. At the extreme northwest tip of this territory lay Xenia.

"Xenia"—the name meant "hospitality," taken from the Greek. Subtitles on the city maps proclaimed Xenia a "city of hospitality," and old-timers, people like Helen Santmyer and Ray Higgins, never got over saying what a marvelous place it was. Santmyer, a retired college professor, had even written a book about it entitled *Ohio Town*—two hundred pages or more of intense description and reminiscence, including whole chapters on the courthouse, the library, and the East End. It was filled with the names of local streets and landmarks and old families, but never once was the label "Xenia" actually applied: it was to be any Ohio town and it could have been. Higgins, a crusty septuagenarian who liked nothing better than a good streaker joke, was editor emeritus of the Xenia *Gazette* and still wrote a twice-weekly column called "Cracker Barrel." There he unabashedly exploited the town's love of nostalgia, writing about things like minstrel shows at the Elks Club or his old Irish mother, but always kept in line by the critical memories of his few doddering peers. They recalled Xenia in its adolescence, when it was a stagecoach stop on the road to Detroit and a friendly farm center for all rural homesteads in neighboring Greene County. Then people poured into town on Saturdays—market days—and the streets were filled with hogs and corn and cattle and wheat. Not until World War II did the patterns change; no one could foresee how abruptly. First the rapid expansion of Wright-Patterson Air Force Base eleven miles away, then the spreading industrialization of all southwest Ohio, and suddenly Helen Santmyer was saying, "You can't believe they're not keeping the library open on Saturday nights any more." Xenia was no longer rural, but it wasn't urban either. It couldn't forgo its distrust of the radical students at Antioch College in Yellow Springs; it couldn't fully accept the encroachment of new subdivisions on the western edge of town; and it couldn't, sometimes, accept new people. The Reverend Robert Von Holle, pastor of St. Brigid's Church, was at his pulpit two years before he felt entirely comfortable. In that way, Xenia remained a small town.

Which is why Jackie Hupman loved it. Jackie was thirty-eight years old, the mother of three teenagers, the wife of camera store operator Dick Hupman, and a seventeen-year transplant to Xenia. "It's like you can't leave," she explained after the storm. "It's a tradition, it's vital, it's the reason we will rebuild here in Xenia. This is a community of old pioneer spirit—we live here for a reason." A short, slender woman with a round face and curly hair, she looked younger than her age but spoke like someone older. She talked of the charter review committee—an assault on the city charter which she had participated in five years before, and of the League of Women Voters, and of her house. Her house most of all. A green Edwardian homestead perched on King Street, it had been her thirtieth-birthday present. All her life Jackie had wanted an older house, something with roots and character. When she finally got it, it cost $22,000—more money than she ever thought she'd see in her lifetime. But it was the most space they could get for the dollars and it was in a neighborhood with potential, worth gambling on.

King Street was the oldest and most elegant of the in-town residential areas, but by the mid 1960s its popularity was slipping.

Jackie Hupman's house before the storm

Newly prosperous Xenians were opting for the more suburban charms of Amlin Heights and Beverly Hills, on the north edge of town, leaving King Street to fend for itself. The Hupmans were the first to rediscover it. After their lead, several more young couples with small children followed, balancing the old, blue blood at one end of the street with new, young blood at the other. Suddenly King Street, with its ancient trees and roots in the past, was a treasure to the entire town. It was as familiar to Jackie as the squirrel that lived by her son's window or the birds that the family watched from the kitchen every evening—silently, so that they could count how many varieties appeared. She talked about her children being initiated into King Street by crawling through creek beds that ran in underground tunnels, and about their proximity to the high school—two blocks in one direction—or to the YMCA, two blocks in the other. She knew her house the way some women know babies. She could talk about the big oak mantel with the terra-cotta tiling, and the sawn oak trim flawlessly matched, and the crown cave molding around the edge of every ceiling. She even knew that the house was built on floating beams —beams that were notched and laid onto plates, not nailed, so that as the framework gave a little the wall would "float" with it, and over the years the house would settle evenly all the way around.

By three o'clock that Wednesday afternoon, Jackie was closing the front door of her house and heading uptown—to meet Dick at the Hofbrau Haus. The day had been alternately drizzly and cloudy, then warm with some afternoon sun breaking through. By three o'clock, in fact, Jackie Hupman was mildly irritated that she hadn't played golf.

In the next hour and a half there were no fewer than fifteen tornado sightings, all occurring within that narrowing band of land between the cold front's 1 P.M. extremity and Xenia. The reports trickled in, but not in time, nor in proper sequence, to suggest how powerful the storm system was. One in particular, from Decatur, Indiana, caused unusual problems at the Kansas City center because there was a Decatur, Alabama, and a Decatur County, Georgia, also. The prospect was confusing.

10

Of course not everybody loved Xenia. There were those who said that most Xenians had nothing better to do on a Saturday night than go down and watch the rails rust, and there were teenagers who looked forward to nothing so much as the day they could leave town. It was rumored, indeed, that some of these kids were beginning to smoke marijuana or worse, and the biggest local news in recent times, a drug bust touching many of their homes, had left policemen wary and parents aghast. Certainly to more sophisticated tastes, Xenia might have seemed bland: the Community Lanes bowling alley and the YMCA were centers of social life; entertaining between three and five on a Sunday afternoon, with Cold Duck and fruit for refreshments, was customary; the U-Tote-Em convenience store, where magazines like *Playgirl* and *Foxy Lady* were beginning to be sold, had a salesgirl who could be heard to mutter, "Now why would people want to read a thing like that?"

And Xenia had never achieved the renown of another Ohio hamlet, Lebanon, thirty miles to the southwest. Lebanon was famed for its Shaker heritage, its streets lined by exquisite houses, its fine antique stores, and most of all for its Golden Lamb Inn, a 171-year-old stopping place that consistently managed to make most lists of America's best country restaurants. Whether it was true charisma, the recent residency of Neil Armstrong, or just good public relations, Lebanon somehow attracted hundreds of people weekly who could not even have told you where Xenia was.

Now it was that time of day when Xenia hung suspended between afternoon and evening. Schools were emptying and highways from Dayton were starting to fill. At Xenia High, that hardy band of thespians which blesses every school was rehearsing the annual spring play, a musical. They were the only ones left in the building. Hundreds of commuters to the Frigidaire and Delco complexes fifteen miles away were returning home to their assembly-line bungalows in Arrowhead ("a planned community full of beautiful brick homes") and Windsor Park. Newsboys were starting to deliver the *Gazette* and police were turning their cruisers townward, anticipating the change in shift. Only firemen, alert to the weather warnings, waited with some sense of expectancy. Storms had strange ways of putting people in trouble—maybe a high-tension wire knocked loose; maybe a tree across somebody's roof. So they watched and stayed ready—trained by their new young chief, John Troeger—in their handsome modern facility at the east edge of town. It lacked only the disaster warning bell tower of the old firehouse, but when that was dismantled in 1961, the authorities decided not to build another because modern fire-hoses don't have to be strung through bell towers to dry.

One block away, at the intersection of Main and Detroit (several of Xenia's streets are named for the cities they lead toward), the central business district dozed. Dozed because it was Wednesday afternoon, a time when most of the local shops were closed. Not the big boys like Kresge's and Penney's, nor even Adair's Furniture, an old family business which had recently added a wine cellar for appeal and won the National Furniture Association's award for the most unusual furniture store in the United States in a town under 35,000. But the smaller shops, the ones like Eichman's Appliances, McDorman's Men's Clothing, and Tiffany's Jewelers were all shut down. The latter, an anomaly, was founded in 1879 by A. Poe Tiffany and had no connection with its more famous New York counterpart. In less than an hour too, most of Xenia's large employers would be letting out. The firms were few and distinctive: Kroehler Manufacturing, regional arm of one of the country's biggest furniture makers; Supervalue, the big grocery warehouse; PHI industries, the highest wages, but generally acknowledged to be the dirtiest (foundry) work in town; and Hooven and Allison, among the nation's most venerable rope-makers, founded in 1869 when the son of a local hardware merchant and the son of a neighboring dry goods family decided to capitalize on the American hemp growing wild in the fields of Greene County.

One of the beneficiaries of their ingenuity was a young man named Ricky Fallis, a jute worker in the mill who had been dismissed from work early because his machine had broken down. At least that's what his foreman had said, but Ricky believed otherwise. Still not out of high school, he had already lost two jobs through hard luck—one at a gas station when the boss fired all the help because one had looted the cash register, and another at the local Cadillac agency where the boss laid all the tough work on Ricky, then took the credit himself. So now Ricky believed he was canned again. He went immediately to the A&W Root Beer Stand, near the center of town, where his fiancée, Diane Hall, was carhopping, and told her what had happened. It was bad news. Their marriage had already been postponed once because Ricky lost the gas station job; now both were apprehensive that the same thing might be happening all over again. There were words—nothing serious, but enough to shake the fragile emotions of a boy of nineteen and a girl of twenty-two. She kissed him and told him she loved him, as she always did, but not with her usual tenderness. Ricky told her he was going home to clean up ("At work I get black as a nigger"), then coming into town to search for a "decent" job.

Actually he had a second job already. He worked nights and on weekends for a TV repair shop—in addition to going to classes twice a week to earn his diploma by June. He was as sincere as he was industrious: he didn't drink, smoke, or swear. He was gentle too, with big brown eyes and a backwoods twang that poured out in a soft purr. His one flaw, which he readily confessed, was an uncontrollable temper that lashed out at the slightest provocation. "Diane," he would say, "is the only one who can control me. I reckon if I got mad enough at someone I could beat 'em to death." Diane had had other moderating effects as well. A Baptist, she had brought Ricky around to a modicum of religion, and had, by now, almost convinced him to be baptized himself. She prodded him into eating, a habit he had somehow never acquired, and always cooked something good for him when they were together. Most of all, she lit up his life. Ricky had had only one semiserious girl before, but now that seemed a dalliance. He had met Diane the summer before, while pumping gas. She came into the station every day, always purchased one dollar's worth of fuel, and left. Finally, he said, "Hey, why do you only buy a dollar's worth?" and she answered that she never had more money, and they began dating. By Christmas they were engaged, with fond memories of hot afternoons at amusement parks and fall nights at the drive-in. In his wallet he carried a picture of the two of them pressed into a snap-your-own-photo booth at the Dayton Mall—he with thick mustache and eyes beaming proudly, she more ingenuous, with eyes wide open and a shy smile.

As soon as he got home he called her. "I'm sorry," he offered. Diane said she understood, as he knew she would. She always said the right thing, always made him feel special. So they made arrangements to meet after she finished work, about five, and Ricky told her he loved her. Later, driving into town, he noticed the sky getting blacker and blacker and blacker.

If he wasn't paying attention to the weather, it was because nothing in his experience told him that he should. For any Midwestern boy who has grown up on a farm, as he had, the prelude to a springtime storm was as familiar as May. The sky, the big sky that covered the flat countryside like a tent, was gun-metal gray and swollen with clouds. The air was tense and still, and you could feel the wet coming on. You knew the wind was going to rise and come sweeping in off the prairie with the rain stampeding behind, and the thunder would crash and the lightning flash and somewhere a barn might light up eerily. Cattle huddled under naked trees and mothers called for their children and dogs cowered in the hallway. You heard the windows bang down and the lights click on and sensed, somehow, the urgency of all activity adjusting to the greater force outside. In the streets, rivulets formed and made flood pools around the drains. Lawns were lanced with bits of branches and somewhere, if it was bad enough, a tree might snap. The fields would be drenched and the stream beds inundated and in the woods wildflowers would start to grow. Yet if it were a storm like most storms, it would soon die. The rain hiss would stop and the wind would falter and eventually the sun might emerge, promising a clear, mellow evening and a resumption of living.

But at the radio station Jay Bracken knew it wasn't going to be a storm like most storms. At approximately 4:10 he received an advisory on his teletype that a tornado might be on the way,

14

turning his day-long watch into a warning, and he began advising his listeners accordingly. Go to your basement if you have one. If you don't, go to the hallway in the center of the house: lie down and put a mattress over you. Every five minutes he issued another bulletin—until the funnel touched down on Lower Bellbrook Road and the power went out and he could do no more. But as a lot of people said later, "We'd all heard tornado warnings for years; after a while you just don't think anything of them."

In their fields between downtown Xenia and Arrowhead, Ralph and John Mallow weren't listening to the radio. The weather was a concern—when was it not?—but they could see what it was doing just fine simply by looking at the sky. Their farm, if you could call it that, was an anachronism. It lay in an area that was prime for development, and many were the contractors who had already approached them. Founded before the turn of the century by their grandfather, the place contained twenty-two acres of apple and peach orchards—more than a thousand trees. It contained four more acres of corn and tomatoes, four greenhouses full of flowers, a barn and a typical Ohio brick farmhouse 140 years old where their mother still lived. Together, Ralph and John had worked the farm since high school, employing one additional man permanently and several Frigidaire retirees every fall. (They came in to pick apples, and to pick up a little cash to get them to Florida during the winter.)

Farming in this part of Ohio, you didn't have the steady cold from Lake Erie that farmers farther north depended on, and you didn't have the mild consistency that favored states farther south. The result was warm days in January and cool days in July, a happenstance which made other Ohioans moan annually about "the crazy weather we're having this year," but which the Mallows met like a lifelong adversary.

This spring, like the previous three, had been rough, handing them an unseasonably warm week in the first part of March, and bringing all the trees to bud. Then followed three weeks of cold, and three separate freezes, leaving the fruit crop in jeopardy with no way to diagnose it. By Tuesday they had finished spraying the trees and, hoping for the best, gone into the greenhouses to work on the flowers. "We figured something was gonna happen," said John Mallow later. "We were looking for a hailstorm. If you're in the greenhouse business, that's what you fear. . . . The last of March, the first of April—when it gets hot and sticky you can figure on hail."

It was hot and sticky that day, with no wind stirring. But when Ralph and John Mallow looked up about 4:35, to locate the source of a distant roar, it was not a hailstorm they saw. It was a swirling mass of black debris with a funnel as big as Arrowhead, heading right for them.

2

THE FUNNEL the Mallows saw was proof positive that Allen Pearson had been right. Pearson is head of the National Severe Storms Forecast Center, an obscure office in the heart of Kansas City whose task it is to track and analyze acute atmospheric disturbances throughout the United States. A cluttered place, full of radar screens and computer hookups, it is staffed by people who talk in terms of recurvatures and convections and who take a professional pride in trying to calculate where storms are going to occur. "Not that we get a thrill out of seeing a bad storm heading for a metropolitan area," one of them said later, "but you would rather it occurred where you warned it would than where you did not."

By the time Pearson arrived at work Tuesday morning, the day before Xenia's appointment with destiny, weather trackers had already noted a marked low-pressure system developing over Wyoming—ominous because such concentrations of cold, dry air can be the mothers of great storms. Simultaneously, the forecasters saw large masses of warm, moist air pushing up from the Gulf of Mexico. Should the two fronts collide somewhere in the Ohio or Mississippi valleys, convulsive weather was inevitable.

"We started then to marshal our forces for Wednesday," said Pearson, "which seemed likely to be a bad day. I sent out messages to our various offices in the Midwest to make sure their radar was up to one hundred percent in view of what we were expecting. This is the only time I've ever done this, but I was confident there would be a significant tornado outbreak. We were working with a system for which we'd never seen a predecessor. Normally the barometric pressure drops to thirty percent. This one dropped to twenty-nine percent. We were surprised at how widespread the damage was, but not at how much."

By Tuesday night the low was pushing rapidly past Colorado, worsening as it went. The Gulf air, unusually wet and warm, kept thrusting north. Early Wednesday morning the storm center sent out its routine teletype message and facsimile weather map to its bureaus (part of the NOAA, or National Oceanic and Atmospheric Administration network) and to the newspapers, radio, and television stations subscribing to its $50-a-month advisory service. The message was brief; conditions were ripe for severe thunderstorms within twenty-four hours in the northern part of Alabama, two-thirds of Mississippi, the upper one-third of Georgia, the boot heel of Missouri, and all of Tennessee, Kentucky, Ohio, and Indiana. Throughout the day, the center issued tornado watches for large swatches of countryside, including southern Indiana, Louisville, and southwestern Ohio. Watches, explained Pearson later, are a sort of "on your mark." They're more urgent than an alert, but not a positive warning that a tornado is actually approaching. Warnings, he said, are the last thing a person hears before heading for the basement. Warnings mean that a tornado has been sighted in the area.

As the weather satellites beamed back photographs and the weather balloons across the country bleeped in data, the storm defined itself and the watches became more specific. At 2:35 P.M. the center could issue its watch No. 98, for the area including Xenia. But this was as specific as Kansas City could get for a town 650 miles to the northeast, lost in the cloud cover on its radar screen. "This amounted to 'get set,' " said Pearson, "and that is where the national center bows out. It is then up to the local offices to issue the 'go' warning that a tornado is a real danger."

In early March, Pearson had gone on the *Today Show,* as he did annually, to explain the storm center's Skywarn program, a system of alerting weather bureaus each morning to the day's heavy weather across the country. "I made an aside to Frank McGee that I thought this year was going to be significant," he said. "I had noticed a shift in the wind pattern. Usually winds are weaker in the north and stronger in the south. This year, in February, they did a flip-flop. They were stronger in the north and weaker in the south. Well, quite a few stations called me about it later. I sat there and squirmed for a month and wondered if I'd made an ass of myself. But if you study the weather every day, pretty soon you start to get a reaction when things are starting to change. It's the way the human computer assimilates things over long periods of time."

The storm system that early April was unusually severe because it was unusually complex. Gulf water is about 75 degrees Fahrenheit, and moisture from it was lifting great amounts of heat skyward. As the advancing power of the low-pressure area to the north began to confront these currents, it sucked their moisture even faster, streaming them northward, creating enormous energy within the Gulf air mass. Now the system began feeding upon itself, pitting cold air moving counterclockwise against warm air moving clockwise, and spitting out turbulence. Far above, the Jet Stream swept to the east-southeast at a height of 65,000 feet, its speed pulling pressure out of the area directly in the path of the Gulf air mass. Here, in front of the storm, the barometer was often a full inch lower than in nearby areas, the lowered pressure helping to force the now colliding air masses forward even faster, creating even greater turbulence along their edges. The air in front of the low pulsed eastward, picking up speed, heat, and moisture until finally the tension exploded in tornadoes.

"Skywarn is just the first estimate of where we think they'll be having trouble," said Pearson. "It's like . . . you see a roller coaster starting to go up but you don't know where the top is. We have found that on the average a squall line lasts six hours; so basically we're trying to get the thing going, let people know, and then get the forecaster to take another look at it later.

"On April third I worked sixteen or seventeen hours," he continued, "then went home and got some sleep. I did AP, UPI—I must have done thirty or forty interviews. I did them till I couldn't stand to hear myself talk. I think this will be the highlight of my career. It's kind of a sad commentary to think of something that killed 331 people as a highlight, but I know that if we had not done what we did, the toll could have been in the thousands."

The reason so much depends on the local weather service, which Pearson did not need to spell out, is that for all the radar screens and computer hookups, for all the satellite beams and weather balloons, meteorologists are still not able to predict just where a tornado will occur. They don't really know what it is that makes one strong storm system produce winds up to 80 mph and hailstones the size of golf balls while another spawns tornadoes. They know only the conditions that foreshadow them and the destruction that ensues, for they've seen it all before, during other upheavals, other springs.

They know that, on the average, the United States is visited by 620 tornadoes a year and that, on the average, 120 people will die from them. They know that the great majority of these monster storms will occur in April, May, and June, but that many will touch down in open pastures and cause little damage at all; most receive only minor publicity. It's the exceptions that make meteorologists wary.

On March 18, 1925, a tornado touched down in Missouri, crossed Illinois, and died in Indiana, cutting in less than four hours a swath of destruction 219 miles long and between a half-mile and a mile wide. It caused property damage of more than $16.5 million, injured 1,908 people and killed 689 more, making it the most homicidal in history. Four towns—Gorham, DeSoto, and Parrish in Illinois and Griffin in Indiana—were virtually wiped out. At Griffin not a single building was left intact; at Parrish only three of the town's five hundred inhabitants were left unharmed.

Other twisters have been less methodical, but more bizarre. In 1931 a tornado whooshed down on the Great Northern Railway's premier express, the Empire Builder, as it sped across Minnesota, and lifted five of its seventy-ton coaches off the tracks. One of them, carrying 117 passengers, was flung into a ditch 80 feet from the railroad, killing one passenger and injuring 57 more. Incidents are told of tornadoes that suck all the soda pop from bottles, impale fragile pieces of straw end foremost into tree trunks, lift herds of cattle into the air, shear the wool off sheeps' backs, and pelt people with grit that tattoos them for life. Tornado chroniclers especially like the tales of Oklahoma City, hit twenty-six times since 1892, or of Baldwyn, Mississippi, struck twice within twenty-five minutes on March 16, 1942, or of Codell, Kansas, assaulted three years in succession—1916, 1917, and 1918—on the same day each time, May 20. (When May 20, 1919, arrived, the people of Codell were underground, but no tornado visited them that year, and none has hit them since.)

Until April, 1974, the worst tornado "epidemic" to plague the United States occurred on Palm Sunday, April 11, 1965. That day, 37 separate twisters ravaged 5 Midwestern states, killing 266 people, injuring 3,261 more, and destroying more than 10,000 buildings. "On that Palm Sunday I was stationed in Washington, D.C.," recalls Pearson. "I went out the next day to see whether the system worked right and if there was a warning system. It was a complete disaster; it was Sunday and people did not pay any attention to the tornado forecast. Communications in Ohio and Indiana were poor. Everything was poor. After five days of examining the area, we made recommendations leading to Nadwarn, which is the Natural Disaster Warning program. It is the basis of many improvements in the old weather bureau and in the Office of Civil Defense."

But the numbers are meaningless because the memories fade. The thousands of individual dramas that make the great storm great are quickly reduced to statistics. Dead. Injured. Property loss. And because the really bad storms occur only now and then —just often enough to tweak a collective consciousness—people are always horrified anew. Who would have thought that wind could do so much? Why don't we have better warning systems? Aren't weathermen learning how to combat these things? Old newspaper accounts of past disasters are trotted out. And all along the path of the storm people begin to read about tornadoes.

Like most laymen, they know remarkably little about the weather—don't know the difference between a hurricane and a typhoon (there is none; if the storm occurs in the Western Hemisphere, it's a hurricane; in the Far East it's a typhoon); don't know the difference between a tornado and a cyclone (a cyclone, in weatherman's parlance, refers to any low-pressure center with winds spiraling around and into it; it may be as small as a backyard or as big as the Great Plains; tornadoes and hurricanes are thus very specific kinds of cyclones); and they don't know that—as in Xenia—they weren't unusually lucky because the tornado set down after four o'clock, when the kids were out of school (more than 23 percent of all tornadoes strike within the two-hour span between 4 and 6 P.M.). But they should know these things, because of all storms the tornado is the most vicious. And in all the world, it likes the American Midwest best. Reason: the broad, tabletop plains spread between the Rocky Mountains and the Gulf of Mexico provide ideal conditions for them since storm systems require two contrasting weather fronts before tornadoes can materialize—an area of warm, light air saturated with moisture, and an area of cooler, heavier air overriding it. In this area, according to meteorological theory, the mountain air is so high that it blankets the warmer front below it. The efforts of the warm air to climb above this cover cause the turbulence that gives rise to tornadoes.

It is a tense situation. Because of the cold-air blanket, the warm air can push itself up only occasionally, rather like an escaping bubble which spurts suddenly to freedom. Rising, it draws the cooler air into its range and imparts to it a high-speed spin which whirls around the upward-sucking interior draft. Almost immediately, the spinning begins to form a column which has to reach downward because the cold air above won't let it go up. The sky, reflecting the tension, is grim; already the meeting of cool and

22

warm fronts has condensed the warm moisture into a heavy cloud cover. Out of this the column starts to emerge, visible now because it drags down particles of the cloud it descends from, while its own wind cools and condenses into cloud the moisture in the air it is slicing through. Thus the infamous funnel cloud curls from the sky and gropes its way toward earth.

"My private nightmare," confides Pearson, "is of a tornado heading toward the Indianapolis racetrack on Memorial Day. I'm worried now because the majority of the American populace is becoming more urban. I guess we've visited over sixty cities preaching the same message: you gotta get ready, you need hot lines between radio and TV, you need mobile homes—and you need an organization that will do all of this in twenty-four hours. Our success varies with the city. You take Huntsville, Alabama, with that big Redstone Arsenal where they store all the missiles. It was hit by three tornadoes within a three-week period. Boy, they got the message quick!"

Contrary to popular belief, the funnel is not black, but white—cloudlike—when it first touches down. It is only air and moisture; there is nothing to darken it. But the outer walls are spinning so fast, the suction inside is so intense, that in fractions of a second it has scooped up enough dirt and debris to discolor it forever: suddenly black and billowing, it surges across the ground. The net effect is that of a vacuum. As it moves along, the racing winds at its base scour everything in their path: trees, houses, cars, people. What they don't suck up, they destroy. Passing over any hollow object, the tornado causes a drop in pressure so extreme that the air within the object bursts it apart. Thus people taking refuge under cars may find themselves pinned to the ground because the tires blow apart, and people hiding in basements may find themselves covered with the canned goods that have exploded.

No one knows how fast the winds within the funnel are revolving. In 1953, after the destruction of some power-line towers in Massachusetts, engineers who knew what stresses they were built to withstand estimated that the winds had to have been blowing

23

at least 335 mph. Other evidence puts the velocity as high as 500 mph. The noise is an unearthly din that comes at its victims like "a hundred freight trains" or "the roar of a thousand jet engines." It starts out as a distant rumble, adds decibels like debris, and pounds down like a cannonade until afterward, when people are asked to remember what it was like, or what they were thinking, they can't recall anything but that unholy racket that seemed to last forever, but was actually over almost before they got to the basement. Some weather experts think the noise results from the crash of thunder within the funnel cloud.

Above all, a tornado is fast. It thrashes across the ground at an average speed of 40 mph and for an average distance of sixteen miles. In no more time than it takes to darken a candelabrum, it can obliterate a neighborhood, uproot a row of oaks, and kill a man. In a few minutes more, it can destroy a city.

"I hear everything," says Pearson. "There's some old Indian legend, or there's a fork in the river, or a bluff, or some lead mine in town. These are the reasons I hear why a city won't be hit. And when we hear that, we remind them of Topeka. It had a bluff on the southwest side that was supposed to protect them. Then, in 1966, they had a tornado rip twenty-two miles through the heart of the city. It affected ten thousand people and up to that time was the most destructive in dollar value in the country. But only twenty-six lives were lost. Their radio tower was on that bluff. It was a classic of good warning."*

Over the years, weathermen have learned to be cautious in their tornado forecasts. They know that if they put out a watch too early, and it lasts too long, people within the affected area start

*Pearson can be downright derisive if the occasion warrants. In January, 1975, four scientists publicized their theory that the U.S. custom of driving on the right side of the road is responsible for a substantial increase in annual tornadoes. At any one time, they said, two million automobiles and six million trucks are on the move, generally on two-way streets. This leads to cyclical turbulence in the atmosphere, and the counterclockwise force that results helps increase the number of tornadoes. Said Pearson, "I'm surprised they didn't find the obvious correlation between tornadoes and X-rated movies. Everyone knows that hot, steamy air is needed for the forming of tornadoes."

to forget it. Like the boy who cried "Wolf!" weathermen can be ignored if they don't substantiate their warnings. Currently, sky-watchers in the National Severe Storms Forecast Center think two to four hours is the proper prelude for keeping people alert. They hark back to 1970, and their experience with the tornado that ripped through Lubbock, Texas, to show how important timing can be. There they spotted thunderstorms over the West Texas plains in the early morning, severe thunderstorms with hail in the late morning, and a steady deterioration by early afternoon. They advised area weather stations accordingly. In Lubbock, meteorologists kept a close watch on the big Texas sky, intensifying their efforts as the afternoon wore on and tornado time approached. By 6 P.M., cumulus clouds in the area indicated increasing ferment; by 7:00, local radar picked up a moderate thunderstorm south of the city; by 7:50 it was bad enough to issue a severe thunderstorm warning.

Local radio stations began broadcasting the warning five minutes later, and at 8:10 a statement advised of grapefruit-sized hail five miles south of the city. At 8:15 Lubbock radar picked up a "hook echo"—trade name for a tornado formation on the radar screen. Shaped like the number "6," it shows up like a curling tail attached to the larger mass of a storm system. The hook echo is whirling moisture or hail, and the whirling creates its "tail." Now the telltale sign was seven miles southeast of the airport, causing a tornado warning to be issued.

That one never hit the city, but the next one did. It came after repeated warnings that a funnel cloud had been sighted, right up to 9:35, when the twister touched down and the weathermen took cover. The storm was a killer, taking the lives of twenty-seven and injuring fifteen hundred more, but weather authorities agreed that it could have been much worse. Without the carefully paced warnings, and their obvious truth for anyone who bothered to look at the sky, people might have written it off much sooner as just another spring storm.

Lubbock was nursed into awareness; Xenia was knocked on the head. The weather that day, alternately drizzly and overcast, was hardly startling. And the radio reports, for anyone listening, told only of bad storms in other regions. At 3:45 P.M., the people of Xenia knew no more than Robert Belesky when he went on duty at the Greater Cincinnati Airport in Covington, Kentucky. Belesky sat down at 3:50 and saw one hook echo already on his screen. Three minutes later he saw five—more than he'd ever seen before.

"You don't think, you react—that's about all you can do," he said later. His first reaction was to call Chester Rathfon, the meteorologist in charge at Vandalia Field, in Dayton, twenty miles west of Xenia. Vandalia had no radar screen, an omission due to expense that is common to most Weather Service bureaus within 150 miles of a major center like Cincinnati. Instead, they receive radar-screen pictures "dataphoned" to them from the larger centers. Vandalia had been receiving these printouts for some time that Wednesday, but now Belesky called to make sure Rathfon had seen the hook echoes. Springing into action, Rathfon called the highway patrol and Montgomery County civil defense units. He sent the same message across the NOAA teletype connected to radio and TV stations. That was what Jay Bracken received at 4:10 and what listeners throughout the Xenia area heard moments after. Eight minutes later the hook echo that was the Xenia tornado first appeared on the Cincinnati radar screen, and at 4:33 it touched down on Lower Bellbrook Road.

Yet even if they'd known all this and heeded Bracken's warning, Xenians still might have been excused for hoping the thing would blow past them. Because for all their frequency, and despite all their historic perversity, the odds that any one community will be struck by a tornado are only once in 250 years.

3

FOR XENIA that once had come. The soybean fields and suburbs were dark in the late afternoon, with a ghastly green glow silhouetting the trees. The big storm was bearing down.

It hit Gayhart Street first. Perched at the southwest edge of Windsor Park, on the line between city and farm, it was a windy place in the best of times and residents had grown used to their treeless vulnerability. Behind them stretched a long, sloping field, bleak now in early April, but lush and full in the summer. Many times they had watched it, like a great, green welcome mat, ushering in the thunderstorms which seemed to build just above it. "I always expected that if any storm was coming here, it would come this way," one of them said later, "and after it hit Bellbrook it was a certainty." Home from work, and listening to their radios and televisions, they were anxious at the increasing intensity of the warnings. Women turned away from their dinner preparations, the men got out of their chairs and children ran inside. Together, they watched through the kitchen windows the sky growing darker and darker, the wind surging and the trees lining the farmer's field rocking crazily.

And then it was upon them—not neat and cone-shaped as the textbooks would have it, but big and black and swirling, like the smoke from a hundred forest fires all roaring down at once. Half scared out of their wits and half determined to do what little they could, they huddled in the safest place available, the center of the house, by the front-hall closet. But these were development homes, of cheap construction and limited space, and they offered little protection against this kind of pressure. Instantly the roofs vanished, the windows exploded, and the walls split apart. Furniture flew and water pipes burst, but miraculously many of the people were untouched. To some, it seemed to come at them twice, slamming their homes with a violence they never thought conceivable, then backing off and slamming into them again. For thirty seconds—or was it sixty?—they lay with eyes closed and eardrums pounding, helpless amid the whirling debris and banshee roar, aware that even if they had tried to scream at the top of their voices, no one could have heard them.

When he heard the noise, Ken Shields was sitting at dinner. Tonight was his first softball practice of the season, for the factory workers' team he played with every summer, and the family was eating early so that he could be on time. Surrounded by his daughters, Laurie, eight, Dawn, six, and Heather, still in a high chair, Ken was saying little. He had been raised to keep silent at meals, a legacy which irritated his wife, Pam, but now it came in handy. He was on his feet in seconds when he heard the front screen door banging—the damn thing never let him alone—and he moved purposefully from the kitchen, in the rear of the house, through the living room to the front door. Opening it, he saw the monster right across the street, toppling his neighbors' fences, and he froze. "Hey, Pam, did you ever see a tornado?" he called, but was too dumbstruck to act. Pam wasn't. She took one look, thought, "I've got to get my baby out of that high chair," and ran. Then it hit.

Pam got as far as the kitchen table, with Heather midway between the chair and the floor, when something struck her from behind and she passed out. Ken lunged for the floor at the entrance to the kitchen, latching onto a leg of the sofa and stealing one last glance at his frightened family before the thing engulfed him. He wasn't sure, but he thought he heard Laurie scream, "Hey, Mommy!" Then, like their neighbors all around, the Shieldses met the wind with faces to the floor and arms over their heads.

28

They'd had no warning, but what if they had? What could they have done, really, in those houses with no basements and no place to hide? Virtually all of them were one-story, with a living room in front and a kitchen in back. To one side were the bedrooms, with a tiny bedroom hall the only truly interior space in the whole structure. Where do you go? The bathroom? The hall? Under the beds? It was the luck of the gods what happened wherever you were.

When it was over, Ken Shields's house was waist high. Not one wall was standing, not one piece of furniture salvageable. Ken was still holding onto the sofa leg, but the sofa was gone and his wrist was broken. His children were scratched and screaming and Pam lay immobile, a peg-sized piece of wood protruding from her neck. Her face was red with blood, "as if she'd been painted," Ken said.

Yet relatively they were lucky. A few houses away Joyce Behnken, twenty-two years old and eight months pregnant, was struck down and killed somewhere in her front hall. Marilyn Miller and her son, Robert, were crushed in a closet while Virgil Miller survived. Around the corner, on Roxbury, young Brian Blakely, seven, was watching *The Flintstones* when his mother threw him under the couch. He was carried into the yard and killed instantly. Michael Ehret, sixteen, was eating a bowl of soup and watching television when it hit. He took cover with his two sisters, Sabina, twelve, and Christina, thirteen, in the hallway, but he was one of the unlucky ones. He died on impact; Sabina succumbed later, in the hospital. Virginia Walls, a housewife, was killed climbing out of the bathtub to get a radio; her head was severed. Prabhakar Dixit, fourteen, a young Indian newly arrived in the United States (his father had worked five years to bring the family here), was struck in the head by their fragmenting house. In one of the most bizarre deaths to occur that afternoon, young Eric Michael Crabtree, aged one month, was torn from his mother's arms and blown outside. His mother, Diane Crabtree, had been home alone and wasn't feeling well. When a friend called and warned her of the tornado, Diane lay down in her front hall and blanked out. When she came to she could feel the house coming down. Then she passed out again, and when she revived the baby was gone. Two days later Eric was found; his father had to identify him by his clothing.

In all, nine people lost their lives during those first few seconds, before the storm passed out of Windsor Park, before it did even a fraction of the damage which made it so infamous. It had grown larger and larger, lapping up whatever lay in its path like so many matchbox houses and Tinker Toy cars. In its wake it left a very few places with walls still standing, but mostly it left piles of rubble—resembling nothing so much as solid-waste landfill—block after block of bricks and boards and trusses and roofing, of insulation and appliances and furniture and clothing. And people with dazed expressions trying to climb out.

For days survivors would argue about precisely what had hit them. It was a tornado, yes, but was it just one? One Windsor Park resident swore he saw four funnels swirling together, suddenly fusing into one mass before they hit. Another said it was six to eight tiny funnels clustering udderlike beneath the clouds. Nearly everyone had his own impressions, and could back them up by the hit-and-miss path of destruction when it was over. If it were only one tornado, they asked, how could it have picked off so many buildings so widely separated from its primary path? Chester Rathfon, Dayton weatherman, provided the answer. "We call it one tornado, but there were several funnels dissolving and reforming. We have pictures of that." In one famous series of pictures, snapped by an amateur as the storm was forming and printed in the Dayton *Journal Herald,* it appears as a huge mass of turbulent white air reaching from the sky to the ground. In another photograph, taken by a housewife in Laynewood, just north of Arrowhead, the image is faint but unmistakable—two gauzy twisters advancing together. In the lore of tornadoes, such a marriage is uncommon but not unprecedented.

Dickson T. Burrows, the Miami Valley Civil Defense Director, had been tuned in to what was happening since precisely 3:59 P.M. He remembered because it was one minute before closing time and he was getting ready to go home. In the windowless, dark-paneled Dayton headquarters of his agency, he had a hot-line connection to both Chester Rathfon at the National Weather Service tower at Vandalia and to the Montgomery County Sheriff's office dispatcher in Dayton. Whenever one of them lifted the receiver, the line rang instantly in the other two offices. The calls didn't come often, but when they did Burrows was immediately on the alert. They signaled heavy weather somewhere and he had to be ready in case it turned into trouble locally. Already this spring he had received several tornado alerts over the hot line. But this afternoon —all day in fact—he had heard nothing about any storm. There seemed no reason to stick around.

Since 1961, Burrows had preached doggedly and without effect the necessity for civil defense preparedness. He had lectured to women's clubs, reasoned with businessmen, and pleaded with officials; no one listened. Oh yes, they agreed, a warning system would be a good thing. But it was like insurance: it was expensive and each year was the wrong year to buy it. Undaunted, Burrows kept after them. A good outdoor warning system was only common sense, he argued. It could save hundreds, or even thousands, of lives. But the more he talked, the more costly and complex it sounded. In all the years he had labored, Burrows had not persuaded a single community to accept his logic.

Now, suddenly, he was vindicated. The call was from Chester Rathfon at Vandalia to the Montgomery County Dispatcher, to say that a tornado watch was in effect until 9 P.M. that night. His voice was matter of fact. It was nothing he hadn't related dozens of times before, and he knew that the message would be dutifully relayed to the city and county patrol cars now cruising their beats. Automatically, a tape recorder absorbed the conversation, as it did every conversation that went through the dispatcher's office, and Burrows was not unduly alarmed. It was only much later, as he spliced together the tapes for a documentary of the day's events, that he noted how dramatically Rathfon's voice had changed by 4:16. It was painfully urgent:

RATHFON: Can you broadcast this in a hurry?
DISPATCHER: OK, what is it?
RATHFON: Tornado warning is in effect for Montgomery and

31

Greene County until 5 P.M. this evening.

DISPATCHER: OK, you just want this broadcast on the radio?

RATHFON: Right. A radar report indicates a possible tornado twenty-five miles northeast of Cincinnati.

DISPATCHER: Twenty-five miles northeast?

RATHFON: It's moving northeastward. OK, can you get going—quick—we have a lot of people. . . .

Hearing it all again, Burrows recalled that 4:16 was when he first became truly alarmed.

The menace was unmistakable as it crossed Commonwealth Avenue and moved into Arrowhead. Advancing with a ground speed of 48 mph and whirling at approximately 318 mph, it threatened everything in its path. Arrowhead was a "theme" development, featuring street names like Wigwam, Buckskin, and Peacepipe, and offering several model homes, all brick ranch-style: the "Chieftain" for $22,050, the "Hiawatha" for $22,980, and the "Roanoke" (the most popular), for $22,700. From the start, in 1962, it had been immensely popular, a placid place with weedless lawns, Weber grills and swing sets in the backyard, the kind of community, in sum, which adjoins every American city—built not for the chiefs but for the warriors of this world. Full of children, it was thought to be an ideal place "for young families starting out." It was attached to Xenia, which to refugees from Dayton must have seemed almost pastoral; it was a twenty-five-minute drive to most Dayton jobs, and the new schools, Arrowhead Elementary and Warner Junior High, were right next to the homes. Arrowhead was the American dream.

Now it became a nightmare. The cozy brick houses, which for most residents represented every worldly attainment, popped like paper bags. Cars were wrecked, appliances were smashed, and through the air sailed all the paraphernalia of modern suburban living: lawn mowers, luggage, and furniture from Levitz, bicycles, bassinets, and Barbie Doll dresses, discount china and fire-sale chintz. At Arrowhead Elementary, the roof vanished and the windows exploded. At Warner the roof buckled, the walls cracked, and the gymnasium caved in completely. In the backyards of Wigwam Trail, young Will Armstrong and his mother, Gloria Chambers, were caught without cover and killed for their carelessness.

"Mom, Terry, are you all right?" The voice was Tammy Hunter's, seventeen, pulling herself out from under the bed, shouting for her mother and brother. "Oh, God! Everything's destroyed! Don't move, Mom, I'll get you out." Eventually, it took five men twenty-three minutes to dig Terry and his mother free, and some weeks later, Terry wrote an account of the ordeal. "We huddled up to the side of the bed shouting to God, 'God be with us! Please Lord, Oh God please!' Those are the words I remember saying. I thought it would never go over our house. It seemed as if it stood in one place and swirled through the house, ripping it into scattered memories."

Other victims talked to themselves and prayed, or closed the door in an instinctive effort to shut the tornado out. They felt every kind of emotion: stupor, disbelief, panic, fright, remarkable calm. Housewife Joyce Scheerschmidt was warned over the phone by a friend of her son. "Oh, sure, Terry," she said. "Good-bye." And she went on preparing her dinner. Later she analyzed her response: "I guess I was stunned. Or else I couldn't believe what was happening." So many people, confronted at last with a horror they had heard about all their lives, were hard-pressed to take it in. "I sat down to read and heard a very peculiar noise," said Mildred Lafollette. "It sounded like millions of bees [several others made the same comparison] to me. I started across my living room and when I got to my dining-room door it was much louder, and as I was alone, I talked to myself and said over and over in a split second, 'It must be a tornado.' "

When the storm reached Mike Kuhbander, he too was eating. The early dinner hour was a long-standing arrangement with his wife, Sheila, who worked four evenings a week at the Kennedy Korners beauty salon, one mile away. Mike would get home from his job at 4:30 and Sheila would have dinner on the table. Ten minutes later she would depart, leaving him with the two children, Kathy, seven, and Tony, two. Since December, however, Mike had been unemployed, permitting a more flexible schedule. This afternoon, for instance, Sheila had gone earlier than usual, to do some errands.

Now Mike was alone with the kids, and he looked around. The house was unsensational—a Hiawatha model—but in the five and a half years since he had moved in, he had added bushes and a backyard fence, thus stamping it with some individuality. The furniture was a hodgepodge, collected from relatives, and on the kitchen wall next to the stove was a plaster imprint of Kathy's hand. The meal was less satisfactory. It was a frozen spaghetti dinner, recommended by a friend of Sheila, and Mike thought it tasted terrible. He made a mental note to tell her so.

At 4:35 the phone rang. It was Sheila warning that a tornado was on the way, and telling Mike to open all the windows and to get into the southwest corner of the house. "For some reason," said Mike, "I did it. I opened the patio doors and the bedroom windows and went back and saw it coming." He saw roofing and debris in the air; then he heard the sounds of nails ripping out, dozens of them, all at once, and he knew it was close.

Throwing Kathy underneath the coffee table and pitching Tory between the table and the couch, he lay down on top of them and watched it happen. Just above his head debris of every description was coming in the front window and flying out the patio door in an endless stream. Like a big jet idling, he thought, then heard Kathy whimpering, "I'm scared, I'm scared." It was over in seconds—always a hard fact to grasp—and the house was still standing, no doubt thanks to the open windows. "Pinch me, Daddy, pinch me, I'm having a nightmare," Kathy was screaming, but Mike was still looking at the funnel, for he lived right at the edge of Arrowhead, where it melted into Mallows' farm, and he could see that the tornado had not subsided. It was heading straight for Sheila's beauty parlor.

At 4:40 P.M. Dickson Burrows had given up all thought of going home soon. He had no inkling, of course, of what was happening in Windsor Park and Arrowhead, but knew now, for the first time in years, that a funnel had been spotted. It was in Washington

Township, in the southwestern part of Greene County, and Rath-fon had extended his warning until 5:30. Burrows interrupted, his tone still professional, but increasingly concerned:

BURROWS: On that last, uh, dispatch, er, uh, call-in from that car —did you have a report of touchdown?

DISPATCHER: Well, he said it touched down about ten miles east of Woodman [Road]. . . . He stood there and said he saw it about ten miles to the east of him and said he's pretty sure it touched down.

RATHFON: Uh, you don't have any direct reports from the area, though?

DISPATCHER: No, nothing. No calls from Greene County.

BURROWS: Well, we better check with Greene then. . . . OK, thank you.

Around him, the normally serene office was in turmoil. Teletype machines, hooked up to the National Warning System in Colorado Springs, were spewing weather printouts. His two assistant staffers were warning communities all over two counties— Germantown, Miamisburg, West Carrollton, Centerville, Bellbrook, anyplace the Montgomery County Dispatcher might have missed. The communications van was put on alert; the rescue crew was notified. Around the city, ham radio operators tuned in spontaneously. In case of disaster, they would work closely with the civil defense unit. It was part of their licensing agreement with the government.

So vast was the devastation in Arrowhead that it became emblematic of all that happened that day. Acres and acres of total destruction, houses reduced to brick piles, and streets obscured by rubble bore mute testimony to the power of the storm. For days afterward, on the bypass that separates West Arrowhead from East, cars slowed and passengers hung their heads out the window to gape. Sightseers descended like locusts, undeterred by the hostility of the residents, magnetized by the catastrophe. They brought their families, explaining that it was important that their children know what might happen. Then they would snap a few pictures, climb back into the car, and head home.

The news media, too, brought their cameras to Arrowhead, hundreds of them snapping closeups and aerials and wide-angles and zooms. Their labors resulted in dozens of reports in the days after the storm, in newspapers all over the Midwest, and in news magazines and on television, many of them emanating from Arrowhead. So much attention, in fact, was lavished upon Arrowhead, that it angered Russ Thompson, president of Mid-Continent Properties and developer of the community. It was inaccurate reporting, he would say; the brunt of the storm in that part of town hit Windsor Park. While Windsor Park suffered more deaths, Arrowhead experienced more widespread wreckage. To the naked eye, it was far more dramatic.

Elsewhere in Xenia, to the naked eye, the storm over Arrowhead was a signal to take cover. People in other parts of town could see it now, towering over the treetops. Most heeded the warning and headed for the basement, but a few had the luxury —or the audacity—to watch without fear of reprisal. People on the north side of town stood in their yards, in their trees, and on their cars and roofs, and stared. Two state troopers, Gary Taylor and Duane Caldwell, were snapping pictures and saying to one another, "Boy, ain't that something!" and all the time it was ripping up Gary's home while his wife and kids hid (safely) in the basement. Rich Heiland, the young reporter from the Xenia *Gazette,* was in the newsroom when it struck. Bolting downstairs and almost into the teeth of it, he took pictures and gathered impressions that led to a news story that made front pages far beyond Xenia, likening the storm to a "demon that had been waiting two thousand years for a victory."

4

As THE STORM moved out of Arrowhead, rooftops and wrenched walls whirled at its apex, looking to many who saw them like giant birds trapped in the updrafts. It fed on the landscape. It passed over the Mallows, in a matter of moments, eradicating the orchards they had spent two decades building, obliterating the farmhouse their mother had been living in, smashing the greenhouses that hail had not harmed, and littering their fields with all kinds of confetti: televisions, two-by-fours, refrigerators, freezers, bedding, blankets, clothes, and a boat. Inside the farmhouse the Mallows were safe, and outside in the ruins, Frank Marsh was too. The farm's one handyman, Marsh had a mind of his own: "I knew where to go. I had studied my *National Geographic.* I told Ralph, 'Right down under that bench, that's where I'm going to get.'" The bench was in the workshop and the workshop toppled too, but Marsh, with a guinea pig for company, rode it out. "I didn't feel scared until a week after."

By the time Frank Marsh had dusted himself off, the tornado had moved steadily northeast, toward the center of Xenia. It had picked up the Simon Kenton School, countless tons of concrete block and steel, and dropped it like a handkerchief on the Cherry Grove Cemetery next door. It had destroyed cocktail hour at the Bon Air Motel as no barroom brawl could have done, first by sending traveling salesmen to the floor, then sending the lounge

37

appointments and rafters after them. It put Frisch's venerable hamburger stand out of business instantly, something a twelve-year influx of fast-food franchises had not been able to achieve, and it left the proprietor of a very prosperous bowling alley next door with three semis on the roof and the pathetic hope that at least his automatic pinsetters could be saved. Even more serious from the point of view of the community, it annihilated the entire Kroehler manufacturing plant, a two-story landmark of stone and steel filled with foam rubber and wood frame piles. The tornado struck forty-five minutes after the last worker had left, so that there were no human casualties, but the brand-new inventory was battered beyond repair, and the fleet of vans in the parking lot were crumpled like so many beer cans.

On West Street, a young Choctaw Indian named Thomas Youngen tape-recorded the storm. An Arkansas native, he had moved to New York City, then to Xenia simply to get away from Megalopolis. That afternoon, he was recording some of the small-town tranquillity to send back to a friend. "There was thunder, so I thought I'd record that," he said later. "But then the wind, rain, and thunder stopped. I knew what was happening. I'm from Arkansas and I know a tornado when I hear one." Running for cover, he forgot the tape, and thereby obtained a rare documentary. It picked up the racket of the foundry near his apartment, a train whistle as it approached Main Street, the rising wind becoming a shriek, nails popping out of the apartment, then the full roar of the storm. It ended abruptly, when the wall caved in.

In Laynewood, Bruce Boyd stepped into the wind to make a movie of the phenomenon. He was sixteen years old, and had never operated the camera before, but asked his mother for permission now. The result was almost three minutes of superb footage showing the tornado billowing and swirling over the town. Six different times Connie Boyd told her son to come in, that the thing was too close; instead, he kept his finger on the trigger and walked from his porch to the sidewalk. By the time his mother finally won out, he had used almost all the film on one reel. Six months later, when an NBC news special of Xenia's tornado was broadcast, the producers spliced Youngen's sound with Boyd's film to make one of the most chilling natural spectacles ever televised.

Ripping through the West End, the storm cut its widest swath, leveling everything between the Mallows' and Main Street, knocking out laundromats and traffic lights, two shopping plazas and forty-one parking meters. It ravaged homes in rundown neighborhoods, and rammed like a locomotive through Kennedy Korners, the burgeoning business founded in 1937 by Xenia's own Papa Joe and carried on by his son Jack. Almost until it was upon them customers pressed their faces to the window, watching what they had never witnessed before. Then it hit, and Jack Kennedy lay motionless on the floor, thinking it would be tough to get it all cleaned for the weekend. But it was not to be cleaned, soon or ever, for the storm wiped out all of Kennedy Korners: the gas station, the beauty parlor (where Sheila Kuhbander was cowering), the drugstore, the post office, and the supermarket as well.

Trumbull Street was in the heart of the West End. A cluster of small, aged houses, it was sometimes called the "Tobacco Road" of Xenia, an uncharitable reference to the poverty of its residents. Most of the people were elderly, and had been there for years, but a few, like David Graham, were newcomers. David was thirty, the father of four, and an employee of the Xenia Foundry. He lived on Trumbull not by design, but because he had been evicted from his former home (the landlord had other uses for it), and this was the first thing he found. Yet he liked it well enough. It was close to work, close to the McKinley School, and there were enough young people for his children to make friends. That afternoon, David and his wife, Sandy, were in the kitchen fixing pizza for dinner. The television was on, as it always was, but no one was listening. The kids were wandering through the house when Bobby, the eldest, happened to go out on the front stoop and saw the twister bearing down. That was the first warning they had. Within seconds the parents had scooped up their children and run to the basement. It was an instinctive decision, and in the best tradition of tornadoes, the correct one. But here it failed. The Graham house, an ancient frame rental, was only one story, forever in the lee of its two-story neighbor. As the winds circled in, they picked up the neighbor and wrenched it apart, discarding the pieces on the Grahams' plot. The house was crushed at once.

Four blocks from the Grahams, in a combination TV repair/beauty salon, Ricky Fallis waited out the storm. The shop was owned by Walt Dingus, and three or four nights a week, after the factory closed, Ricky did part-time work for him. But now he was just visiting. "I got to hang around somewhere until Diane gets off work," he had said to Walt, and then he started to talk about the wedding. "You'll be there?" he asked, and Walt had responded in jest: "I didn't want to go to my own and I'm sure not going to yours!"

It was then that they heard the roar, and heard the firemen yelling (the shop was adjacent to the West Second Street branch of the fire department), and Ricky stepped outside to have a look. He knew instinctively what was happening, panicked at the thought of Diane, and told Walt he was leaving. The stocky repairman grabbed him by the shoulder and yelled so that there would be no argument, "Get in that bathroom behind the beauty shop and don't come out until it's over." Dingus gathered the two beauticians still on duty, both worried for their families, and forced them in behind Ricky. He sat on the women, literally. Later he found their claw marks on his back.

For the employees of the A&W Root Beer Stand, it was twenty minutes until the change in shifts. In the front room, Betty Marshall, the genial manager, was fixing drinks and handing out food; in the back, her long-time friend and fellow worker, Dorothy Rowland, was getting ready for the evening crew. Diane Hall, the only carhop on duty, was waiting on two customers in front. "We always tried to have everything out for the dinner shift," Betty explained later. "We had the cole slaw made, the hamburgers stacked in the freezer and the french fries in their trays." They did all this because no one on the night shift was over eighteen years old—to Betty's consternation—and they wanted things to run as smoothly as possible.

40

Now, Dorothy was listening to the radio, and she called to her friend, "Come here and listen to what they're saying." It must have been after 4:40 because when Betty heard, she opened the rear door and saw the twister at Kroehler's coming toward them fast. Corraling the customers, the other employees, and two visiting boys, she directed as many as she could between the refrigerator and the ice machine, in front of the wall that separated the two rooms. In a totally unprotected place, it was the best shelter available. Dorothy Rowland lay down across from the others, by the counter that held the root beer syrup, and Diane Hall remained a flimsy partition away, in the "carhop room," a small area in the front of the building where the girls could rest between customers. It was on them in seconds. First the awning ripped loose, then a ferocious roar, and the whole building collapsed.

By the time the storm struck the center of town, the streets were deserted, with a few last-minute stalwarts shouting to stragglers to come inside. In the absence of other shelter, people crouched in their cars. Basements were packed, with women sobbing or screaming—as much for the safety of their children at home as for their own. The sky was coal black, and the basements were too because the tornado had already clipped the city's electricity. Coming across the fields, it had demolished all three of the 345,000-volt lines bringing power to the city.

Sweeping down Main Street, the tornado picked up the rear section of a fifty-seven-car freight train—the 4:40 from Detroit to Cincinnati—and lay it like a Lionel all over the road. It dealt St. Brigid's a fatal blow, leveling a landmark that had stood for 123 years and leaving Catholics with no place of worship. "The church was in very good shape," Reverend Von Holle said later—he had had it thoroughly checked out when he came to Xenia, and noted with satisfaction the hand-hewn beams. "It was as good as any new one, maybe better."

In seconds the winds flattened the McKinley School, target of five generations of adolescent abuse, and slammed into the Steele Building and the Xenia Hotel simultaneously. The "theatrical heap" was left with a gaping hole in the back of its upper stories;

its windows were exploded, but the foundation held. With that, the prestigious law firm of Cox and Brandabur, which for years rented the whole top story of the Steele Building for $140 a month, was deprived of perhaps the last great bargain in downtown real estate.

The hotel (its employees were in the basement and Hal Black was at the top of the stairs, apprehensive that his daughter was out joyriding with her boyfriend) lost its roof, leaving the entire upper story and all its antiquated contents open to the rain. Its walls buckled imperceptibly, and the floors sagged in consequence, leaving everything downstairs imperiled too. But so far its treasures —the fifteen Northern rockers, countless marble-topped dressers, and the bed William McKinley had slept in—survived intact.

So too did the Courthouse. Battered and bruised, its roof tiles loosened and its clock face shattered, it somehow stood tall and weathered the storm. Visible now even in Windsor Park, where houses had formerly blocked it, it was to become a symbol of communal endurance. Also spared was City Hall, an art-deco delight straight out of *Dragnet,* and the Greene County Building, a sort of footman to the Courthouse. The hub of Xenia's government could still function.

Ray Higgins was at the fringe of the assault. He lived on South King Street, in the mustard-colored house his wife's father had built for them decades before, when they were first married and South King was still "one of the nicest streets in town." He had just returned from the Neeld Funeral Home (the son of one of his employees had died), and now he was seated in the kitchen reading the paper.

"What's that noise?" asked his wife.

"Wind," said Ray.

"I never heard wind like that," said Janice, getting up to look.

She went to their screen porch, adjacent to the living room, and opened the storm door. Instantly she was sucked out against the screen, where she saw the massive black cloud foaming above. She did not hear the chimney topple, nor the arbor crack, for she was fighting her way inside again when Ray said, "My God, it's a tornado." They moved helplessly about, not knowing where to go or what to do, but it didn't really matter, for the heart of the storm was moving four blocks to the north, and they were not harmed.

Inside the Hofbrau Haus, Jackie Hupman had been sitting at the bar, trying to persuade the friend who did her wallpapering to get busy with her dining room. Her first inkling of the tornado came when a passerby ducked in and said, "Come on out and look at the wind blowing over Kresge's—you won't believe the crap it's picking up." Jackie poked her head out and said she wasn't going anyplace.

"You could just barely hear the roar," she said later. "But then you could really hear it and feel it, and you knew it was there. Dick was out on the sidewalk, and when he saw it, he screamed, 'Oh my God, it's a tornado!' From the way he screamed other people knew he was telling the truth, and they got off the street. He ran in and called the kids and told them to get to the basement. Then Don told everyone to get in the beer cooler, that it was lead-lined and double-reinforced. So we followed him in, about twelve of us, and I remember that everyone had cigarettes. Someone said to put 'em out, because if the building blew in on top of us we might need all the oxygen we could get. Then it was like your hair was standing up on your body, and your ears felt like they were going to blow up, and people were grabbing their ears and trying to blow out, or yawn, or something, and I remember my friend Candy Ireland starting to giggle—she giggles when she gets upset."

While Candy giggled the tornado battered large shops and small. It left Eichman's Appliances beyond restitution and McDorman's Men's Clothing indiscernible beneath the bricks. In Tuffy Snider's pharmacy, the pills rattled and the medicines rocked, but the foundations held firm. It left Tiffany's untarnished, and the Hofbrau Haus safe, but destroyed Dick Hupman's camera shop. In the firehouse on the east edge of town, John Troeger and his men watched the thing coming, gesturing at it to take another direction, like bowlers waving their balls toward a strike. When it didn't, they flopped on their stomachs until it passed.

ONE OF THE PEOPLE marveling that day was Jack Jordan, the feisty editor of the *Gazette*. Jordan was standing in the door of the *Gazette*'s offices at 37 South Detroit Street, and thinking, "Now where are all those big trees coming from? There aren't any big trees downtown."

Since 1950, when Jordan had become managing editor of the paper at the age of twenty-nine, he had been immersed in civic affairs. He was president of the local Chamber of Commerce, chairman of the American Legion and the YMCA, all before he was thirty. "My generation came along at a time when we were following a lost generation," he would explain. "This was caused by the men ahead of them holding on too long. Suddenly, when these others let go, the ones in front of us let it slide." So he and some others had stepped in to fill the void, which had worked out fine, except: "Suddenly, when we passed into our mid-forties—the time when we should fall into it by maturity—God, we were tired ourselves."

Around town Jordan has a reputation for aggressiveness, crusading, and irascibility. If the issue is worthwhile, he will stop at nothing to promote it; if the item is newsworthy, he lets nothing stand in the way of its publication. "Just remember," he was told when still a cub reporter by old Jim Chew, publisher of the *Gazette,* "people never forget what they think you did to them for printing the facts." Many times since Jordan had found that to be true. Recently the paper had been instrumental in establishing the Greene County Vocational Center ("It was defeated a couple of times, then I personally went out. . . .") and it had caused a major stir over the makeup of the Greene County Memorial Hospital board. ("The board didn't want the paper to cover its meetings. I said 'no way,' so we denounced it and we were off and running.")

His office, overflowing with memorabilia, reflects his personality. On the walls are journalism citations, civic awards, and naval documents from his service during World War II. There are pictures of his family, pictures of colleagues, caricatures of himself, and, above the mantel over the fireplace, an aerial view of Xenia. In the corner, behind the door, is a cartoon of a Marine, with the inscription: "Yea though I walk through the valley of the shadow of death, I shall fear no evil; for I am the meanest son of a bitch in the valley." It is a small office, with green walls and the desk in front of the fireplace. In it, Jordan overwhelms. He looks about the way he ought to look: usually tieless, big, with white, shaggy hair, sideburns, a wide smile, and a ruddy bulbous nose that is almost a parody of itself.

"Now I'm not a premonition-type guy," he said later, "but being an old navy aviator, I knew turbulence. I was uneasy; the girls in the front office were restless. By four o'clock the sky was very black, and I realized we were right in the line of this thing." He called his wife, who was upset too, and told her to go to the basement, then said to the girls, "Let's get this place secure." Jordan began herding the *Gazette* employees into the basement, then pulling in people from the street. The last thing he remembers is trying to close the double doors to the outside, feeling the suction, then scrambling behind the steel door at the top of the stairs. The door had a glass window in it and he watched from there.

In the bank, Cart Hill wandered downstairs at 4:25 P.M. because it was close to quitting time and he wanted to speak with his vice-president, Tom Teeters, before he left. He noticed the black skies outside, and saw some of the secretaries scurrying to get into a car before the rain fell. Then someone told him that his West

45

The view up North Detroit

Branch manager had called to report a tornado.

"We shut the door and told everyone to get in the basement," he recalled afterward. "Then Roger Arey and I stood in the doorway, mesmerized, and watched it come up the street. We saw it take the roof off St. Brigid's, blow up the McDonald's, and then we ran too. The doors exploded inward behind us." Above him, two employees were trapped on the second floor. They had tried to come down, but when they opened the door at the bottom of the stairs, the glass blew out of the adjoining street entrance door, and the vacuum forced them back. In the basement, Hill found no more room in the vault, so stood outside, next to a postage meter machine. "I thought, 'If this thing goes, it's gonna tear me to pieces,' but then I looked at that vault full of girls and thought, 'What a way to die.' My ears cracked six times—the last one so bad it made the back of my navel hurt."

46

The Xenia high school

Meanwhile the tornado was moving into the city's oldest neighborhood with a vengeance. It humbled North Galloway by knocking the houses off kilter, as if collectively they had gone on a binge and could no longer stand straight. It played havoc with the historical complex, leveling the Snediker Museum and the Galloway Log Cabin, and the Moorehead House and Glossinger Center as well. In a doll collection of fourteen fine china figures, it left only three uncracked, and in a miniature-soldier collection of 150, only a handful were saved. Yet it scratched not a crystal on the Moorehead chandelier. Some of the older houses survived, like the old Chew mansion, where ninety-three-year-old Jessie Chew, widow of the late publisher, clung grimly to her wheelchair in front of the great stone fireplace while above her, the Gainsboroughs and Reynoldses, the Constable and the Turner trembled on their hooks and, outside, the swimming pool filled with flotsam.

47

But the house stood. Jackie Hupman's did not. All along King Street the big trees were reduced to roadblocks, the houses ripped through like orange crates.

Flailing up North Detroit, the tornado didn't actually level Central Junior High, but it mutilated the structure so badly that middle-aged Xenians who remembered graduation day there could only shake their heads sadly. It sideswiped the Xenia library, removed the upper story of the Masonic Temple, and then zeroed in on Xenia High, where a brush-up rehearsal for *The Boy Friend* was in full swing.

The show had been performed twice the previous weekend, to crowds of nearly four hundred a night, but even more were anticipated for the coming Saturday and Sunday. Five minutes before the storm struck, Gene Foiles, the music director, had gone home, but David Heath, the drama director, was still holding forth. Suddenly, in a half-jesting tone, one of the girls at the rehearsal said, "Would anyone like to see a tornado?" It was impossible to see anything from the auditorium, but Heath rushed to the front hall to have a look. In seconds he had twenty teenagers huddled in the front hall, though none were too worried and some still laughing, until the first winds hit. They heard the windows shatter and the steel girders rip, and then they felt debris flying in. The particles stung and the soot clogged their nostrils and they began to pray. When it was over, there were three buses on the stage where they had been rehearsing, and a steel beam on the Steinway piano where Foiles had been playing. The roof of the auditorium had dropped to within a foot of the seats. The school was gutted; only its shell remained. It was a two-block mass of twisted steel, with the only safe exit menaced by chemicals leaking from the laboratory above it.

For most Xenians, the loss of the high school was the single most striking evidence of the tornado's power, maybe because the school was only seventeen years old and such a point of pride, maybe because it was such a poignant testimony to how much more unfortunate they might have been. "What if it had struck an hour earlier, when the school was full?" they kept asking. "What if we hadn't been on daylight saving time?" (Ohio is at the western end of the Eastern Standard Time zone, and there is perennial controversy about it. When the tornado struck in Ohio, it was dusk in New York City.) Whatever the reasons, Xenians continued to point to their school for weeks after the storm, until the Corps of Engineers finally carted it away. "Did you see the high school?" they asked friends and officials. It was Exhibit A.

But there were other things they marveled at too. Like the way the tornado could destroy an entire room and leave a glass of water standing on a table, or fling a penny into a plywood wall, or float a policeman's badge to Jamestown, ten miles away, and wham it into a tree. There were instances of personal checks and family photos, swept up from the desks and coffee tables of their owners and deposited as far away as Chagrin Falls, Ohio, a suburb of Cleveland. But the main subject of discussion was death—the way the storm picked off people as arbitrarily as buildings.

Ruth Palmer died on her couch, eyeglasses at her side—was she asleep?—in her Trumbull Street home. The house had crashed inward. Clara Pagett was killed trying to close her office door at the local chapter of the American Cancer Society. Ollie Grooms was killed when the chimney of her house fell in on her basement, not far from David Graham's. Clyde Hyatt, a switchman for the Penn Central Railroad, was killed when he left the pint-sized green tower where he worked and tried to make his way home on foot. The tower wasn't touched. Linda McKibben and Richard Adams were crushed in the Elbow Supper Club on West Main Street. And, Johnnie Mott, Xenia's resident photographer of children, who was at home when she heard the warnings, drove, at her husband's request, to his office, which had a basement. She made it, but the basement windows exploded, and she was killed by an airborne two-by-four that hit her in the back of the head.

When people heard stories like these and related them to their own close calls, it was like a tonic. They would say over and over that they just couldn't believe more people weren't killed, and, indeed, had you driven through Xenia for several weeks after the storm, the scope of the destruction lent validity to the wonder. When you saw where some of them lost out, and others did not, you had to believe that luck was the final arbiter. In house after house survivors would point to a jagged piece of bathroom wall, or a lonely closet amid the rubble, and say, "Thank God I was there; if I'd a been anyplace else I wouldn't have made it."

As the tornado passed over the high school, it was heading almost straight for the Greene Memorial Hospital, Xenia's primary medical facility. Had it continued on course, the results in increased death and injury might have been enormous, but capriciously, it did not. It veered slightly to the right and caught the Xenia fieldhouse instead. A big, white, Mayan temple of a building, it was known as the "snake pit" to opposition basketball teams throughout the West Ohio League. For thirty-five years the rabid Xenia fans had screamed and stomped in wooden bleachers that crowded the court, demoralizing their visitors and winning three-quarters of their games. Now the fieldhouse was in shreds. Ken White, who lived four blocks away and who played basketball on the championship team in 1942, was on his way home from work as the twister approached this scene of his triumphs. He had just taken cover when it destroyed his home in Pinecrest too. With it went six hundred trophies on display in his garage, all belonging to his son Dale, a two-time National Champion baton twirler (1968 and 1970). The garage had been his showplace.

Pinecrest was on the eastern edge of town, an agreeably affluent subdivision with streets named after Miami Beach motels: Doral, Saxony, Eden Roc. Now the tornado tore at its ranch-style houses as relentlessly as it had torn at Arrowhead. It brushed up against Harvey McClellan's house, the only place in Xenia with an actual underground bomb shelter, and busted all the windows on the second story. Harvey was asleep while his wife, Virginia, was sitting on the north side with the shades drawn. The storm funnel passed directly over one house, where the wife kept $1,600 in twenty-dollar bills stowed in her top dresser drawer. She didn't trust banks. That day she lost her house and her savings, and she still had to tell her husband what she'd been hiding.

Within a ten-block area, the tornado literally wiped out everything in its path, and on Doral Drive, the last outpost of possibility, it killed two more people. They were Theresa Cross, two, and her babysitter, Ivra Taylor, thirty-four, caught for some indiscernible reason in the Crosses' garage. With that, the monster storm struck out across the fields toward Wilberforce and Central State University. It had gone approximately eight miles, killed 28 people, totally destroyed 1,297 buildings and badly damaged 3,300 others. Its momentum was still undiminished.

CART HILL laughed in spite of himself. Running from the bank down South Detroit just seconds after the storm, he passed two drunks in front of the Hofbrau Haus. "Hell, I don't know," the one was saying to the other, "but it wasn't like this when we went in." With that, they went back to their beers.

Jackie Hupman, emerging from the Hofbrau about the same time, must have felt a similar befuddlement, because her first comment was "Gee, Dick, you lost your sign." The sign over his camera shop. He had never liked it anyway.

Ricky Fallis burst from the bathroom and went for his car, behind the repair shop. "I've got to get to Diane," he yelled to Walt Dingus, but of course his car was smashed and the driveway was blocked and he couldn't get anywhere. In that first moment, no one knew how to react.

For one thing, the silence was overwhelming. Not a bird chirping, not a trace of air stirring, not a person to be seen. For many Xenians, just beginning to crawl out from the rubble, this was the most frightening time of all. The stillness mocked them with its impersonality. They took in, as best they could, the ruins of their neighborhoods: the uprooted trees, the dislocated houses, wires dangling, and debris-covered streets. They saw the second-story bedrooms exposed like stage sets to the public gaze. They smelled (unexpectedly) the smell of freshly severed wood and of gas from the broken jets. And they agreed with an aged shopper caught at Kroger's: "I actually didn't know how I got out of the store, and when I did I was in a new world; I was not adapted to what I saw."

Very quickly, a steady rain began to fall, soaking the contents of roofless houses, and people began to take stock. "Mom, are you there?" "Paul, are you all right?" "Help, over here—my sister's buried under this board." Most were to some extent in shock and not entirely conscious of their actions. They picked up bits of debris, examined them, and threw them back down without really knowing what they had held. They stared at the objects suspended in trees and tried to comprehend that their houses and everything in them had been destroyed. Some were afraid to move, not knowing that the "live" wires were already dead. They hugged neighbors they hadn't spoken to for months, hailed friends who answered quickly, then promptly forgot whom they'd spoken to. When they searched for pets amid the rubble and couldn't find them, some went to pieces, making a lost dog the scapegoat for all their emotions. Children screamed, and some could not stop throwing up.

A wail of sirens pierced the rain, traffic started up tentatively, and men who hadn't run since high school took off half-crazed to see if their families were all right. At Main and Detroit people with broken or bloodied limbs looked for help, were piled into anything that would move, and driven to the hospital. Yet almost as soon as traffic started, it was stalled by the gigantic trees, chunks of roofing, and crushed cars that littered the streets. Drivers who had been thankful moments before that their engines even turned over now abandoned their autos and made their way on foot.

For John Troeger it was especially frustrating. No sooner were his men off the ground than they had two ambulances and two pumpers charging into the streets. Having watched the storm so long from the firehouse, they were almost certain Arrowhead had been hit, but they couldn't get to it. In addition to two large trees and countless fragments of buildings, the overturned freight train created a dead end beyond which passage was impossible. His ambulances picked up whomever they could east of the train, then headed back up Detroit toward the hospital. Simultaneously, the hospital was calling the firehouse. "We're in dire need of your emergency generator," came the voice, as if from another planet; Troeger dispatched it on his hook and ladder. Minutes later, he was called by the city manager: "Go across the street to the phone company; have 'em contact the governor and ask him for the National Guard."

Ricky Fallis ran terror-stricken to the A&W Root Beer Stand. He saw the destruction. "Diane!" he screamed, "Diane, are you there?" He saw some movement beneath the cement blocks—and then Betty Marshall was talking. "I know she's all right, Ricky. She's right here with us."

Betty was lying with the heavy metal order ring on her chest, her feet caught beneath broken boards and cement blocks. When Ricky arrived, she was still trembling from the shock of live burial. Vaguely, she wondered what had happened to the loudspeaker apparatus, a large piece of equipment that had been hanging over her head. Then the place was overrun with people trying to help, and Ricky and two other men pulled her free.

Not quite one mile away, Diane's two younger brothers, Terry, twenty-one, and Ronny, eighteen, were driving, as best they could, to the A&W. Both had seen the twister heading directly for it and, with their mother, Juanita Hall, had taken cover in the basement. All their thoughts centered on Diane. The only girl, she was the light of her mother's life and beloved by both boys. When they came upstairs, they ran three abreast for the car. Suddenly, though, Ronny thought better of it. "You wait here, Mom," he said. "We'll bring her home." Their neighborhood, just south of Route 42, had been out of the path of the storm and their car had not been touched.

Nearing the A&W, the Halls shuddered. The place was a chaos of rescue workers crawling over rubble, rescue vehicles pulling up and bodies lying on the ground. A crowd was forming, and the two boys had to muscle their way in. The Wisecup family, a young mother and father and their infant child, had just been dug out. All three had suffocated. Dorothy Rowland had been blown across the concrete floor, her stomach torn open, her body limp.

54

Diane's body was the last found, thirty minutes later, under a mass of wreckage and the mammoth refrigerator that had stored hamburger meat. Still in the brown pants and white blouse that were her uniform, she lacked only her shoes and her glasses. Her face was almost purple, which caused some to wonder if she had first been felled by a heart attack, and one of her eyes was bruised.

Ricky became hysterical, wringing his hands, shouting and crying. He would not talk, would not be comforted, but moved fitfully around Diane's body, kicking at the cars. Finally, he sat down beside her, and refused to leave. Her brother Ronny was hardly more composed. He screamed and cursed and, Betty said later, "had to be held by the cops to keep him from hitting people."

Juanita Hall, who had remained at home for thirty minutes, could stand it no longer. She set off on foot, getting more and more apprehensive the closer she came. The sight of Kennedy Korners, no higher than her chin, put her in a panic. By the time she got to the root beer stand, she could see her daughter's body, but Juanita did not give up hope. "She may not be dead," she thought. Three times she asked Ronny and got no answer. "She's not dead, is she, Ronny?" Finally he ran to her and threw his arms around her. "Oh, Mom," he cried.

In a paroxysm of grief, Juanita fell to the ground and had to be lifted into an emergency truck. Diane's father, Grady, had been at work at Xenia's waste-treatment plant at the time of the storm, but as soon as he arrived home he headed for the root beer stand. Heartbroken, he saw there was nothing he could do and went home to comfort his wife.

Ricky stayed at the stand until Diane's body was finally taken away that night. He had closed her eyes and then stood silently above her, not saying anything. Betty Marshall, Walt Dingus, Ronny Hall—all tried to talk to him, but got nowhere. Much later, around 9 P.M., he accompanied her body to the Old Soldiers and Sailors Orphan (OSSO) Home's temporary morgue and then to Greene Memorial Hospital. At last it was decided that the body should be transferred to the city morgue in Dayton, and there, close to midnight, Ricky said goodnight to Diane.

David Graham could see nothing. The ceiling of his house was suspended eighteen inches above his head, blocking out all daylight. Silence surrounded him. He was pinned solidly, his left leg in front, his right in back. His right arm was locked at one side and he couldn't feel anything with the left. The only option was to swivel back and forth, which he did until he was finally free enough to pull himself out.

"Are you all right?" he called to Sandy, getting a faint affirmative response.

"Yes," she said. "But hurry."

David inched his way out, noting that his back was aching and his face bleeding. He looked up and down the street. Destruction, everywhere; dazed people, everywhere. It took him a few minutes to persuade neighbors that his problems needed their immediate help. From ground level, no one could see Sandy and the children, nor could they crawl under the ceiling to look into the basement. The only course was to lift the ceiling, which was not going to be easy. It was heavy. Lifting would require sustained effort from several men. With his back injuries and lacerations, David could not be one of them.

For the next three hours, rescue workers pulled and tugged. Because some had families of their own to look after, the personnel kept changing but the job never stopped. Part of the ceiling was supported by an armchair at the edge of the wreckage—if that should give way the whole thing might fall inward. "Look out for that chair," the man in charge kept yelling to the crews, and to David, "Why don't you get in an ambulance and get those cuts taken care of?" David refused. He wasn't leaving until his wife was released.

Finally, well after dark, four-year-old Sherry's body was brought up. Bobby was next, found near his mother, safe but unconscious. His mouth was open, and nearby, water from a broken pipe was flowing into the space around him. Had the rescue operation taken much longer, the water almost certainly would have gone into his mouth and drowned him. Sandy came last, her knee swollen badly, but otherwise unharmed. The two

56

remaining children, David, eight, and Billy, six, were left in their makeshift crypts until morning. It was late now, and the rescue teams knew they were not alive. Their efforts could be better spent elsewhere.

Just before David climbed into the ambulance, one of the rescue workers pointed out to him that the stairwell area was untouched. If only he and the family had stopped there, they would have come out unharmed.

This was one of the major tragedies of the tornado, aggravated, if possible, by the fact that David Graham had undergone a vasectomy almost three years before and thus would not be able to beget any more children. He had made the decision because his wife was a diabetic; childbearing was complicated for her, and they had lost a fifth baby in childbirth. Rather than risk more of the same, David had gone ahead with the operation.

Of course it had not been so fatal for everyone. Ray Higgins and Janice looked at each other, looked at the house, and felt very lucky. Then, "The cats, Piggy," Janice said (forever she had called him "Piggy"). "Where are the cats?" With that, four furry heads peeked out from beneath the pleated slipcover on their living room couch, and one "meow" emanated from the fireplace. Princess, the one white cat, was black from the grit that had blown down on her.

An hour or so later, they walked uptown to survey the city. They talked to Paul Grant and his wife, who was crying because their clothing store was ruined. They passed Donge's Drug, where Ray always got a senior citizen's discount, and Tuffy's Corner Pharmacy, where he did not, and crossed to the *Gazette,* to see if all was well. By the time they returned home, they had been gone nearly two hours, and both were drained. But astonished, too, by what Janice had done. Ravaged by arthritis, she almost never ventured from the house alone and seldom walked far. Even on Fridays, when she went to the beauty parlor, Ray walked with her —to provide mental, if not physical, support. Tonight she had moved like a track star, over trees and around fallen walls and across perilous streets. Piggy was proud of her.

In the lobby of the Xenia Hotel, Wink Black thought she might never laugh again. A half-block up the street, her house looked like a trapezoid, and here debris muddied the mosaic, lapped at the legs of the rosewood piano, and clogged the entrance to the dining room. Above, the upper two floors seemed to have crashed partially onto the balcony, and the skylight was shattered. Rain poured through. "All I want to do is get out," she said to Hal. "There's not a thing we can do here tonight, and we'll just depress ourselves looking at it."

Hal agreed. As he looked around, his vision of a fine country restaurant seemed absurd. It was difficult to tell if the place could be saved, but he was hardly optimistic. The employees, except for Les Cyphers, the maintenance man, had fled. "I suppose you're right," he said to Wink. "If Les here is willing to stay and watch the place, we'll go on into Dayton."

Les was perfectly willing. An ex-railroad man, he had lived in the hotel for fifteen years, and could not imagine that Xenia would have much better to offer tonight. Grabbing two jackets from his room, and a blanket from the linen closet, he took his place by the front door, rocking back and forth like Sitting Bull. He thought about the future; he might be out of a job, but that might not be all bad. For the first time in fifteen years, he could start collecting his railroad pension.

Two miles away, in a battered brick farmhouse surrounded by eight hundred splintered fruit trees, Ralph and John Mallow also stood guard. They were in the living room on the east side of their house, where the damage had been least severe, and their only companion was a lone bucket, registering the drips that fell from the ceiling. Never much on conversation, John had said it all when he first stuck his head out the window and exclaimed, "My Gawd, we haven't got nothing left."

Their immediate concern was their mother. A lady in her seventies, she had suffered cuts on her arms, face, and legs when she tried to shut the glass-paned front door at the onset of the tornado. "If she'd a stayed back with us, she'd a been all right," Ralph said.

Her two sons had wrapped her in towels, and looked for help, but it was at least a half-hour before anyone came up the driveway to offer it. Finally, an ambulance from New Burlington, one of the many that had begun to pour in, took her to Greene Memorial.

Meanwhile, the brothers had begun to notice the people from Arrowhead flooding across their fields, picking through the shoes and boards and broken appliances in the ridiculous hope of finding their own lost possessions. They could hear the shouting, and they heard the gunshot when one man shot his dog because the creature's leg had been crushed in the storm. And very soon, they saw dozens more filing up Bellbrook Road—persons trapped in town when the storm went through, but now struggling to get home. All evening the procession continued, like mourners filing into a wake, reminding the Mallows that their misery was shared.

For hours Cart Hill did little more than try to keep order in the bank. Many of his employees, finding they couldn't drive, had returned. These he ushered into the basement, where they would be safe, and safely out of the way. Later, with additional tornado warnings, and more people seeking shelter, the basement filled. Periodically Cart would go below to see what was happening; once he discovered a woman with a glassy-eyed stare who appeared to be dying. Learning that she needed insulin injections every hour, and that she had been without one since 4 P.M., he spread word that he needed a life squad pronto. Remarkably, he had one in ten minutes.

At 6:30 P.M., his son Tony arrived to say that the homefront was safe. Worried about the new warnings, Cart sent him immediately back to bring Marilyn, his wife, uptown. In case of more wind, she could be secure in the vault. He then turned his attention to sealing the bank, boarding up the three double doors and adjacent windows that gave entrance to the street. With tools and plywood rounded up by Tom Teeters, his vice-president, and working with the portable emergency lights that had been installed only two months before, he was finished before dark.

Tony returned with Marilyn two hours later. They had taken the road as far as traffic would permit, then walked the rest of the way. Marilyn, an instinctive Florence Nightingale, arrived with pockets filled with sandwiches for Cart and a heart full of frustration that there was so little she could do. But that night there was nothing. They waited another half-hour, when police said it was safe to leave the bank, and then another hour after that, until the last person was gone. The Hills were home by 10:30, and Cart had just settled down with a drink when Captain Sharp and several other Salvation Army officials arrived on his doorstep. The ensuing meeting lasted until 12:30 A.M.

More than anything, Jackie Hupman wanted to find her children. Cheryl, the eldest, was supposed to have been at a church on Second Street, at a guidance seminar, and now Jackie turned in that direction. "No, you don't," said her friend Gary Neff. "We'll find Cheryl. You go to the store." So with two other close friends at her side, Jackie headed for the camera shop, and Dick ran home.

Later she remembered sitting in the window of the store, its Pentax display unaccountably missing, and drinking drinks supplied by the Hofbrau Haus. All night the bartenders gave free drinks to anyone who wanted them. "I was told that all of the color had gone out of my face, that I looked terrible," she recalled, "but at the time I couldn't understand what they were talking about." Like a mirage almost, Cheryl suddenly appeared, and the two of them embraced and cried. Cheryl asked where her father was, and then, looking steadily at her mother, asked, "Do we have a house?" Jackie said she didn't think so. "How do you know?" her daughter pursued. She knew because, minutes before, another friend from King Street had walked by and said not to bother going home, that there was nothing left.

In time, Dick reappeared, and all the children were accounted for. One by one they took off again, to search for friends, and Dick joined Tuffy Snider on a rescue mission to Kroehler's. But not before Jackie had had a chance to ask him about the house. How bad is it? she wanted to know. Can we save it? The response was not encouraging: "It's too soon to say, but I can tell you this: the

60

clothes from your bedroom are hanging in the living room." Jackie swallowed hard.

For the next couple of hours, as twilight turned to darkness, Jackie did what she could to help whomever she could. When the baker around the corner discovered that he still had enough gas to bake, she helped pass out the donuts he produced. When Gene, at Gene's Corner, announced that he had hot coffee for anyone who wanted it, she helped spread the word. And when Tuffy showed her which cartons contained what supplies, she helped pass out medical equipment to the emergency vehicles streaming past the pharmacy. Even though she was only three blocks from home, she never got there that night. She was too busy. At one point, she remembers, an officious-sounding stranger told her to get off the streets, that they were imposing a curfew and she was to take shelter. "Listen, mister," she fired back at him, "I own a business here, and it's gone. I own a house and that's gone too. And if I can help anyone else, I'm staying." The last thing she remembers is a conversation with her mother in Dayton, over the telephone in Tuffy Snider's pharmacy. For some reason, it could still work for outgoing telephone calls, and Jackie quickly put it to use:

"Hello, Mother?"

"What do you want, dear?"

"Well, I just called to say that Dick and I and the kids are all right, but we don't have a store or a house."

"Jackie, what are you talking about?"

"Haven't you heard about the tornado?"

"Yes, but the news reports said it only hit the edge of Arrow-head."

"Well, try half this town."

"Oh, my God . . ."

7

IT WAS a world where the things that normally mattered not only didn't matter, but suddenly didn't exist. While other people were safe at home reading *How to Be Your Own Best Friend,* Xenians were crawling through the wreckage of their neighbors' homes. While others waited on Watergate, Xenians wondered where they might spend the night.

At first they had trouble assimilating the full extent of the damage. At Kennedy Korners, Jack Kennedy wondered why no one had rushed to help his stricken establishment, little realizing that people all over the city were wondering the same thing. Partly because communications were nil, and partly because nobody had ever heard of a tornado that went from one end of a city to the other, downtowners knew nothing about the periphery and Windsor Parkers were unaware of Pinecrest.

But there was another reason why they could not comprehend it—even after the physical disaster was evident: the concept of catastrophe was something they—like most of us—scarcely ever thought about. Hurricanes, earthquakes—they were things that happened in other places, usually on television. Add to that the chaotic aftermath of a natural disaster, and it's almost impossible to keep in mind that this mangled washing machine once washed that tattered shirt to keep that frightened child warm as he played. Most Xenians walked around in a stupor, unable to face or make the decisions hanging over them.

But somebody had to take charge and quickly, and that was Bob Stewart, the city manager, crawling out from a pile of people in the basement of City Hall. A tornado had been the last thing he had been looking for. Wednesday, April 3, was his anniversary, his twentieth in fact, and at three o'clock that afternoon he had called his wife to discuss it. "Come on down after work and I'll buy you a drink," he had proposed. From there, they would decide how to celebrate properly. But then the warnings started, and the skies darkened, and at 4:30 he was back on the phone with Yvonne, telling her to take the kids to the basement. "In about two minutes all hell's gonna break loose," he screamed as he headed for the City Hall basement.

Stewart knew too well. Formerly the city manager of Madeira, a small municipality outside Cincinnati, he had been hit with tornados there in 1969, and knew something of the emergency measures that would have to be taken. A thick-waisted man, with slick black hair, spectacles, and an indoor complexion, his face is only now beginning to show some lines. He looks like a Xenia businessman, moves energetically, enjoys excitement, and delights in making decisions. He has a reputation for putting people above politics, for treating small-timers and tycoons with equal concern, for taking time from his schedule to explain water bills to widows, and for occasionally joining Tuffy Snider's crew in the Hofbrau Haus after work. In two and a half years, Xenians had come to like and respect him, an implausible combination for any government official, but true.

Stewart had come to Xenia in roundabout fashion, starting out as a policeman in Clarion, Pennsylvania, then moving to Silverton, another of Cincinnati's satellites. "I liked to consider myself a progressive law-enforcement officer," he recalled later, "so when they started the police-science course at Chase Law School, I applied." Paying for the nighttime course out of his own none-too-handsome paycheck, he had to sacrifice considerably; dining out twice a year became a treat. Yet he graduated number one in his class, tied with Carl V. Goodin, the future police chief of Cincinnati. He was promoted to sergeant, then became police chief in Madeira, and was made acting city manager when the regular one moved away. He served as city manager for five years before leaving to be a civil engineering consultant with a private firm. But that was short-lived. "One of the biggest problems with engineers," he would say, "is they think of legal, political, and financial concerns." One year later he answered a trade journal ad for the city manager's post in Xenia.

When he was accepted, he knew it was a conservative city, and that he would probably have to ruffle some feathers. "I knew there'd be periods when I'd have to put my job on the line," he said. "When I was hired in Madeira, someone said to me, 'What if we don't like you?' I answered that my father had a dairy farm in Pennsylvania and I supposed I could always go back there. I felt the same way when I came to Xenia." But so far things had gone very well. He and his wife, Yvonne, liked the town—the Courthouse and the cannons reminded them of Clarion—and the people had been extremely friendly. The day they moved there, the city employees had dinner ready for them at their new home—a rental, one block from the office. But that had been way back, long before he went down to the basement and surfaced to a city in ruins. "When I saw what had happened," he said, "I knew that Madeira was a snowstorm by comparison."

Stewart's first step was to establish a command post in the Greene County Building, across the street and one block east of City Hall. Of the three government structures, it had clearly weathered the storm best, and he knew he would need such a headquarters to coordinate all the jobs that required his immediate attention. From his Madeira experience, he also knew he would need a portable radio, a yellow pad, and a pencil. In the wake of the storm, it was important to note what was not hit; and while the lack of communications made that difficult, eventually the reports trickled in: two schools, Cox and Shawnee Elementary, were OK. Ditto the YMCA. The hospital had survived too. And that was about it. True, large residential sections remained intact, and, scattered here and there, some commercial outlets too. But

64

the guts of Xenia were gone. About 40 percent of the city, as it turned out.

Stewart began to plot the general outlines of the damage on a map. At the same time, his police and fire chiefs reported in automatically, and detailed their initial rescue efforts. He knew that broken gas lines all over the city posed an immediate danger, that looters would run rampant without the National Guard, and that the water supply was more than likely to have been contaminated. One broken sewer line would do it. At this point it seemed impossible that there would be fewer than three hundred deaths; emergency morgues would have to be set up. He needed emergency generators to provide light and heat, emergency telephones for communication to the outside world, and emergency shelters for the hundreds of homeless. He asked to have a perimeter control established around the outskirts of the city, to keep out all but emergency vehicles, and he told Joe Harner (in charge of streets, water, sewers, and sanitation) to round up every chain saw in the area and the fuel to run them. Then he and Joe began discussing what resources they did have.

Help from Wright-Patterson Air Force Base, the mammoth military installation just east of Dayton, was already rolling in. General Irby B. Jarvis, Jr., commander of the 275th Air Base Wing, had been in the base weather room when the twister struck, and he lost no time dispatching his people to Xenia. Medical staff, supply corps, and engineers—all were available at once. Had the tornado waited twenty minutes, most would have been off duty, and he would have been hard pressed to recall them. A medical command post and intensive-care section was set up in Arrowhead, where state highway patrolmen were estimating seventy-five to one hundred dead. By 7:10 P.M. the base was calling for blood, and nearly five hundred donors lined up in the rain to give it.

Simultaneously, the first large convoy of heavy equipment— dump trucks, bulldozers, etc.—began the eleven-mile trek from the base to the stricken community. All were essential for the immediate task of clearing paths for emergency vehicles. Later a second procession took off, that one including emergency

65

generators, flatbed trucks with floodlight sets, and hundreds of containers of bottled water. It was the beginning of a caravan that lasted for several days, bringing more water, more floodlights, and, soon, the fuel to sustain emergency operations.

Highway 235, the one link between Xenia and Wright-Patterson, is a two-lane road that meanders peacefully through sloping fields and woods, but that first week in April, it looked more like the supply route to a combat zone. "The military help was the most immediate help we had," Stewart said later, "and its contributions were enormous."

Xenia was also blessed by its proximity to one of the most remarkable rescue operations in the country, the Box 21 Rescue Unit. Centered in Dayton, this was a group of forty men finely trained in the art of emergency aid. It was, in a manner of speaking, their hobby. Teachers, businessmen, and lawyers, they were all deputy sheriffs, equipped with two-way radios in their cars and homes, ready instantaneously for a crisis. Each had under his belt 270 hours of police training; twenty-two were paramedics and the rest were alumni of the state's Emergency Victim Care Program. They owned $250,000 worth of equipment, including ambulances, trucks, and boats, and four years previously had received an international rescue award for the recovery of four people from an overturned boat at the crest of a dam in the Big Miami River. In 1974 they responded to well over a thousand calls. Xenia was one of them.

They took off for Xenia automatically. Ted Howell, their chief, simply turned his car around as the report came in over the radio; the others followed, bringing everything but the boats. All that night and the next they worked hand in hand with Dickson Burrows and with the dozens of emergency vehicles pouring in from all over southwestern Ohio until the rescue missions were terminated. "There was a complete lack of communication," Howell said later. "We were fine, but we never did realize the extent of the tornado until we'd cleaned up Arrowhead and started into downtown."

Dickson Burrows likes to claim that he was in Arrowhead fourteen minutes after touchdown. "We were the first to arrive," he said later. "We started to organize things, keep people from smoking, and try to guide recovery of bodies, advising people not to move the dead or injured, but to mark where they were. In less than five minutes, we had found five dead." Within the hour, his communications van received word that it was needed in Xenia proper—up to that point its crew had thought the housing development was the only place hit.

Moving downtown, Burrows ran smack into Bob Stewart.

"Where's your command post?" he shouted.

"Right here," came the response. "You're looking at it." The last thing Stewart wanted now was the uninvited expert telling him what he should be doing. "We've done everything you say," he continued. "We're in control." And he meant what he said.

Burrows set up shop just outside the Greene County Building command post. His role was crucial that night because both the city and the county had lost their radio frequencies in the storm. With his sophisticated equipment, and with the help of two experienced ham radio groups—the Miami Valley FM Association and the Radicom React, a citizens' band—Burrows was able to maintain contact with the outside world. He could talk with both the state highway patrol and Montgomery County officials, and through them he sent requests for water all over the state. Coordinating ambulances, rescue workers, and initial clearance crews, he also set up ham operators' centers in the YMCA, Cox School, and Blue Moon Dance Hall—all designated shelters. Most important, perhaps, Burrows dispatched a group of the amateurs to erect a temporary antenna to restore the Xenia police frequency. Were he the type, the civil defense director might have taken a certain I-told-you-so pride in his services that night. But he wasn't.

Soon a network of temporary shelters began to emerge—primarily in the basements of churches and public buildings. Before nightfall they were filled to overflowing. Cramped and stuffy, the smell of hot coffee mingling with sweat and medication, they were hardly anybody's ideal port in a storm. But, as Yvonne Stewart's experience demonstrates, they served their purposes admirably.

Yvonne is a soft-spoken woman with piled-up blond hair and a pale face that frequently breaks into a smile. Shortly after the tornado, she encountered her husband on the street and gave him the bad news. "The house is gone. . . . Bobby's back watching it. . . . we've got to get to the Y, to find Lisa." Surrounded by four of their six children: Kim, thirteen, Pam, fifteen, and Pat and Mike, the ten-year-old twins, she explained that Lisa had driven a friend to the YMCA just before the storm.

The city manager was almost too preoccupied to listen. "One fire station is gone," he stammered, "the police radio is out, there are no communications—you can't believe the destruction I got." Yvonne remembered Madeira—four days without seeing her husband—and she didn't plan on anything different now. Quickly she pushed on for the Y and, just as quickly, Bob Stewart forgot he had ever seen them. Hours later, at the command center, Rich Heiland asked the city manager how his family was and, fleetingly, he seemed close to tears as he replied he didn't know.

By the time Yvonne arrived, the Y had already evolved into Xenia's primary shelter. A low-slung, brick and yellow panel structure, of the early-sixties variety, it looked solid and secure. Although its gymnasium and rear quarters were badly damaged, the building as a whole was fine, and word of mouth made it a haven within minutes. Upstairs, the familiar "multipurpose room" had been converted to an emergency medical center. In the fading daylight, sutures were made, casts set, and hundreds of tetanus shots given. In a back room, WGIC began broadcasting lists of people safe in the Y. (The station took a positive approach; injuries and casualties were not announced.) And at the front door, Janet Schmidt, the Y's office manager, stood for hours answering the endless appeals: "Have you seen so and so?" "Do you know where my son is?" As she listened to the anguished voices, she ached for the comfort she could not give, thinking, "Can't I find *somebody* on the list so I can say yes to their relatives?" But that whole night she never did.

Yvonne found Lisa immediately, fresh from the basement of the Y. During the storm, Dale Leverson, the director, had kept his clientele downstairs, and then asked them to remain there until some order could be established above. Mostly they were young boys in bathing suits and teenagers from gym class, and they had sat for more than an hour afraid in the dark, until Leverson told them to go at their own risk. Now Lisa fell into her mother's arms. They embraced and exchanged stories, then faced the fact of no home for the night. After some discussion, Lisa proposed the Y. Sure of its womblike security, she said it was more than adequate in lieu of anything better. Yvonne agreed.

Turning, they entered the shambles of people looking for their families, of wounded trying to find first aid and homeless seeking shelter. They passed quickly by the medical activity (Yvonne had to struggle to keep the twins moving), and headed for the stairs to the basement. A vast, subterranean cavern, it looked big enough to house half a city, yet she was not surprised to see it fill rapidly.

They were hungry, frightened people, most of them, as they settled in for that first night away from home. They had no idea where they would go or what they would do. Many were still without their families and most were in a state of partial shock. At approximately 6:30 P.M., nearly two hours after the storm, there had been another tornado warning, washing away whatever feeble equilibrium they had achieved after the first attack; now they were limp. The place was raunchy at best, with low ceilings and no ventilation, no electricity, and no water. There were no windows, so candles had to suffice. Toilets were unusable, but people used them anyway, and the stench began to mount. For a long time, no drinking water had been available, but when someone finally provided some, Yvonne could not stop drinking it. She was surprised at her thirst, but the increasingly frequent trips to the bathroom made it an uncomfortable trade-off.

"I'm sitting there and thinking 'Where do you go with six kids?' " she recalled later. "I thought of my sister-in-law in Mason, about thirty miles down the road, then I heard it had been hit too." By eight o'clock, sandwiches were available in the cafeteria and a serving table was set up downstairs. About the same time, an emergency generator restored light to the first-aid room; much later, a second one was installed for the basement. People sat in clusters—it wasn't a time to be alone—and talked nervously of their experiences. Warmed by body heat, they were comfortable enough, but sleeping was difficult. Even when the Red Cross provided hundreds of cots, they could only stretch out and lie still. As far as Yvonne was concerned, it was almost inappropriate to sleep at a time like this anyway. That the woman right next to her could rest as soundly as a baby was almost as disturbing as the young boys running rampant, smashing cookies into people's hair.

So it was diverting, as well as reassuring, when John J. Gilligan, the Governor of Ohio, visited the shelter later that night. Gilligan had arrived in shirtsleeves several hours earlier and reported directly to the command post. His customary Irish grin was gone, and his wide eyes and lean face reflected the gravity of the situation. David Spahr, the assistant city manager, was wryly bemused to see Gilligan at all. Earlier that afternoon—years ago it seemed —he had gone with some other Xenia officials to Columbus to put their proposal for a new sewer trunk line before the governor; he had been too busy to see them and they had dealt with an aide. Now the great man himself was right here in their godforsaken command post assuring Bob Stewart that whatever he wanted he could have, asking what he might do to be of service.

In the YMCA shelter, Gilligan moved through the crowded basement slowly, seeming to stop and talk with every family, cheering them as much by his official presence as by his genuine concern for their plight. When Mike Stewart asked him what he was going to do about their lost home, and school and bicycles, Gilligan promised restitution on all counts. And gave Mike his autograph. It was an extraordinarily effective goodwill mission. For the haggard refugees, the authority figure was just what they needed—an assurance that guidance was forthcoming. Directionless themselves, they wanted to be led away from danger; Gilligan was the first sure sign that they would be.

70

Upstairs in the emergency medical center, fading daylight had been replaced by the light of lanterns, candles, television cameras, and, finally, electricity. All night the room had been a mass of dirty, scared patients, medics in civilian clothes, and civilians who had found their way to the Y to offer assistance. Somehow the first aid had been administered—wounds bound and anxieties calmed —but at great mental and emotional cost to the health-care workers themselves. Throughout the emergency phase of Xenia's tragedy, this problem of stress among disaster workers came up repeatedly, but that first night, in the Y, Ruth Wilcox might have had a monopoly on it.

Ruth was a registered nurse with the Dayton State Hospital, and a columnist for the Dayton *Daily News.* Five days a week, in print, she answered letters that asked everything the writers always wanted to know, but couldn't find out in Dr. Reuben's book. In her role as sex advisor, she was on her way to Xenia to address the Child Conservation League when the tornado struck.

Brought up in Kansas, she had had more than her share of twisters already; in 1957, while she was still in nurse's training in Topeka, a tornado touched down upon her dormitory and killed eleven people. Nine years later, in the much greater Topeka tornado, her grandparents' farm had been destroyed. The experiences had left her wary; indeed, had she known that the dirty sky over Route 35 was carrying a tornado just south of her, she would have turned around and gone home. But by the time she knew, it was too late. Cars were lined up all over the roadside, a police blockade had formed, and a uniformed trooper was asking her her business. Immediately, she was directed to the Y. Driving in and surveying the damage, her estimate matched Stewart's: there would have to be two or three hundred dead.

She thought of how ill prepared Ohio was for anything like this, and how cautious Kansas was by contrast. There the hospitals had more tornado drills than firedrills; there a nurse wouldn't think of leaving her post without seeing that the patient on a respirator was plugged into emergency power. She remembered how as children they were trained to respond in a tornado; they knew where to go, what wall to crouch against, and to avoid the gymnasium at all costs; parents knew they were not to go to school to get their children if a warning was issued. Periodically, the civil defense units passed out area maps, so that people would be able to chart a tornado's approach should one occur. At night, Ruth remembered, should a storm be sighted, emergency vehicles would fly down the streets with sirens ringing. And, knowing that, you could always sleep peacefully.

When she arrived at the Y, the Red Cross was supposed to be organizing, but there were no experienced people on hand. Supplies were coming in, but no traffic plan had been worked out. No one was in charge of lost children; no one kept tabs on who had been treated and who had not; no one had thought to identify the patients with tags telling what medicine they had received. Because the cleanup had not been started, the mud and, later, the cables for emergency power, mingled on the floor beneath the wet feet of people drifting in and out of the rain. At first there were no tranquilizers, but later, some phenobarbital arrived.

Ruth set up a traffic plan, routing the wounded one way and the lost or emotionally distraught another. She used adhesive tape to tag the wounded and tried to establish priorities among people who needed attention. Whom to service? The seventy-five-year-old man with no physical injuries but badly in need of some spiritual comfort? Or the woman dying of cancer whose painkilling medicine was buried in the storm? Whatever she did, the stress was acute. The room was dark, and the noise level ferocious. When people are afraid, she knew, talking becomes their release; because they are excited, their blood pressure is up and their voices rise accordingly.

"You just knew a long night was ahead," she said later. "I didn't know another person in the room. The nurses were all in street clothes, so it was hard to tell who was who. I didn't know the capabilities of the others, and I didn't know what was going on outside. But you sensed that there was death all around." She was stretched to her limit by the situation. "I was dripping wet from carrying people in from the street and, really, the need for a cup of hot coffee was overwhelming. You had enough adrenalin to keep you going, but after a while, fatigue wears down anybody's system."

Most of all, Ruth wished she had somebody to talk to. "If you're isolated like that, the need for communication is intense." Assuming that the storm victims could only be feeling worse, she was reminded anew that people need a place where they can vent their emotions. She thought, too, of the constant exhortations during her nurse's training to keep calm in a crisis, and how quixotic that was when the crisis finally happened. Under these conditions, it was all one could do to keep going.

Later, Ruth discussed with a local psychiatrist her reaction to the forty-eight hours she spent in Xenia, and he assured her that health-care workers needed relief from the stress almost as much as the disaster victims. His own prescription: go into a back room and make passionate love. With anybody. Nothing could be more therapeutic, he said. Pointing out that in wartime sexual activity always increases markedly, he attributed it to the tensions of battleline living. And, as Ruth already knew, it was a medical fact that sexual release of any kind—in pairs or in groups—decreases tension substantially. Ruth agreed that the theory made sense— her experience in Xenia was easily the equivalent of war. But that Wednesday night, six hours after the largest tornado in recorded history, she didn't know all that. She settled with the utmost gratitude for a Big Mac hamburger, donated from Dayton.

THE STORM left one road after another blocked by abandoned cars or water. Cars were everywhere and so were cops, directing traffic, redirecting drivers, telling them that their destinations were inaccessible. Passing them all were hundreds on foot, with dazed or panicked expressions, trying to find their families or discover if their homes were still standing. Flares burned everywhere, ambulances screamed. On clogged Route 35, motorists kept having to pull off to the side to make a path down the center of the divided highway for ambulances and rescue squads from townships and counties that Xenians had never heard of.

Into this melee Ken Shields wheeled the battered Volkswagen he had borrowed from a neighbor. In the car were his wife, Pam, the jagged piece of wood still jammed in her neck, the three girls, cut and scared and crying, and Mary Hofferbert, a neighbor who wanted to help. Pam's pretty young face was drawn; the splinter was fully eight inches long and she kept raising her arm to pull it out. Ken restrained her, fearful that it would hemorrhage. He jerked the car out of Windsor Park, onto Lower Bellbrook Road, and headed into town. When a fallen pole blocked his way, a policeman told him to go back to the bypass and try Route 35 instead. On 35, he hopped into and out of lanes, driving down the shoulder or the median strip, his one thought to get Pam to the hospital before Mary Hofferbert could no longer prevent her from pulling at the splinter. At the intersection of Allison Avenue, he was detoured again, this time by piles of debris and a volunteer traffic director. Turning north from the highway, he slammed the car in and out of gear in a frenzy, driving down sidewalks and across the remains of yards. Then he stopped. A dead end, a downed tree, and a snarl of traffic signaled that he could go no farther. Whipped, Ken slumped across the wheel. In front of him spread the ruin of Galloway and King streets; behind, the destruction was unrelieved to Windsor Park.

He felt as though he were living in a dream sequence. Here he was five minutes from the hospital, his wife very probably dying next to him, and he helpless to do anything. Looking around, he thought it grimly appropriate that the nearest vehicle should be a hearse, but he appealed for help anyway. "We're in the same fix you are," someone yelled back. Scores of people seemed to be standing around, he thought, apparently no better equipped to deal with the situation than he. Then, over the same route he had come, a Greene County Sheriff's car pulled up, red lights flashing. Orders barked out: "Get sheets for that woman. You, you, and you, move that tree." In seconds Pam was wrapped in sheets, the tree was gone and the dream sequence was over. The Shieldses were in the hearse, speeding to the hospital with siren flashing. (The borrowed Volkswagen was left behind. Three days later its owner found it with three flat tires.) One of the first families to arrive, they found a staff already in gear and doctors who said Pam would have to be operated on at once. It was 5:15 P.M.

The Greene Memorial Hospital is a modern brick complex, rising fortresslike among the ranch styles of Xenia's fanciest suburbs. Its corridors are close and cramped, hospital green throughout, and they reek of hospital smells. When the tornado warnings began, gynecologist José Ensenat was in his office on Monroe Drive, just across the street. He had finished his office hours, and he bounded over to the hospital to check on two bedridden patients—who weren't in the least alarmed. "You should be a weatherman instead of a physician," one of them said as he kept moving between her bed and the window. Another, not in his care but in the same room, balked when he suggested she take cover in the bathroom. "But I haven't been out of bed since my operation," she protested. Ensenat convinced her that the time was at hand. Then he watched the storm go by.

He marveled at the way it sucked up roof tiles and sent sparks flying from utility wires. But he was terrified too. Ensenat was a Puerto Rican, his wife a Texan. They had come to Xenia in 1966 after three years in the Philippines with the Air Force. Unable to decide between his home base or hers, they had compromised by returning to the area near Wright-Patterson where they had first been stationed. Initially the distance from their respective families had seemed appealing, but there were times now when Mary seemed to long for Texas. Ensenat's thoughts flew to her. (He thought also of his new partner in gynecology, just moving into Xenia that day.)

"God, please, God, help my family," he prayed silently. The storm was coming from Beavercreek, where he lived, and he had no way of knowing whether they were dead or alive. Nor was he to find out soon. Just as quickly as the winds subsided, he was approached by Herman Menapace, Greene Memorial administrator, and asked whether the code-one alarm—the all-out disaster code—should be sounded. Ensenat didn't think twice before saying yes. But it meant that he would be totally involved in the hours to come. He took off his coat and rolled up his sleeves.

Four months to the day before the tornado, Greene Memorial had rehearsed its disaster drill, and José Ensenat had been designated "triage" officer. (The word sounded strange and impressive in those days before the world food crisis brought it out of storage.) His job was to meet patients at the emergency room door and distribute them, sending those not expected to live to one room, those requiring surgery to another, and those with minor injuries to a third. Within minutes the first casualties arrived, on doors, boards, and tabletops. Smashed cars cluttered the driveway, motors were still running, and people with towels wrapped around their heads stumbled in for treatment. Some appeared burned, but turned out to be covered with caked-on mud. Others had pieces of wood or glass embedded in their skin. Most common was the multiple skull injury. But what could have been bedlam was re-

76

markably orderly. "There were a couple of instances where I could see someone was gonna break up—you could see the face twitch—so I tried to calm them down," said Ensenat later.

Rapidly patients filled the low-ceilinged emergency room, spilling into the corridors and out into the rest of the hospital. Ken Shields was one of these. After watching Pam wheeled away for surgery, he sat down with his girls and waited. Several times he was moved down the corridor, and finally ordered to an elevator to go to the second floor. Only then did he feel his wrist throb and sense that it was broken. But the girls were crying for something to drink, and that became his priority. Signaling a nurse, he got some orange juice, along with an admonition to drink it slowly, and, at long last, medical attention.

The girls' cuts were sewn up and Ken was taken off to X-ray. "What about my kids, what about my kids?" he screamed in the confusion, until finally a woman he had never seen before assured him she would take care of them. Still hollering, he was carted away and the girls disappeared. Later that night he learned that Pam was all right; she was to remain in the hospital for another week and would come out with an almost colorless face and a six-inch scar running from her earlobe to below her neck. But she'd live. And, good as her word, the stranger who had commandeered his children called Ken's father the next day. They were delivered safely to his door.

For an institution unschooled in crisis, things fell into place almost miraculously. When Xenia's lights dimmed, the hospital's emergency generator automatically came on. Just as abruptly, hospital personnel switched from ordinary to emergency operations. People without specific duties went to the cafeteria and doctors on call went to the emergency room. "You weren't thinking," Ensenat said later. "You were just attending to what was going on then and there. It was all happening too fast. But once in a while you'd think about your family."

When the telephones went dead, the hospital fell back on its ambulance radio system, installed nearly two and a half years before as an emergency link to area rescue squads. When the water-cooled emergency generator blew a fuse, the hospital countered ingeniously. Rick Roskos, chief engineer, knew that the problem had arisen when Xenia's city fathers, fearing contamination, shut off the water supply. He suggested, therefore, that by cutting off all valves to the city, Greene Memorial could create its own cooling system. Water was pumped from a tank truck through the water-softening system and into a generator. Fifteen minutes after they faded, the lights came back on. Meanwhile, surgery was performed by flashlight and X-rays were read by twilight.

Throughout the night, the hospital took in approximately sixty physicians and a hundred nurses from surrounding communities. Still there was no way to handle the overload. So, in a once-in-a-lifetime break with procedure, the crowds of people waiting outside—some of them nearly hysterical—were allowed into the hospital to search out their injured relatives. Nurses handed them compresses as they entered, told them to find their family and hold the dressing against the wounds. Blood-spattered shirts, bloodshot eyes, and day-old beards made a decidedly unclinical spectacle, but it may have been the wisest decision all night. It freed the doctors for more crucial injuries, and it relieved those waiting from the agony of wondering.

Humaneness was the order of the evening. Patients with minor injuries hung back, imploring the doctors to treat those more seriously injured. In fact, the toughest cases seemed to have arrived first. At one time there were four near death in one room, two of them young children with crushed skulls. Dr. Edward Call, the surgeon in charge, tried to resuscitate them but couldn't. "I don't think we lost anybody that we wouldn't have lost anyway," he said later, recalling the extraordinary conditions: the diminishing sterile areas around the operating tables, people without masks standing nearby, X-rays that wouldn't print because the automatic developer wasn't hitched to the emergency generator. "And you have to remember that we were not necessarily the center of the action. Because we're a small hospital, we didn't get many of the more serious injuries. In Dayton and Springfield, there were neurosurgeons who worked all night on a single skull fracture."

In all, Greene Memorial treated and released 436 people for

disaster-related injuries between six o'clock that night and 6 A.M. the next morning. Not one of them was charged a fee. Of ninety patients admitted for more extensive treatment, only those with medical insurance were asked to pay. Through it all, teams of doctors and nurses worked without a break. Only when they felt the regular Greene staff would be able to handle the remaining cases did they start to leave.

José Ensenat left about midnight. His feet were swollen and he was dog-tired. But his family was safe. Sometime after sundown Mary had gotten through to the hospital switchboard to say that she and the three girls were all right. A fourth child was away. So now Ensenat went back to them, to the house he had wondered about. He put his feet up and swallowed two shots of wine. Before going to bed, he told Mary the story of his ordeal. "And the next day," he recalled later, "I had tickets to Opening Day and we went."

Away from the hospital, elderly couples, afraid to abandon their homes, sat through the night in sodden bedrooms with candles burning, afraid of looters, afraid that they would lose their houses, afraid of tomorrow. Little children kept asking their parents if the choo-choo had gone, and parents would assure them it had, although they weren't sure themselves. It was as if the tornado had turned their minds inside out, working a kind of aversion therapy on their normal responses to life. When the second warning sounded at 6:30, people panicked openly, running helter-skelter for cover like mice in an electrically charged cage. One family lay down in a cornfield, faces pressed to the earth, and did not get up for several hours. When yet another warning came through, at 2 A.M., most people were in basements or some kind of shelter, but psychically they were on an open plain.

For state trooper Ken Martin, the worst part of the night was his stint at the temporary morgue, set up at the OSSO Home. He was used to death, to the bad auto accidents on narrow highways, and to the stares of the morbidly curious. And he had seen some pretty bad maulings. But not like this. As the bodies came in without identification, they were tagged male or female, black or white. Martin saw a young boy with a brick stuck in his head, and then, pulling the blanket back from a female corpse, he saw a head with a triangular trench from the mouth through the skull. It was unlike anything he'd ever seen on the road, and he was almost sick. That was the last body he looked at that night. He went home with an extraordinary perspective on what a tornado could do to soft flesh.

But of all the ordeals that night, perhaps none lasted longer, or took more bizarre turns, than Mike Kuhbander's search for his wife, Sheila. It began almost at once, when he ran out of his house and saw debris still falling, flames leaping into the air from gas lines and a truck on fire across the street. As quickly as possible, Mike deposited his children with a neighbor, carried an amputee to safety (the man was sitting in rubble up to his stubs; Mike first thought he had lost his legs in the storm), then took off across the field to Sheila's beauty shop, three-quarters of a mile away.

Like so many others, he felt as though he were acting in a TV show, passing unreal scenes to reach an improbable destination. The beauty shop was a pile of concrete blocks, and Mike thought instantly, "There's no way she could have survived." But from behind some wreckage the owner appeared to say Sheila was all right so he ran back across the fields, thinking she might have headed for home. There Mike saw his father, white as a ghost, viewing the destruction. But no Sheila.

"I came from Dayton as soon as I heard and . . . my God, son, are you all right?" said Anthony Kuhbander.

"I'm OK, Dad," Mike replied, "but I can't find Sheila any-where. If you want to help, put the kids in the car and take them back to Dayton. I've gotta keep looking." His father agreed and Mike returned to the beauty parlor—again found nothing and again returned home.

By this time his brother Ron had arrived from Beavercreek, having run three to four miles across the fields to help. Hearing that people were being housed at Cox School, they walked and ran the mile to its door. At no sign of Sheila, they borrowed a car from Mike's former employer and tried to go to Dayton for some searchlights. But by now the stream of traffic and emergency

80

vehicles was so thick that they hadn't a hope of getting out.

"You stay with the car," Mike said to his brother. "I'm going to cut cross-country to Don's and try to get some flashlights there."

Don Markland was an old and close friend who lived in Sugarcreek. Beneath a darkening sky, with rain pouring and lightning flashing, Mike ran to his house, got the flashlights, and could not stop Don from going on with him. The two of them hitched a ride on an ambulance back to Arrowhead.

The sight that greeted them was unbelievable. There in front of Mike's house were his brother David and his father, and two horses saddled for action. David owned a riding stable in Beavercreek, and the two of them had ridden the horses cross-country, leaving Mike's children at David's house.

"You have to be kidding," Mike began. "How are we supposed . . . ?"

But David had it figured out. "Let's don't waste time. Just where do you think we oughta be going next?"

Mike thought their best bet was the badly damaged Supervalue warehouse on Bellbrook Road, not far away. He'd heard victims were sheltered in vans there and he wanted to look. Accordingly, the two brothers turned their steeds in that direction and picked their way through the debris. They searched every van by candlelight and Coleman lantern, but Sheila was not there either. Fearful that the horses' hooves would be torn in the rubble, they returned to Arrowhead, and Mike's father and David took the animals back to Beavercreek. Markland stayed with the house and Mike climbed onto a bicycle he dug out from beneath the bricks.

It was 10 P.M. He rode into Xenia, found nothing, came back to Arrowhead for the fifth time that night and waited. And rode around some more and waited again. The plan was for Mike's father to return with a car, but as the hour grew later and the weather worsened, Mike began to lose heart. He was about to make one last swing through town when Anthony reappeared.

"What in hell took so long?"

"Mike, you wouldn't believe the traffic, the roadblocks, the police—I'm lucky to be here at all."

It was 12:30 A.M. now, and pitch dark and windy. Gas lines were off and fires were out. As Mike said later, "It was the spookiest part of the whole night. There was almost no one else in Arrowhead, debris was whistling around the yard, and it was pouring rain. Just then a police cruiser goes by with its loudspeaker blasting out another tornado warning. 'Let's get out of here,' I yell, and Dad and Don and I headed off for Cox in one big hurry."

Staying only until the warning had passed, they went on to the hospital, learned that Sheila had not checked in there, then drove back to the YMCA Red Cross headquarters. They searched the basement, where Yvonne Stewart lay awake, then got lists of all the places refugees were staying and kept going. It was early in the morning by then and the traffic was relatively clear—a nine o'clock curfew had helped that. The Kuhbanders stopped at the sheriff's office, then, with the rain flooding down, pushed on to the Second Street Church. There they were urged to remain for the night, and to resume the search in the morning.

"We're not stopping anywhere until we find Sheila," Mike snapped.

The last place on his list was the Blue Moon Dance Hall, a cavernous cement-block pavilion on the south edge of town. It was subdued when Mike arrived, with hundreds of people on cots talking quietly or trying to rest. It also impressed him as the most organized place he'd seen. There was a register at the front door and Sheila Kuhbander was listed. She had been there, but had gone to a friend's house and left the address. They were reunited at 4 A.M., she having given him up for lost when she heard that Arrowhead had been destroyed, he having run steadily for ten hours trying to find her. Sheila began to cry, and Mike only barely managed not to.

By 7:30 P.M. a single-lane path had been cleared through the downtown portions of Main and Detroit streets. To Rich Heiland, the young *Gazette* reporter just returning from his own losses in Arrowhead, even that much progress was impressive. Somebody, obviously, had gotten a handle on things and was moving ahead.

82

Much less impressive, he thought, was the response of two fellow staffers who had opted to leave town after the storm and not return until the regular time on Thursday. It struck Heiland as grotesquely unprofessional. The *Gazette* was facing the biggest story in its history, with a roof leaking and the electricity out. At such a time, it went without saying that you redoubled your efforts to beat the odds. Heiland had watched people all over Xenia who were doing just that—people who normally would have been finishing the dishes and watching TV—so that his scorn for the deserters was conspicuous and symptomatic of the communal resolution already surfacing.

In that spirit, Jack Jordan had indicated he wanted a paper produced for Thursday. His decision was to write the stories in Xenia, by flashlight if necessary, and to print at the Middletown *Journal*'s plant, fifteen miles away. For the initial take-out, Heiland started for the command post to see what progress he could report. As he walked up Detroit, the town was lit by the flashing red lights of dozens of emergency vehicles and by a floodlight that the Air Force had erected on the Courthouse lawn. Many of the stores were boarded up, and Gene's Corner restaurant was pouring out free coffee by candlelight. Residents from other parts of the city were drifting in to see what damage had been done, and Air National Guardsmen—940 men from the 128th Attack Fighter Group and the 251st Mobilization Group at the nearby Springfield base—from Springfield were starting to arrive.

Heiland learned that the command post had (pretty well) mapped out the extent of the damage, and that various city officials were acting spontaneously to carry out the initial search-and-rescue/debris-clearance efforts. To his "cynical city hall reporter's eye," they seemed to be working with "cold-blooded efficiency." He had wondered, frankly, if Stewart's men had the mettle to meet this challenge, but after a few questions and observations in the command post, he was more than satisfied. He wrote the story of Xenia's first tribulations with a flashlight cocked beneath his chin and water splashing all around him, feeling as though he were on a sinking battleship.

"I will cry a hundred years from now," he began, "no matter

how many memories come and go, when I think of what this wind did to my city and its people. Yes, my city, now more than ever, though I have absolutely nothing left to show for my existence here except the most important thing of all—life. My life, and the lives of my children and wife. We should all be dead today, as, sadly, too many are. But we are alive, and we will be back . . . although many of us are homeless and must now dig through the wreckage of our dreams for bits of furniture, mementos such as a family photo album. And dig we will. And survive we will, dammit."

In truth, Heiland's concerns about the city's leadership were understandable. Not because its administrators were weak—historically they had been very adequate—but because the task before them was so great. To an outsider coming in that night, or the next day, it looked insurmountable. How to coordinate the outside help, clear the roads, care for the wounded? Who should be in charge of each and what priorities should be assigned? What to do about the homeless families, the roofless homes, and the businesses shot to hell? Where to store the truckloads of supplies and what to do with the hundreds of volunteers? How to procure water, warmth, and waste-treatment facilities for half a city in the middle of the night? How to do any of it when communications were all but nonexistent?

As it happened, a lot simply came together by instinct. In the heat of the crisis, people seemed to open up like sunflowers in June, giving everything they had to restore order and comfort to their neighbors' lives, forgetting themselves and acting spontaneously for the common good. In Arrowhead, one call for help could bring as many as forty kids simultaneously. They swarmed across the broken homes like ants, pulling up the prefabricated walls and extricating neighbors in seconds. So thorough were they that the rescue teams had little to do when they came through several hours later. People began cleaning their own streets right away, sawing their own trees, and finding shelter for themselves. At the Y, the supplies of donated food were so generous that refugees were surprised at the abundance. They were surprised too that so many strangers could act so selflessly. And they would have been pleased and proud if they had known how systematically Stewart's men were stitching the city back together again.

Already Troeger's search for victims had scoured much of the city. With rescue vans from Yellow Springs and Washington Township, he had been able to maintain pretty good radio contact with his ambulances, and had completed the downtown area. Fanning out from the center, his men continued to search for people and gas jets until 2 A.M., when darkness and exhaustion made further effort futile. Harner too had been active. Turning first to the freight train blocking all east-west traffic downtown, he saw it partially cleared after a Penn Central official radioed a switch engine to pull away all the cars still on the tracks. With that, Harner put volunteers to work on the trees and rubble still cluttering the intersections; by nine or ten o'clock he had Cincinnati Avenue opened—the first so distinguished. The four railroad cars overturned on Main Street proved to be more troublesome; Harner tried first with his front-end loader, then with some heavier equipment from Wright-Patterson. Another Penn Central official appeared to say he preferred to move his own cars, and could he have one hour to do so? "You've got sixty minutes," responded a tight-lipped Colonel Hartman. And in sixty minutes, by means of some gigantic cranes equipped with countervailing weights, the cars were gone. Within three hours of the storm, Police Chief Jordan had twenty-seven of his thirty-three-man squad on duty, primarily controlling traffic, but with an eye cocked for looters. Tom Fister, Xenia's new young building inspector, was out at once too, looking for all signs, walls, and poles that seemed in imminent danger of collapsing. Each of them, he knew, was a public safety hazard, and would have to be cleared immediately.

Sometime that night, between 1 and 3 A.M., Stewart gathered them together around a table in the command post and made it all official. Troeger would coordinate search and rescue; Dave Lyon, the city planner, would handle damage assessment. (At that point, they believed, erroneously, they had to come up with a total estimate of the damage within seventy-two hours in order to qualify for a disaster declaration.) Fister was to handle inspection for safety; Jordan to provide security and traffic control and Harner to continue street clearance. The others had general responsibilities, with Stewart at the command post. The meeting was matter-of-fact, conducted coolly by men with haggard eyes and overloaded minds, but it was not without humor. A field phone set up between the command post and the civil defense disaster van outside (Burrows was in the meeting) was nicknamed the "Cricket" because it buzzed incessantly with questions about trivia. Buzz, buzz, and "Where do you want these hammers?" or buzz, buzz, and "Do you need a dump truck from Piqua?" It was farcical.

By 2 A.M., Xenia was fully launched toward recovery. Its officials had done everything they could to take care of immediate needs and had plotted their strategy for the upcoming days. Refugees were on cots or with friends, and nothing more could be done until morning. The governor was there, the National Guard was arriving, and the President had been alerted. The city had been sealed off from the curious and emergency aid was pouring in, literally by the ton.

When the meeting finally adjourned, Bob Stewart had his first chance to survey the destruction firsthand, and he moved through the cluttered streets carefully, not allowing himself the luxury of astonishment. When he had absorbed enough, he stopped at the YMCA, made his way through the crowded corridors, downstairs to the stuffy basement and, between the bodies and the cots, to his dozing children and drowsy wife, and greeted her belatedly: "Happy anniversary, honey."

9

THE TORNADO that raged across Xenia proved to be just one outcropping of a storm system that brought death to dozens of households and disaster to scores of communities from Guin, Alabama, where twenty-three died, to Windsor, Ontario, where a curling rink lost its roof and eight players lost their lives. It was, according to the Satellite and Mesometeorology Research Project of the University of Chicago, the worst outbreak of tornadoes in the nation's history, spawning 127 twisters and claiming 329 lives. But statistics generally fall flat. People are impressed, briefly, when they learn that an outbreak was unusual, but then they recall that natural disasters of one sort or another occur with modest regularity, and their attention wanders.

Not so the privileged survivors of that gray day in April. For them it was an indelible experience which they would recall as minutely as we recall the day John Kennedy was shot. It would take weeks for the full impact to be felt, days and weeks of retelling and reliving. Now they stared and responded numbly to the help coming from every direction.

It came first from Washington, in the form of Vice President Gerald Ford flying low over Xenia on his way to Cincinnati to throw the first baseball of the 1974 season. "The destruction, the devastation is unbelievable. I have never seen tornado damage where it just literally tore apart buildings . . . it made matchsticks out of them," he was quoted as saying when he landed. He also said that unless President Nixon had declared Xenia a disaster area by the time he returned to the capital that night, he would urge that such action be taken.

Yet even before Hank Aaron had slugged his 714th homer, Nixon moved. Less than twenty-four hours after the storm, he declared Ohio, Kentucky, and Indiana federal disaster areas, making Xenia eligible for all kinds of federal assistance programs crucial to its recovery effort. The President had moved exceptionally fast, sidestepping the political dickering which frequently attends such decisions. As one Red Cross official explained, "It wouldn't seem difficult. You only need the city to ask the governor of the state, and the governor to ask the President to apply for the federal declaration. But when you get a city manager or mayor that the governor doesn't like, or a governor that the President doesn't like, it can take weeks." Normally, the federal declaration takes at least one week. Because it came through so fast for Xenia, emergency recovery was greatly accelerated. How greatly no one could foresee at the time.

On Friday, Xenians were visited by Ohio's two Senators—the Democrat, Howard Metzenbaum, and the Republican, Robert Taft, Jr. Like all politicians in strained circumstances, they worked hard to say the right things, to talk about stiff upper lips and aid forthcoming, without making promises they couldn't keep. "It's the most overwhelming thing I've ever seen in my life. . . . Emotionally I don't think it will ever be rebuilt," said Metzenbaum. Taft was more direct. He called current disaster-relief programs "totally inadequate" and predicted quick Congressional approval of the stepped-up disaster bill which he had introduced in the Senate a year previously. He even went so far as to say it was "incredible" that victims could only hope to be approved for 5 percent loans to rebuild while President Nixon pledged as much money as necessary "at no interest to victims of last year's earthquakes in Nicaragua."

Strong stuff, but it fell largely on deaf ears. Hewlett A., alias "Moon," Mullins, the towering black who was head of the City Commission, called the Taft-Metzenbaum dialogue "a Howdy

Doody show," saying that the Senators spoke to no Xenia officials, but simply posed before cameras. At that point, Xenians weren't ready for anything that sounded at all political, however well-intentioned. With good reason, they responded best to the tangible aid pouring in, to the people and supplies they could see, and they warmed to anyone able to empathize with their trauma. In that respect, both Taft and Metzenbaum scored: they appeared visibly shaken by what they observed, as if they had not been briefed adequately, and they stayed longer than planned. The townspeople took note.

They were sensitive because they had suffered a variety of losses they felt no one else could comprehend and no one could help to alleviate. Jackie Hupman had lost her house. The Mallows had lost their livelihood. Ricky Fallis had lost his love, and the David Grahams had lost three children. No political promises or Red Cross relief could compensate them.

President Nixon arrived in Xenia on the Tuesday after the tornado, in the midst of his Watergate woes. The visit was a surprise, denied by the White House up to three hours before Air Force One landed at Wright-Patterson. But its impact was strong. Flanked by Congressman Clarence Brown, a Republican from Ohio's Seventh District, and Governor Gilligan, Nixon moved swiftly from Arrowhead to the downtown command post to the YMCA to Shawnee School. Along the way he talked with the people thronging his route with hands outstretched, and he commented continually on the destruction: "The worst I've ever seen . . . similar to the San Francisco and Alaskan earthquakes . . . devastated physically but not spiritually." It was just what Xenians wanted to hear. Like Gilligan's visit to the YMCA shelter the night of the storm, Nixon's tour was a sign from on high that help was coming, an official recognition of the town's travail. "Just the fact that it was the President who came to see us . . ." Bob Stewart said later.

The happiest memories, perhaps, were the occasional encounters of the townspeople with their Chief Executive. "Fight it out. Don't give up," Nixon told Norman Corbett, a homeowner whose house on Main Street was badly battered. "Did you see Hank [Aaron] hit number 715? Maybe if Johnny Bench stays well for twenty years he'll break it again!" For Beverly Pearson, director of Xenia's Red Cross chapter, Nixon's twenty-minute visit to the Y was an oddly tense experience. "At the time, I had a lot of other priorities. I wanted to get shelters firmly established in the Wilberforce area—I had been there that morning trying to stifle the media's impression or desire to make Red Cross assistance in that area a black-white issue. [Wilberforce and Central State University are predominantly black institutions.] But I was told to be at the Y for Nixon. You have mixed feelings about the President. It's so easy to make up your mind—then you see him in front of you as a normal human being and . . . well, after that I was a lot more critical with the things I was reading about Nixon."

It was a sentiment shared by a lot of Xenians. Like most middle-grounders, they had not found it worthwhile to worry much about Watergate. The *Gazette,* as was its policy on national issues, had declined to take a stand. ("Who am I to presume wisdom at the national level?" Jack Jordan would say. In 1960, the paper stopped endorsing presidential candidates.) Nevertheless, Greene County had grown increasingly Democratic in recent years. That, combined with the mounting evidence against the President, had been enough to predispose most Xenians against Nixon. In their destitution, however, those feelings were forgotten. Said one woman, living across from Shawnee School the day of his visit, "Last week I said I wouldn't go across the street to see him, and here I am, right across the street and looking at him. But he's here to help us."

Genevra Hunter, who, with her son Terry and daughter Tammy, had been buried in Arrowhead, didn't even need that much rationale. Missing the presidential caravan in Arrowhead, she pushed and shoved her way to Shawnee until she was at the forefront of the ropes holding the crowds back from the officials. When Nixon arrived, she thrust out her hand, which must have been shaking, because the President asked her if she was all right. "I told him he was a good man and I'd been praying for him," she said later, "and he smiled back." At which point Genevra's husband snapped the best picture he could. "It was the most thrilling thing I've ever had happen in my whole life. I can't explain how I felt; it was wonderful," recalled Genevra. And in her living room today is a forty-by-sixty-inch blowup of a tanned and smiling President Nixon, with white trench-coated Clarence Brown next to him. In the foreground is Terry Hunter's hand groping toward the President, and off to one side a fluttering bit of pink scarf—the one visible reminder that Genevra Hunter was there.

Nixon made very clear his intention to help Xenia rebuild: "This town will come back and be better and stronger than it was before, and it was a very good town before the tornado. The spirit of the people here is heartwarming. Everyone I talked to said they will stick it out. People like that should get all the help their government can provide." The President promised to do "everything that the law allows" to rebuild the city, to cut the red tape and speed up disaster relief. As if to support his statements, he pointed to James Lynn, Secretary of HUD, and Thomas Dunne, FDAA administrator, close by his side. The pledges were taken to heart, which was fine for the moment; but later in the summer, when the red tape proved as intractable as ever, they came back to taint the memories of that visit. "It didn't mean a damn thing," Jack Jordan said later.

The President's visit had one further effect, and that was to solidify the community's growing resentment toward the national media. The friction had begun almost at once, that first Thursday night, when Stewart granted a press conference at 6 P.M. and was instantly bombarded with such questions as "You mean Xenia had *no* warning system at all? Isn't that shortsighted?" Or, "Could you detail your emergency plan to us?" It wasn't so much what was asked as how, and under what circumstances. The questions came from national correspondents in well-tailored suits, leveled at a beleaguered city manager who had better things to do than be fall guy for the eleven o'clock news. When it was over, Moon Mullins was heard to comment, "That wasn't a press conference; it was an inquisition." Throughout those first days, the contact between townspeople, their officials, and the media was unrelentingly abrasive. To Beverly Pearson, reporters seemed to have no interest in what was going well—they only wanted to know where the Red Cross wasn't doing its job or what victims weren't receiving prompt federal aid. One lady, in Windsor Park, would never forget the man from Channel 7, in Dayton, who stood in front of her house with his camera crews and said, "There's nothing up here—let's go over there; there's a bunch of dead people there."

It had all come to a head during Nixon's visit. Jack Jordan and Cart Hill were both appalled, when the President was at the command post, to see a number of national television cameramen climb onto the top of somebody's car to get a better angle, and refuse to get off even after they dented the roof. "It was unbelievable," Hill said. "The lady asked them please, please to get off, that they were ruining her car, and they wouldn't budge." When they did budge, said Jordan, the car was a shambles. And there was an embarrassing incident just before Nixon departed. "Hey, Mr. President," a reporter cried, "how about some words for the local media?" The local media, it should be said, had been rudely shunted aside in the face of the national press corps that followed Nixon like bloodhounds. Now its representatives were asking for their chance and Nixon consented. He told them how difficult he knew the tornado was for local media, because they depend on local advertising, and he said that he hoped revenues from local advertisers would not be cut off too long. When finished, he said, "Thank you, gentlemen, and good luck." To which a national correspondent blurted out, "We don't need the good luck, Mr. President. You do."

Jackie Hupman had spent the night after the tornado at the home of some friends in Amlin Heights. "You've never seen such a bunch of scared adults," she said later. "There were about twenty of us, physically shaking and trembling. We knew more tornado warnings were posted, and nobody could sleep. We just sat around the radio listening to weather reports until 5 A.M., when the 'all clear' was sounded." At that point everybody collapsed—everybody except Jackie. Still frightened and concerned about her house, she tossed and turned until 7 A.M., when she got up and made coffee for the others. Then she took off for King Street. The sun was shining, the air crisp and clear—a mockery of the day before—but tears were streaming down her face the whole way. Not for the houses, which deteriorated as she approached home, but for the trees, the huge trees completely uprooted as if a flood had washed through. They would not be replaced in her lifetime.

When she reached her house, she sized it up carefully. The façade was intact. She climbed the steps and removed one of the porch pillars which was blocking the front door. Stepping in, and closing out the chill behind her, she looked around. Debris and dirt were everywhere; the windows were broken, the furniture soaked, and the terra-cotta tiles loose. The blue shag carpet was jagged with glass and the walls were stained by moisture. But no structural damage that she could see. "Not too bad," she thought, and jumped up and down on the floors to see how solid they were. Satisfied, she began to clean. She pulled glass out of the carpet, piled debris in the corners and put dishes in the dishwasher. Upstairs, she discovered that she could not get into her bedroom, so she crawled from the window of her daughter's room across a short section of roof and came in from the rear. It was, as Dick had warned, chaotic. Dirty, sopping clothes littered the floor, chests were overturned and all the pictures had been knocked from the wall. Her jewelry box was wedged between the floorboards and the south wall. In the fireplace, her grandmother's rocker looked as though someone had tried to shove it up the chimney. Her bed was flung up against the door, stripped of its covers and stark against the woodwork. Jackie removed it and stepped back into the hall, her footsteps thudding eerily in the silence.

She climbed to the attic, where she was surprised to find much of the roof still in place, and she felt strangely proud that it had not cracked. But the view was shocking. For the first time ever, she had a clear shot of the high school, now a focal point in the diagonal wasteland spread beneath her. *Dear God in Heaven.* Yet she remained optimistic. At that point, she intended to move back within two or three days.

Dick was more pragmatic. "You may as well accept the fact that the house is gone," he kept saying. "The roof is crooked, the chimney is broken, and the south wall is bowed." These things were undeniable, and they contributed heavily to the city inspector's decision to condemn the building when the first team came around. But Jackie was adamant. "I don't care," she replied. "We can strip the wall, we can rebuild the chimney." On Friday, she corraled her father-in-law, a cabinetmaker and former home builder, to get his opinion. He said it was too far off plumb to bother with, but if they really wanted to save it, they probably could. Jackie was encouraged, but still Dick refused to listen. Persuading her that the furniture was going to have to be stored, at least for a while, he enlisted a couple of trucks (freely offered by scores of helpful outsiders), and they began the painful process of emptying their home.

"I guess that's when I really started to have some doubts," Jackie said later. "By Friday, most of the things were gone, and I remember all of a sudden I couldn't stand to be alone in the house. I sat on the front steps, and I didn't know what I was going to do, when suddenly I thought I heard something. I started walking around the house crying 'Here Pepsi, here Pepsi,' when some National Guardsmen appeared. They must have thought I was crazy, but I just knew our cat was there. I asked them to lift up the side of the garage, and when they did, Pepsi ran out." It saved her from despair.

On Monday, the Hupmans got the final word. In a last-ditch effort, mainly because he knew Jackie would never rest without it, Dick called in an architect friend and asked for his assessment. The verdict: it might be saved, if the Hupmans were willing to spend between $75,000 and $100,000. The foundations had shifted; so the house would have to be jacked up while new ones were built. They would have to find a man who could plaster over wood lathe, virtually a lost art, and another who could take out the ancient woodwork while the walls were replastered. The chimney would have to be rebuilt, the south wall reinstated, and all the terra-cotta around the fireplaces recemented. Again, craftsmen for such jobs were rare. It was a crushingly expensive proposition, with the outcome anything but certain. Old houses, it seemed, were never dependable once the original foundations were violated.

Overwhelmed, Jackie capitulated. Dick waited until the day before the deadline to sign the release which would allow the Corps of Engineers to clear it away; meanwhile, he and Jackie retrieved fixtures and molding. They took it all, even the oak front door: 8 feet high, 4 feet wide, and 3½ inches thick. The house was demolished the second week in May with Dick recording it on film. Jackie couldn't bear to watch.

For the Mallows, acceptance came more easily. Maybe it was because they were farmers, and farmers are more rhythmically attuned to regeneration, or maybe it was just simpler. Certainly one factor was the appearance, the morning after, of the salesman from the company that built their barn. "Boys," he said, "we got a new barn coming free of charge." The metal structure had been guaranteed to withstand any wind; now the firm was making good on its promise. To the Mallows, it was like a call to arms. That same afternoon, with five men working by hand, they began clearing the land to make ready for the summer's crops. In two weeks they had three acres prepared for planting the middle of May: tomatoes, beans, sweet corn, squash, onions, and beets. " 'Bout as much as usual," Ralph drawled with his usual lack of excitement. Indeed, to listen to him talk, it was difficult to discern that anything had disturbed him. "Oh, we're gettin' there," he would say. "There's shortages of this and shortages of that, and I don't know when we're gonna get those greenhouses back, but it's comin'. Here, take a coupla these tomatoes home with ya." Only when he was directly questioned about the tornado did he sound faintly beset. "Well, that morning we didn't know what to do. We just walked around here in a daze."

Considering the damage, it was a calm reaction. The two brothers had lost all the peach trees, most of the apple trees, the barn with eight hundred apple crates, and the greenhouses filled with

95

flowers, ready to sell. The buildings were insured, of course, but not the lost trees and not the lost income. Which hurt. The orchards had accounted for the major portion of their business. Nevertheless, they were untempted when three realtors offered cash to buy them out, undaunted in their resolve to replant the orchards: twelve hundred "whips" two feet tall that would take five years to bear fruit, ten years to be productive.

Three weeks after the storm their new barn stood before them. One month after the storm the Corps of Engineers arrived and began clearing—it took nearly two weeks, but both Mallows were extremely pleased with the results. Afterward, passersby observed how much they missed the old brick farmhouse. It left a gap, no doubt. But how much more they might have missed if the Mallows had walked away. By planting as usual, the farmers had reassured them—in ways they could never articulate to themselves—that the rhythms of the earth had not been interrupted.

Through it all, Frank Marsh, the Mallows' man Friday, had stuck by his old friends, and now he had a story to tell too. Soon after the tornado, a Dayton radio station had held an airwave auction to raise money for Xenia. One of the items was a major-league baseball bat autographed by every member of the Cincinnati Reds. "Goddamn my hide," Frank thought to himself. "I'm just lucky to be alive." Out of gratitude, he started the bidding at $50. He finished it too, winning the bat for $375.

For Ricky Fallis, the hours and days since the storm had been tormented. He spent Wednesday night with Diane's family, in the basement, and the next day rode into Dayton with Grady Hall to identify her body. It was a solemn trip. The two of them got along well—they had been rabbit hunting together several times—and Grady liked his future son-in-law. "I'll tell you just what my wife's father said to me," he had said when Ricky asked for Diane's hand. "You're lucky. You're getting a fine girl and I hope you're both happy all your lives. But if you ever think you can't treat her right, just bring her back where you got her." But now there was nothing to say. They rode in silence.

At the morgue, Grady lost control for the first time. "I just about broke down. I went on my knees, and I said, 'Oh God,

Diane.' They had her under a sheet, and I didn't want to identify her. If she was hurt that bad, I didn't want to know it. But I reached down and felt her hair, and then Ricky raised the sheet. She looked beautiful to me. . . . I think I kissed her toes." Ricky said very little. He kissed her once, and the two left.

That afternoon he returned to Dingus's repair shop to retrieve a picture of Diane which he had in his car. He'd had her camera too, and now he wanted that—he wanted everything that had belonged to her. As he pulled the items from the auto, Walt saw him kick it violently, as if it were to blame. Returning to the Halls', he was there when his own parents came to pay their respects. "We really thought a lot of that little girl," Ricky's father said, and the four of them began to talk—for the first time ever. Juanita Hall had met Ricky's mother once ("and she seemed nice"), but that was the extent of their acquaintance. Now they mourned together, but nothing they could say helped Ricky. Friday night at 10 P.M. he was picked up by the police for being out after curfew. He had been at the A&W site, staring at the ruins when they found him. It took six men to get him in the car, but finally they did, and delivered him to the Halls', where he was spending most of his time.

It was a modest place, wood frame covered with asphalt shingle, but it was a constant solace to him. He had sat there so often with Diane, talking to her parents, eating a meal or coming in from the laundromat, that to return there now was to be close to her still. And it was a comfort to Diane's parents. "We felt it was nice to have Rick here, to be close. We felt like we were all suffering together," Juanita said later.

Ricky insisted on spending those first nights in Diane's room, in her bed, thinking about the plans they had made, the furniture they had bought for their apartment, the names they had picked out for their children: Melinda Marie, Misty Thomas, Aaron Thomas, Jason Thomas—he never had liked the middle name, but Diane had insisted. Now Diane's room was, in a sense, Diane. Small, painted in alternating sections of blue and red pastel, it reflected her everywhere. In one corner was a teddy bear Juanita had bought her when she was eleven, and on either side of the bed, the Mediterranean coffee tables that she and Ricky had purchased together. There were pictures of rock 'n' roll stars on the walls, and, strewn about, the stuffed animals Ricky had won for her at fairs. Even months later, the faint scent of her perfume was still discernible. "She loved her room and wanted everything in it," Juanita Hall explained. "She wanted to keep her bed when she got married, and when I told her she could have it all, she hesitated because she said there'd be nothing left."

Diane was buried on Tuesday, in Woodlawn Cemetery, after a small family service in the Bible Baptist Church on West Second Street. When her parents purchased a gravesite, Ricky borrowed $155 from his mother to buy one next to it. His family thought it wrong, but couldn't stop him. Friends who went to the funeral home reported that Ricky stood over the open casket like a sentinel; every so often he would grab Diane's hand, or look at her as though her eyes were about to open. The service was short. As the minister spoke, Diane lay in an open casket, dressed in her wedding gown. Ricky put the wedding band on her finger, and took one last picture of her, on her bier. He carried it with him all summer.

David and Sandy Graham got out of the hospital two days after the tornado. David was fine, but Sandy's knee had required some attention, and he had stayed with her until she could leave. Bobby, meanwhile, remained in bed for almost a week—a smashed muscle in his leg required therapy before his release. The family stayed with Sandy's parents in Xenia, generally a happy place, but strangely somber now. "They almost acted like it didn't happen," David said, noting that both in-laws and friends took every opportunity to avoid talking about what was uppermost in their minds. Even his own thoughts seemed more mechanical than mournful. He had to make funeral arrangements, had to think about a place to live, had to look after Bobby. His house, he quickly learned, had been gone over thoroughly by friends and relatives; they had found a few pictures, his Bible, and his bowling ball. Nothing else. His car, a '65 Ford, had been smashed, leaving David free to get the one positive thing that came out of the storm for him—a "new" '70 Oldsmobile.

98

David also learned that his father-in-law, Curtis Brown, had encountered unusual difficulty locating one of the three children, Billy. On Thursday morning, hearing that the two boys had been uncovered and taken to the morgue, he went to the OSSO Home to identify their bodies. He found David at once, but was told that none of the other victims remained unclaimed. Protesting that the two brothers had been dug up side by side, Mr. Brown insisted that they would have been brought in together. No, he was told, there was only the one boy. Possibly he should try Dayton. It was the beginning of forty-eight hours of intense anguish for Curtis Brown—"the worst part of the whole thing," he said later. Back and forth he went, to Dayton, to Greene Memorial, and even to morgues in outlying counties. On Thursday night, with the aid of others in the family, he recombed the wreckage of the house. But Billy Graham was nowhere in evidence.

The Montgomery County Morgue, however, did have an unidentified child. As he continued to search, Mr. Brown became more and more convinced that someone had mistakenly identified his grandchild for their own, and that if he could only get a look at the "identified" children, he could prove his point. For a time, the Montgomery County Coroner refused him permission to see pictures of the others. It was "against policy." But finally Mr. Brown prevailed. It took him only a second to know that the body identified as Will Armstrong, the boy who had been killed in a backyard in Arrowhead, was in truth his Billy. He recognized the shirt.

"You'll have to have better proof, some kind of identifying mark," the coroner said to him. Someone in the family recalled that Billy had a scar on his head, received six weeks previously when he had risen up while crawling out from beneath a bed. The coroner relayed this to the attendant at the OSSO Home, where the boy still lay, embalmed and dressed, ready for burial by Will Armstrong's family. Leaving the phone to look, the attendant came back moments later and said he could find no such scar. "Look again," said the Montgomery County man. "It might be a scar on a scar." The man looked again, and found it.

Kindly, Curtis Brown had not told his daughter of the trouble they were having. He solved the mystery on Saturday morning, the day Sandy was to be released from the hospital, in time to pick her up and tell her that it would be necessary to identify Billy. Only a parent could make the final claim. Sandy and her father went into the OSSO Home and looked at the child. His face was so swollen that the mother could not be sure, but finally, remembering Billy's habit of sucking on his left forefinger, she looked at his hand. The finger was slightly disfigured, and she knew conclusively that it was her son. She went home, Curtis Brown recalled, and wept for four days.

David, Billy, and Sherry Graham were buried on Wednesday after a triple service at the Williams Funeral Home in Cedarville —held there because the Neeld Funeral Home, in charge of the arrangements, had been destroyed, and traffic in and out of Xenia was still impossible. In their grief, David and Sandy Graham had turned heavily for solace to their religion, the Nazarene Church of God. "If a man has a problem and takes it before God, and he's serious, God'll help," David explained. "I know when I ask God something I'll get an answer—if you pray for something and He sees fit, you'll have it." Sometime before the service, David was approached by a man from ABC with a request to photograph the caskets as they came out of the church. The footage would be used for the special Reasoner report on Xenia. "He caught me off guard," David said later. "At the time I thought it might benefit somebody else, but if I had it to do over, I wouldn't." Sandy agreed. But undeniably, it was powerful viewing for the television audience—first the three small caskets leaving the funeral home. Then the scene at the graveside: the mourners seated by the freshly dug holes, the caskets borne from the hearse to the grave, and in the background, three grave-liner vaults, one pink and two blue.

One week before, these people had shared almost nothing. David Graham had never heard of Ricky Fallis, and Jackie Hupman had never met the Mallows. Now, suddenly, they held one goal in common: to set themselves rightside up again as solidly and as soon as possible. It helped only slightly that thousands of others were similarly engaged. Each individual's experience with the tornado was intensely personal; it followed that his adjustment in

100

A funeral procession for one of the tornado victims

its aftermath would be equally so. But with only themselves and their families to think about, and with dozens of specialists to help them, they could, at least, recover in private, taking as much time as they liked. The city officials were not so blessed. Saddled with the well-being of the community as a whole, they had no time for their families and less for themselves. On call twenty-four hours a day, they were endlessly immersed (and occasionally swamped) in the rigors of reactivating the city. It was hellish hard work, and it created special tensions all its own—as Bob Stewart was learning.

Bright and early Thursday morning he found himself arguing with Cart Hill. The bank president had risen before dawn—at 5 A.M. the return of power had snapped on all the lights in his bedroom—and had come into town to begin sorting what was left

101

of his West Side branch office. Wading through ankle-deep water, he fished out most of the records, finally salvaging everything but $300 worth of traveler's checks, two weeks of Christmas Club payments, and a few personal checks. But he was worried about looters. They were all over the West Side branch, he said, and he went to the command post to demand that the city manager dispatch some Guardsmen for protection.

"That's not true," Stewart countered, "we haven't any looters." Whether he did or not, he was determined that they not become a public issue. It would only rile people further. But Hill persisted, until each man thought the other was responding hysterically. The interview was finally terminated when Stewart said he would have to lock Hill up if he didn't shut up. No sooner had Hill left than an attorney friend of Stewart's walked into the command post and began making his own loud and irrational demands. Stewart put his arm on his friend's shoulder and talked softly into his ear: "If you've got a problem, we'll talk. But if you're gonna scream, I'll throw your ass into the street."

If he had any ability in that kind of situation at all, Stewart believed, it was in divorcing himself from the experience and doing what needed to be done. During his years as a policeman, he had been involved in enough auto accidents and witnessed enough gunpoint situations to know that he had to stay rational. "If I'm in the uniform, but don't keep control of myself, how can I expect others to?" But that day he was too accessible to do the kind of job he wanted. The command post was smack in the center of town (later perceived as an error by most of those involved) and almost anyone who tried hard enough could get to him. "Bob, I need your help in getting into my store; the Guard has the street blocked off," or "Bob, the hotel says all its food is going to spoil and what should they do with it?" Many of these intruders would complain about the tough time they had getting into the command center, and Stewart would snap back, "You're here, aren't you?"

Almost by default, Stewart was the hub of the wheel. To him came all the outside agents seeking to help; from him radiated all the directives to city officials. Whether or not he wanted the job was moot; there was no one else to take it. The mayor was a figurehead, and the City Commission, though always the final word, was a committee. And if ever one-man rule was warranted, this was the time. Fortunately, the commission seemed to realize it. "I would like your permission to make emergency status requests over $1,000," Stewart said. "Done," they cried in unison. "I request that the Miami Valley Regional Transit Authority be put under contract to provide emergency transit services to the city," he continued. "Done," again. The image of that first Friday afternoon meeting, in the commissioners' chambers on the second floor of City Hall, with the wind whipping through the glassless windows and everyone bundled in overcoats, was engraved on Stewart's memory. Somehow it seemed to dramatize the unity and urgency they all felt.

Trying to do a hundred things at once, the city manager found that his days became a blur. Weeks later, he could remember little that was specific about the fortnight after the tornado, only that it was relentless, and that he tried to anticipate as much as he could. He started by declaring a state of emergency, meaning, among other things, that no intoxicating liquor could be sold in the city. (As it turned out, the tornado had not so altered people that they wouldn't take a drink. The Hofbrau Haus was closed for three weeks, but Don Hilgeford, its proprietor, noted gloomily that "bars on the outskirts of town were doing a booming business.") Stewart authorized the distribution of store permits to owners of businesses in the downtown area so that they would have some proof of identity for National Guardsmen who questioned their presence. Looking ahead, he signed a contract between the City of Xenia and the Supporting Council on Preventive Effort (SCOPE) to supply emergency funding up to $45,000 for low-income disaster victims. He appointed the Miami Valley Regional Planning Commission to coordinate applications for federal and state assistance in the restoration of city services and, importantly, to begin to develop a long-range strategy for Xenia's recovery. It was administrative detail, the nitty-gritty of emergency operations, and he agonized that he was not doing enough. "What else should we be thinking about?" he wondered aloud. And to himself: "Why didn't you anticipate something like this?"

But his answer was always the same: "Because the average individual doesn't experience enough crises to motivate him, and who could have imagined this anyway?"

By 1:30 Thursday afternoon the search-and-rescue efforts had been completed. One hundred and eighty men, including Troeger's firemen and scores of volunteers, had convened at 7 A.M. and fanned out in groups of thirty to conduct the search. Nothing new had been found—a testimony to the localized efforts the night before. It was also a victory of sorts for Troeger, who had come to Xenia for the challenge of the bigger job when he already had a very good future in his native Battle Creek. "If I don't go now I never will," he had thought when the opportunity arose. With the tornado, he proved his mettle a hundred times over. Eventually, of course, hospital casualties swelled the death toll, but almost no one could believe it was as low as it was. Rumors circulated that officials were keeping the real truth secret, and only the impossibility of pinpointing any missing persons finally quelled them. Ray Higgins was shocked that he knew none of the thirty-two killed. Had Xenia really gotten so big?

A second rumor, again false, pertained to contaminated water. Joe Harner had noted almost right away that water pressure was off, leaving open the dangerous possibility that they could not fight fires should one occur. Obviously, some pipe somewhere had burst. So Joe did the only thing he could: he cut off all the city's water mains and then walked through town on a street-by-street basis, turned them back on one at a time, and looked for the leaks. "I don't know where we would have stood if we'd had a major blaze," said Harner, an unflappable pro who had been on the job ten years. "But by Friday the water pressure was back up." In three days he got only three hours of sleep and, for the foreseeable future, he had to give up bowling, his one hallowed hobby. Normally Joe played in a league three nights a week, with an average of 190, but it would be well into the fall before he would see the lanes again.

When he wasn't checking water mains, he was overseeing street clearance. Dividing the city into ten work sections, he established three checkpoints for volunteer equipment and one checkpoint for personnel. Each section was manned by a foreman familiar with the area, and route priorities were established. As best he could, Harner supplied four end-loaders and fifteen dump trucks to every section, and he ruled that right-of-ways would extend from back of sidewalk to back of sidewalk. The debris was heaped in residents' front yards, from the sidewalk to a line even with the front of their houses. With nothing but kind words for his crews, Joe still liked to tell one story above others:

"There was this detachment here from Wright-Patterson under a Colonel Hartman. They'd been working their way in from the west side of town, but finally they met up with the others. So Hartman comes into disaster control and says where do you want us now? Well, there was this section of 68 North I'd been holding off on, just because there was so much stuff here. It even had a house blown out over the street which the people propped up with two-by-fours so's it wouldn't collapse. That alone was a major piece of work. So that's where I sent 'em. And do you know he went all the way from Church Street to Ankeny Mill in one afternoon?" It was a phenomenal performance, and Harner shook his head in disbelief whenever he recounted it. The military, he explained, simply had better crews, better equipment, and better organization than his volunteers. And what about the house leaning over the street? "It wasn't there when I looked again—that's all I know."

The workload was staggering—the kind of thing people in safer havens sometimes contemplate merely to savor their actual security: "What if . . . we lost all our schools, or the power were knocked out, or the phones went dead . . . how would we act?" Xenians were playing for real now and, to their astonishment, doing very well at it. They first got their stomachs filled and their houses emptied. (On Thursday, Sergeant Craig of the Xenia police force helped one penurious homeowner retrieve $50,000 in cash from its hiding place in the flue of his chimney.) They then saw the streets cleaned, the water turned back on, and an emergency public transit system installed (later retained as the "X Line," which serves Xenia today). Within two weeks, service was restored to ten thousand telephones. (Many were never out; Ohio

Bell had simply thrown a switch so that during the emergency only certain phones belonging to doctors, public officials, and emergency services could make outgoing calls.) Within ten days, 95 percent of the habitable homes had electricity and 90 percent had gas. In the process, Dayton Power and Light crews had relit approximately thirty thousand pilot lights. (The weather was so bad that unions agreed to suspend their rules about working under inclement conditions.)

10

NORMAN STEINLAUF was driving home from work in Livingston, New Jersey, listening to the six o'clock news, when he first heard about Xenia. A deputy director for the Federal Disaster Assistance Administration, with headquarters in Manhattan, his thoughts raced automatically: "Who's gonna handle it? Do we have enough people?" Such questions were routine because he had been in the disaster business, if you could call it that, for over two years. In 1972 he had ridden into Elmira, New York, on a cargo plane filled with port-o-johns to assist recovery operations in the wake of Hurricane Agnes, and he knew the kind of effort required even to begin to put a community back on its feet. But the best way to know Steinlauf is to listen to him talk:

"My reward for doing a good job in Elmira and Corning was to be sent to Wilkes-Barre for a month to handle the flooding. That was between Thanksgiving and Christmas in 1972. Then I was home until March and Lake Ontario started to act up. The community up there screamed for assistance, to recover from the damage done by heavy winds and rainstorms and off I went. From there, in July, I went to Boston; there was flooding in Vermont and New Hampshire and I was to be acting regional director. In August, while I was on vacation at the Jersey shore, I picked up the paper to see that there were six dead in a Jersey flood. That afternoon my boss, Tom Casey, came by on his way to see the governor. I just looked at him and said, 'What the hell are you doing here?' "

Steinlauf is big and burly, with black curly hair that forests his head, bulging eyes that seem forever darting in different directions, and a mustache that obscures his mouth. He exudes perpetual motion, looking to the people who work with him like a movie tycoon handling three deals at once. But that is perfect for his job. Disaster work, especially in the initial stages, is hardcharging business: eighteen hours a day, missed meals, a thousand decisions and the most adroit diplomacy in dealing with a dozen federal agencies and umpteen state and local officials whom one has never met before. He thrives on it, and like most people who find an unusual niche, he fell into it quite by accident.

In 1967 he had joined the Office of Economic Opportunity under Sargent Shriver and later moved to the Internal Revenue Service. When, in August, 1971, Nixon announced his wage-price freeze, and the Office of Emergency Preparedness was given the responsibility for implementing it, Steinlauf was drafted from IRS to OEP, where he soon learned that disaster victims were as much his responsibility as disconsolate capitalists. In July, 1973, the President again reorganized the office, this time creating the Federal Disaster Assistance Administration (FDAA) out of the Office of Emergency Preparedness, and making it responsible to the Department of Housing and Urban Development (HUD). It was the first federal agency committed solely to disaster work, and Steinlauf was in on the ground floor. "I like this work very much," he would say. "It's exciting, it's helping other people, and I've always had jobs like that. We train for something like Xenia constantly, always reviewing procedures to improve performance, so we're keyed up all the time. It's a challenge, and when done properly, it's very rewarding."

Because FDAA has ten regional offices, each of which can usually handle its own problems, Norm had never been away from his northeast base. But now, in the late hours of this early day in April, the country's disaster services were strained as they had seldom been before. Tom Casey phoned at 12:30 A.M. that night and told him to have his bags packed. "I think they want you in Ohio," he said.

Three hundred miles to the south, in Alexandria, Virginia, Don Hannah listened to the same six o'clock news and girded for action. The Red Cross damage and assessment officer for the eastern United States, he went to work at once dispatching survey teams to Dayton and alerting Red Cross reserves throughout his region to stand by. Even more than Steinlauf, he was an old hand at disasters, and could fascinate fellow workers for hours with his tales of the 1970 tidal wave in Pakistan which killed almost half a million people (the largest natural disaster in modern history), or the 1972 dam break at Buffalo Creek, West Virginia, when 125 people were killed in the oozing black sludge that buried the town. Now he scrutinized his office walls, where, on huge maps of the United States covered with Plexiglass, markers were superimposed to indicate storage areas for Red Cross vehicles and locations of reserve workers. Hannah charted the area around Xenia in ever-widening concentric circles, planning the resources he would tap as the magnitude of the destruction became known. On Saturday, he flew to Xenia.

A handsome, rugged man, with a reddish-gray Hemingway beard and sleepy eyes that belie his almost mythical energy, Hannah has always been respected and renowned, and occasionally loved, among fellow disaster workers. "He has an incredible amount of energy, can assess a situation in an instant, is always covering his feelings, always being positive," said one. "Whenever I suggested that he do something, no matter what, he'd already looked into it." What makes Hannah the special person he is? "I suppose all of us have some do-gooder streak in us," he will theorize. "I don't like to say this, because it never sounds right, but it's especially rewarding in a life-death situation, where you can actually save lives. It gives you almost a godlike feeling, like you're really doing something for someone."

Above all, Hannah has come to believe that speed is the essence of effective disaster relief. Get that aid—the hot coffee, the cots and blankets, whatever—in there as fast as you can. In minutes if possible, in hours at worst. That's when the people need you the most; that's when an awareness that you're there will have the greatest psychological benefit. That Wednesday night he was frustrated because he hadn't been able to get his initial-damage survey teams on a flight until 6:30 the next morning. By Saturday, he too would be in Xenia.

In Plain City, Ohio, five hundred miles to the west, Eli Nissley listened to his radio and heard about the Xenia storm. A Mennonite, he didn't own a television, for reasons he was happy to explain: "I believe it could be used to good advantages, but in its present form it detracts from more important things like Christian literature and the word of God." For years, as a member of the Mennonite Disaster Services, Nissley had practiced what he preached: in 1964 he helped rebuild a complete village on Kodiak Island, Alaska, after an earthquake sent it plunging into the sea. In 1966 he rebuilt underinsured churches in Mississippi after racially inspired firebombings (a risky business—at times the Ku Klux Klan had threatened his life). Now a retired carpenter, he fully expected to be called in again. Aside from his manual skills, and the time to spare, he was an experienced administrator. On Thursday, he awoke to see heaps of aluminum and dry wall scattered about the fields behind his house—Plain City was only fifty miles from Xenia. On Friday he got the word: could he come to Greene County and supervise the Mennonite operations?

At the Steak and Shake Drive-In in St. Louis, Charles Betterton was in the middle of lunch when it started to hail. The wind was incredible, he noted, but it subsided without incident and he went back to work. That was Wednesday afternoon. The HUD director for long-range recovery from the Mississippi floods which had ravaged parts of Missouri and Nebraska in April, 1973, Betterton may have been the wunderkind of the department. Only twenty-five years old, he had joined HUD straight out of the Peace Corps after a rash of tornadoes hit his native Mississippi in 1971. Since then he had held a number of disaster-related jobs in increasingly responsible positions, thanks, no doubt, to his ability and his absolute confidence in himself: "I think I'm as capable, if not more so, than anyone else I've run into," he would say. But more than that, he epitomizes an almost religious dedication to the improvement of disaster handling in the United States. His creed: "There is a chain link between all people in the world. When I was eight and my sister was six, our father was killed. My sister climbed into a pine tree out behind our house and raised hell with 'Uncle Universe' for letting it happen. Her phrase stuck with me, maybe because it was so unspecific. Uncle Universe is not God, or any one being. He is the sum total of all people past, present, and future—all actions, thoughts, and deeds. My plans are to serve Uncle Universe in whatever capacity he wants me to fulfill." On Friday Betterton received a call from the Chicago office: stand by for duty in Ohio or Indianapolis. He was to be a disaster field office director, his first assignment to full responsibility during emergency operations.

They were all different and all kindred spirits, these four and dozens of others like them who came to Xenia. They were part of a special disaster subculture that lies dormant in the United States most of the time, but is ready to respond at a moment's notice. Its members know how to provide and cook hot meals for ten thousand, how to clothe an army or house a city. They know how to be soft and solicitous to families still quaking with fear, and how to be hard as hammers with the rip-off artists who try to trade on their good graces.

Working out of drafty gymnasiums and converted church lounges, they impress the toughest critics with their competence. Most of the year they sit at desk jobs, in publicly supported agencies where the paint peels and the pressures are unremarkable. But then, when the earth cracks or the winds roar, they spring into action en masse, descend on the stricken community almost like the storm that has preceded them, expend their peculiar energies, and leave. They'll work twenty hours a day, if necessary, living on coffee and cigarettes, to bring the emergency to an end. One sets up application centers and trains local volunteers, another procures food. A third specializes in finding housing for the aged, a fourth coordinates damage surveys for public buildings. They tromp through the wreckage in combat boots, and sit behind desks for hours, interviewing victims, telling them what kind of aid they can expect and where they can go to get it.

They are like a fraternity, or the election addicts who live from campaign to campaign, and know one another only by face and function. In between they go separate ways, but come the crisis and it's almost a homecoming. They nod to faces they haven't seen since Buffalo Creek or Rapid City, and talk about those previous disasters the way film buffs might recall DeMille epics. It is a fast, frantic existence for two to six weeks—depending on the scope of the calamity—but eventually it slows. For the disaster crews, that's the signal to depart. Fueled by adrenalin, they grow restless when it's no longer called for, and begin to want to leave as soon as possible—back to the local chapters, regional branches, and home offices that sent them out.

Norman Steinlauf drove into Xenia before noon on Thursday. He had come down from Columbus, making a "windshield check" along the way, and summed up his impressions as "sheer horror." All he could hear was emergency generators and the rumble of heavy equipment—bulldozers, pickup trucks, and tree-shredders. Around him, glassy-eyed people walked the streets, crushed cars littered the curbsides, and venetian blinds swung crazily in the Courthouse windows. Overhead, helicopters criss-crossed the wreckage. But through it all, Steinlauf was looking for something else. Were the people already working to clean up the mess? Experience had taught him that if they were, he could count on his federal aid being accepted in the right spirit—as support, but not salvation. So now he looked, and what he saw was encouraging. Behind the rubble, within the broken homes and battered buildings, Xenians were scurrying like ants. The last thing they were waiting for was his arrival. Steinlauf even had trouble searching out Bob Stewart. "I told my people to find him, and tell him that if he needs help we'll give it to him."

The aid he tendered came in two forms: assistance to the town and assistance to the victims. Steinlauf was empowered to provide

100 percent grants to replace whatever public facilities had been damaged—be they paltry as parking meters or important as sewage plants. On a more personal level, he was coordinator for all the federal benefits that would accrue to individuals: temporary housing, unemployment benefits, food stamps, Small Business Administration loans, and the like. All the king's horses and all the king's men, trained to put Humpty together again. It was, and is, a remarkably comprehensive program, designed to alleviate a community's psychological and physical apprehensions almost before they are realized.

And like a lot of the federal government's paternal initiatives, it was as unheard of ten years ago as it is taken for granted today. In 1960, for a *Holiday* magazine article entitled "The Controversial Red Cross," Richard Harter wrote, "No doubt Government will eventually take over the financing of disaster relief so that persons who suffer through no fault of their own can get help as a human right rather than as a gift, with the bills underwritten by the entire nation rather than by those who donate to the Red Cross. Eventually, however, is a long way off. Although a considerable fraction of the population would probably favor immediate acceptance of this responsibility by Government, there is no organized movement in that direction." But all that was a long time ago, when *Holiday* was still printed on 11-by-14-inch paper, and the Great Society had not been born. In 1960, the government had no ongoing disaster-assistance program. Its only provisions were for partial (50 percent) restitution for damaged public works and low-interest SBA loans to qualifying individuals.

With the outbreak of Hurricane Betsy in 1965, Congress passed emergency legislation that permitted the "forgiveness" of $1,800 on whatever loan a family obtained from the SBA. In other words, whether a family borrowed $2,000 or $20,000, it would be forgiven the repayment of $1,800 of that loan. In subsequent years, as other disasters occurred, the legislation was renewed and the forgiveness sum began to rise; in 1969, at the time of Hurricane Camille, it was $2,500. Still, the legislation was temporary: each measure passed was for a specific emergency period only. When that ran out, the country was again without a disaster program.

Finally, in the aftermath of Camille, Congress passed the Disaster Relief Act of 1970. A thorough and comprehensive document, it pegged the forgiveness gesture at $2,500 and, for the first time, wrote into law the federal government's 100 percent financing of rebuilding of damaged public works. As Richard Harter had predicted a decade before, Uncle Sam had entered the disaster business in a big way. The new act even made provision for food stamps, legal services, unemployment assistance, and twelve-month rent-free housing—all items traditionally handled by the private sector. But disaster relief, as politicians and professionals are wont to point out, is an emotional thing. The greater the destruction, the louder the cry that Congress do something, and the more likely that it will. In 1972, that is precisely what happened.

That year—an election year—in the face of the unprecedented destruction caused by Hurricane Agnes, Congress was persuaded to boost the forgiveness feature to $5,000 and to drop the SBA interest rate to one percent. When it was all over, and the returns were in, the President's disaster fund had disbursed $714 million in relief—almost $500 million more than it ever had before. The handwriting was on the wall: in 1965, with Hurricane Betsy, federal inputs compensated for 12 percent of disaster losses; in 1972, they had risen to 88 percent. It was costing the government a fortune and, clearly, it couldn't continue.

In April, 1973, a repentant—and newly elected—Congress abruptly rescinded its generosity of the previous fall. It dropped the forgiveness feature entirely and hiked the interest rate on SBA loans to 5 percent. So rapid was the changeover, indeed, that Jack Look, an SBA lawyer in Springfield, Missouri, found himself applying two sets of standards to the same county. In early April, after a flood in Harris County, Texas, he was able to offer victims $5,000 forgiveness and one percent loans. Two months later, after another flood in the same area, he offered no forgiveness and 5 percent loans. Which is exactly what Norman Steinlauf was offering in Xenia.*

*In May, 1974, a new Disaster Relief Act was passed, as Senator Taft had predicted. Under its provisions, victims who had been turned down for an SBA loan, and who had

By Friday morning Steinlauf was surveying the floor plan for his FDAA control center; by Saturday noon he was in it. The rooms were makeshift, on the second floor of an out-of-the-way storage hangar at Wright-Patterson, and with their gray-green walls and flimsy partitions, they seemed to float in a vast sea of space. In the morning they were empty; eight hours later they contained desks, supplies, and ringing telephones. Phil McIntire, Steinlauf's young individual assistance officer, and Mike Chavinski, his public assistance officer, supervised the setting-up. Relative newcomers to the federal bureaucracy, they are about as far from the stereotyped bureaucrat as two people could get. At twenty-six, Chavinski's shoulder-length hair and beard make him a dead ringer for Rob Reiner, Archie Bunker's son-in-law. At thirty, McIntire looks Ivy League, with sandy hair, a friendly face, conservative clothes. Both are college graduates and working toward an MBA at night, both highly skilled and highly paid (salaries can range to $22,000), and both New Yorkers to the marrow: they loved the challenge of the disaster, but thought the Midwest potentially monotonous. Chavinski is shy, McIntire more effusive. "There's a certain anticipation about knowing you're going into a crisis situation," Phil said later. "It's hard work and hectic activity; the first two weeks I worked seventy-six hours overtime. But I have a strong personal commitment to helping people. When I look back, it's been tremendously rewarding."

Now they were running a marathon against time: to pick up material at the airport and office equipment from other sections of Wright-Patterson in order to get the control center completed as quickly as possible. They had to be briefed by Red Cross officials and military personnel on the gravity of the situation; they

---

exhausted all other resources, including the Red Cross, could apply to their state government for an outright grant of up to $5,000. The gift would be financed by both the federal government (75 percent) and the state (25 percent), but the state would be responsible for both selecting who was eligible and for administering the funds. In essence, it was a way of providing for the truly destitute. Too often, under the old forgiveness/low-interest clauses available to everyone, disaster victims had claimed excessive losses on the premise that they would be compensated at little or no cost to themselves. For example, an old couch lying unused in the basement might be included on their lists. Now, under threat of having to pay 5 percent for the money to buy a new couch, they would be less eager to claim such marginal losses.

had to make telephone calls to other federal agencies to tell them where FDAA would be. Shortly a representative from each of those agencies—from HUD, HEW, IRS, GSA, and the Air Force —would set up a desk of his own at the control center, and would act as Steinlauf's liaison to that agency in the field. (Thus the HUD representative at Wright-Patterson was Steinlauf's contact with Charles Betterton at the HUD field office.) But the point was to hurry, always hurry.

"FDAA's whole thrust is to get things restored quickly," Steinlauf never tired of saying. "We're here to cut through the red tape, to get the job done efficiently, effectively, and economically. We are a mini-government. We have absolute authority over the other federal agencies. If HUD says to me, 'We'll be here a year,' I say to them. 'Don't give me any projections like that. The law says we may provide help for *up to* one year. If we can get people back to a normal life in less time, we're going to.' If the Corps of Engineers says to me, 'We can be finished with debris clearance in six to eight months,' I say, 'We're going to be finished in ninety days and what do you need to get the job done?'"

He could be especially churlish on the subject of mobile homes, a perennial bone of contention in every disaster area. Why? Because people demand them. They are immediate; they can be placed near the victim's former lot, and the government owns many hundreds of them. What could be simpler? Steinlauf explains: "Our purpose is to get things back to normal as soon as possible, and that's the reason for our reluctance to use mobile homes. It creates a mobile-home bureaucracy. You have to be concerned about maintaining them, about hookups, and then about carting them off—all of which costs. And sometimes people get comfortable. After a year we're required to collect rent. Then we get called by the utility companies and told we should pay those bills too. I tell the companies, 'The hell we do; you collect!'"

Each day in the control center there was a press briefing at 10 A.M. FDAA representatives gave situation reports of what each agency was doing, including figures on temporary housing efforts (how many people had been relocated to date), damage surveys (mandatory before any federal money could be released), and Red Cross undertakings (meals served and victims aided). At 4 P.M. there was a staff meeting for FDAA and all the agencies, wherein all current business was discussed. For example, IRS might report that people had lost all their financial records; they would get an extension on their income tax deadline, only days away. Others might have filed early but need their refunds quickly; IRS would speed them up. Or HEW might report that Central State University needed temporary storage space because of all the buildings it lost. Norm said he would find it, and did.

With so many government agencies working under one roof, the atmosphere was surprisingly civilized. What friction there was seemed more amusing than malicious (at least to an outsider), and it surfaced only in whispers. Mostly it had to do with what the FDAA officials perceived as the excesses of HUD. And to understand that, you had to understand the FDAA's pride in itself: "We're very lean and trim," Steinlauf would say. "Not myself personally [pointing to an ample waist], but around the country we have only sixty to seventy people in all. Our administrative expense is three percent of our total disbursements."

Thus the FDAA had two cars in Xenia. HUD had eleven. The FDAA, of course, had the sparest of headquarters. HUD was encamped in the spacious recreation lounge of the Faith Community United Methodist Church, with dozens of desks, several copying machines, and a complexity of telephone lines—all courtesy of the federal government. HUD's field office signs were carved by the Greene County Park Department—yellow lettering on brown wood, such as one might see at the entrance to Yellowstone. One FDAA observer even went so far as to say that when all the others were eating standard Red Cross dinners—fish, mashed potatoes, bread and butter—the HUD people somehow wangled salad too. But there was another reason for the joshing: at home, when there were no disasters to handle, the FDAA was only one part of the whole Department of Housing and Urban Development, and was responsible to its chief, James Lynn. In the field, however, FDAA officials were supreme. In Xenia, for exam-

117

ple, it was Steinlauf's responsibility to see that HUD was doing its job; he wondered privately if that wasn't just the least bit irksome to HUD disaster officials.

The emergency operations spread every hour, enveloping the city like a thousand hands reaching for a single drowning man. In fact, so much was happening so fast that no one could have tracked it precisely. Phil McIntire's "one-stop center" was one of those hands. Crux of any emergency phase, the center was just what it sounded like—a place where disaster victims could go to receive, all at one time, advice and direction for every conceivable need. If a person needed clothes, or shelter, he would learn where to find both at the one-stop; if he was concerned about rebuilding his house, which might mean a city permit and a government loan, he could see about both at the one-stop.

But first, Phil had to find one building big enough for the center and its ancillary services—the baby-sitting, hot meals, and nurses on duty that always went with it. "You have to get in there fast," McIntire liked to emphasize, "to give the people something tangible. It shows them that help is coming." On Friday he learned about Shawnee Elementary, a school that sat just north of the path of the storm; on Saturday he confirmed it. Volunteer crews spent all that day and night clearing the auditorium (salvageable equipment from other schools was already being stored there), and by ten o'clock Sunday morning they were ready for business.

The variety of booths was mind-boggling: food stamps, Social Security, Internal Revenue, HUD and Veterans Administration, Department of Agriculture, Volunteer Services, welfare assistance, legal aid, Small Business Administration, home loans, personal loans, business loans, and job placement. But to anyone who remembered the haphazard arrangement of such things prior to Hurricane Camille, when SBA might have been in one office and Red Cross in a different one across town, and most of the others not available, it was a marvel of efficiency. It even had a director of its own, Gordon Wenger, and an FDAA "how to" manual with complete instructions for its smooth operation.

For most Xenians, it was the next best thing to Santa Claus and

118

they flocked to it. One young father reported that as he sat waiting between booths (which reminded him a little of boot camp), he was approached first by a Catholic priest who wanted to know how he was doing emotionally, and then by a black social worker, who asked about the well-being of his family. Finally came a "kid" from Antioch College in Yellow Springs (with long hair) who wanted to know about his children's education. A staunch Baptist and admittedly biased, the Xenian was surprised at the evaporation of all customary prejudices in the bonhomie of the center. He talked as if these were his long-lost brothers ("You couldn't believe how nice they was, and so concerned, really . . .") and he noted with amazement that the collegiate long-hairs were as pleasant as house pets. The one-stop was good to him; he received groceries and clothes vouchers from the Red Cross and signed up with HUD. Like many others, he had come in not really knowing what to expect and he left not knowing what more he could ask.

"The tough part is separating your emotions—you have to be a little hard at times because you have to get things done," Phil McIntire would say about disaster work in general. "You don't have enough time to do the job as well as you'd like; you have to cut corners, have to rely on people without checking." But with the Xenia one-stop, he had no such reservations. At its height, the center processed five hundred people a day. They learned about it from newspapers and radio, and streamed in from ten every morning until six at night, when it closed for curfew. By the time it was terminated, on April 26, it had processed 6,500 registrants in all, with scarcely a wait for any of them. It was, in Phil McIntire's estimation, "the best of its type I've ever seen."

The hand that Mike Chavinski extended was twofold: primarily, it sought to survey and assess the damage to public facilities, so that the FDAA could authorize funds for rebuilding. Based on Mike's estimates, first of a community's emergency needs and then of its long-term requirements, the FDAA could advance local authorities 75 percent of the cash needed for repairs. In that way it speeded up the recovery process considerably.

Yet before any of this could occur, Mike had a second responsi-

119

bility which required his immediate attention. This was emergency debris removal. When he arrived in Xenia, buildings were in imminent danger of collapsing, roads were strangled, and people's lives were endangered. In all disaster areas, debris that presents a health and safety hazard of this nature—which was virtually all the debris in Xenia—is removable at the federal government's expense, via the FDAA. (This is a point Steinlauf likes to make loud and clear. During his time in Xenia, he ran into Ike Pappas, the CBS newscaster, who was covering the Midwest and did a story on the tornado. Although Pappas and Steinlauf were college classmates, they hadn't seen one another in twenty years, so it must have come as something of a shock when Steinlauf said that the show was lousy. Why? "I didn't like him saying that state and locals clean up the debris. The *feds* clean up the debris. The point is that the individual doesn't have to be concerned.")

In Xenia, Chavinski coordinated the cleanup of this debris. He went first to the city to get emergency clearance approval for the most crucial jobs, then to the Corps of Engineers to sign an emergency contract for removal. City permission was necessary because, as FDAA representative, Mike did not have the authority to determine which debris was a public safety hazard and which was not. That was up to Xenia's officials. When a hazard was found, the city then had the power to authorize its clearance without the owner's permission. In all other cases, owners had to sign releases before the city could enter their property. But in no instance could Chavinski order the removal first.

The Corps of Engineers was designated the official contracting agency for all debris removal. While the Corps itself does not own heavy equipment, it has numerous contacts with private and military contractors who do. Backed by FDAA, it is able to hire and pay as many contractors as it needs to complete a job. In Xenia, it hired all kinds, and they came from as far away as California, New England, and the Deep South. The job was that big. There was not, however, an inordinate number of the emergency problems that Chavinski first looked for. It was more a matter of getting *all* the debris removed as quickly as possible. With the

120

incessant rain and snow that began falling the Friday after the tornado, more roofs sagged and more walls buckled and there was no telling when a building might become a public nuisance. The fire at Cherry's proved that.

11

CHERRY'S WAS a furniture store, founded in 1913 by the father-in-law of A. G. "Bert" Fath, Jr., its present proprietor. Located at 56 West Main Street, just two doors from the Steele Building, it contained three floors of modestly stylish wares, catering to conservative tastes. The brick building was badly damaged in the tornado, losing all its roof and a big chunk off the back of the second floor. Whether it could be saved was questionable. Fath had visited the place immediately after the storm and toured the two lower floors; he had not been able to get upstairs, but had seen enough to arrange for salvagers to move approximately $100,000 worth of damaged goods on the following Saturday.

The night before the salvagers were to arrive, Friday, April 5, Air National Guard Second Lieutenant Carmine Forzono made Cherry's headquarters for his night patrol. In command of twenty men, he was to cover one quadrant of the downtown area—about ten square blocks radiating northwest from Main and Detroit. As was the custom, Forzono would send out three three-man patrols on foot and two men (usually including himself) in an army truck. The others would wait at headquarters, and every hour the shifts would rotate. Guardsmen in Xenia much preferred this downtown duty to the suburbs because in their off-hour they could relax under some kind of shelter. Patrol squads in Arrowhead and

Pinecrest had no such refuge—the best they could do was huddle in trucks.

Friday night was particularly bitter, with temperatures dipping into the twenties, and Forzono was pleased when the command post pointed out Cherry's as a possible shelter. It was large, approximately 60 by 120 feet, with access through the display windows on either side of the double front doors which were bolted tight. He made a complete inspection, noting happily the nests of sofas and chairs, but warning his men that the basement was off-limits. Its low-slung ceiling of accoustical tile was leaking badly, and he feared it might collapse. With headquarters thus established, the night progressed without incident. At one time one of the men pointed out that the basement was really a lot warmer than the upper floor, so Forzono took another look at it, but stuck with his original ruling.

Much later, some men from one of the National Guard's floodlight crews said they were going to the basement; Forzono said it was prohibited for his men, but they could go at their own risk. They declined. At 3 A.M. he checked back in at the command post, and learned that six of his men were to be pirated for roadblock detail, beginning at 5 A.M. These roadblocks were to guard against weekend tourists, and Forzono knew that whoever he assigned would be on his feet for four or five hours without respite. Accordingly, he reduced his patrol squadron to three two-man teams, and allowed the others to rest. It was 3:30 A.M.

One hour later a National Guard colonel and a sergeant came through for a check. Seeing the men catnapping in the cold, and noting the rain and sleet outside, they took pity. Would anyone like to come over to the command post? No, came the response, even this was better than that cement floor. At 5 A.M. the trucks for the road crews came by and Forzono picked six men. At the same time, the patrol shifts changed, and Forzono grabbed the opportunity to take a nap himself—his first all night. Lying down on a couch midway toward the rear, almost buried in the ski cap, gloves, rubber bib pants, and boots he wore to keep warm, he thought to himself, "If anybody found me like this they'd think

I was dead." As it happened, they almost did.

About twenty minutes later—for no ascertainable reason—he awoke to see a column of flame five feet in diameter spreading rapidly in front of him. "Fire, fire, we're on fire," he yelled to others still dozing around him, and looked to see if they were responding. He saw Staff Sergeant William Wolfe running to the very rear of the store, to where the cellar stairs were located, and start screaming. In seconds the fire was covering the ceiling and Forzono had no choice but to dive for the front. Safe on the sidewalk, he peered back into the inferno, only to realize that Wolfe and another sergeant, Walter A. Radewonuk, were still trying to escape. The latter, apparently, had been in the basement all along, and Wolfe had gone back to warn him.

In a panic, they tried the bolted doors first, forgetting that they wouldn't budge, and so lost maybe five crucial seconds. They veered to the left, and made for the broken windows, Wolfe crashing through first and rolling on the ground to smother the flames which were spewing from his shoulder. Radewonuk was right behind him, but his whole back was ablaze, and he hadn't the strength to get up from where he landed. Screaming for help, he lay beneath the second-story overhang, which was blocking the flames as they crackled upward, forcing them to whoosh out just above his head. Into this holocaust Forzono lunged, taking with him another man's coverlet to blanket the burning man. It worked at first—he got the fire off Radewonuk—but when he lifted his head to drag the man out, the force of the flames bursting beneath the overhang hurled him backward. The heat within Radewonuk reignited him instantly, and Forzono was helpless. He wanted to go back, but Airman First Class Gregg M. Mills was restraining him, and he was pulled out into the sleet against the roar of the fire and Radewonuk's agonized cries.

The whole sequence, Forzono later estimated, took well under two minutes. He was placed in an ambulance, taken to Greene Memorial, and treated for second-degree burns. The building continued to blaze until 7:30 A.M., when firemen brought it under control—a total loss—and Forzono returned to the command post to make a report. Fortuitously, he had kept a list of the men

124

on his patrol, and all but one was accounted for. As bulldozers began clearing away the rubble, rumors spread that this second man was dead in the fire also. They were confirmed the next afternoon when the charred body of Sergeant Jerry L. Regula, twenty-two, was found in the basement wrapped in carpeting. He was near the front of the store, and the building's façade had apparently fallen in on him. Publicly, none of the Guardsmen could explain why the two men had been in the basement; privately, and reluctantly, they speculated that both had disobeyed orders and sneaked downstairs for the extra warmth.

Also missing was a sure explanation of how the fire ever started —Troeger believed, after an inspection, that it probably began in the basement, maybe from a cigarette, a candle, or even an open fire. He was insistent that neither gas nor electricity had caused it because both lines were shut off. And while it is conceivable that pockets of gas can be trapped in tornado debris, he did not think that had happened here. More likely was Bert Fath's explanation: he blamed it on the elevator. On his tour of the store the day after the storm, Fath noticed that the store's old hydraulically operated elevator had dropped from the first floor to the basement, thereby rupturing the oil reservoir that lay at its base. Oil was all over the tile around it. He reasoned that the fire started with a careless spark—maybe from a cigarette, maybe from a candle—and spread rapidly up the greased elevator track to the cracker-dry beams which supported the second floor. Beyond that, the issue was closed. Except that on August 9, the day President Nixon resigned, Governor Gilligan came back to Xenia to award the Distinguished Service Cross to Airman Mills and Sergeant Wolfe for their valor the night of the tragedy. To Carmine Forzono, he awarded the Ohio Cross—a state equivalent of the Congressional Medal of Honor. It was the first time it had ever been bestowed.

The fire at Cherry's cast an additional pall over the community, as if to remind them that the storm was only the beginning. It roused Bob Stewart and John Troeger after only three hours of sleep—the first they had gotten since Tuesday—and it necessitated a cordon of Guardsmen around the afflicted block all day Saturday and Sunday. The lines of soldiers, six feet apart, looked mean and militaristic, but officials were afraid of another fire and they were taking no chances with strollers. Uncertainty over the fate of the second Guardsman deepened the gloom; the discovery of his body confirmed it. Bert Fath said, "I feel heartsick that a man gave his life to protect this junk."

Now more than ever, there was the urgency of debris removal. Since Thursday, building inspector Tom Fister had been working out a strategy. He set up a structural status center in the Greene County Building, above the command post, and he began making surveys of the greatest damage. It was no mean assignment. Fister was thirty-one years old, a relative newcomer to Xenia, and still green at his job. But he had a feel for it. If he questioned whether a building was a public hazard, he would clear out a space on the sidewalk in front of it. Then he would come back the next morning; if bricks had fallen into the space, the structure would be added to Chavinski's emergency list. Real Estate Data Inc., in Miami, Florida, donated six complete sets of Greene County's plat books (a $350 value), showing boundaries for every piece of property in the city. He got three hundred rolls of Polaroid film the same way. All necessary to identify and record the hundreds of properties his department would have to inspect.

By Friday he knew he would need thirty inspectors plus a staff to correlate their findings. By Saturday he had them, all certified architects, engineers, or inspectors, from Dayton and Fairborn. They traveled in teams, some by car to scan the minor damage, but most on foot, checklists in hand, to scrutinize the major destruction. One can judge how strenuous these inspection tours were from the fact that they took only four days to complete and revealed 3,300 buildings damaged. Of these, 1,257 were deemed structurally unsafe.

There were appeals from winners and losers: some wanted their approved houses torn down and some wanted their condemned houses saved. But Fister took it as a mark of the inspectors' thoroughness under pressure that the reversals were few and far between. Meanwhile, he began the long process of evaluating the

126

reports, drawing up the demolition permits, and securing the releases.

Once granted, a large R (or one of two other conditional designations) was slashed across any wall left standing and the contractor knew he could bring the bulldozers in. But the delays were endless. Either a family couldn't agree that its house was unsalvageable, as the city inspection team had determined, or its insurance company hadn't settled, or it mistrusted the Corps of Engineers. Virtually all homes in Pinecrest, Arrowhead, and Windsor Park had been built without basements, on cement-slab foundations that contained all gas and water pipes. If a bulldozer ran wantonly across that slab, as, rumor had it, quite a few did, it would sever the pipes and the homeowner would have to tear apart the cement in order to reinstall them. An expensive undertaking.

As a consequence, there erupted in all three subdivisions a rash of signs saying "SAVE THIS SLAB" or "BULLDOZERS KEEP OFF." Contractors were doubly stymied because they needed the go-ahead on several contiguous dwellings or it was not practical to begin work. They wanted to clear a whole block at once, not pick and choose. So Steinlauf stepped in with the solution: a deadline. "May first. Either they release by May first or they pay for removal themselves." The ploy worked; either fears of the contractors' carelessness proved groundless, or homeowners yielded to the greater fear of having to pay for something that could be gotten for free. Xenians began to sign. Eventually the deadline was extended for hardship cases, so that very few didn't sign when it was all over.

Yet the problems of debris, for which Steinlauf had to find solutions, didn't stop with individuals. Maybe the traffic patterns thwarted its removal. ("We have the entree with the state to say, 'Look, we're having a problem moving the debris.' So we say, 'It's your state and your problem, but if the pattern slows us up, let's get an alternate route.'") Or the dump site would be inadequate. ("So we establish another dump site. That's more effective and more efficient; now we've got trucks moving two ways.") It was so simple to hear Steinlauf talk about it, but the paperwork and coordination were endless.

For weeks and weeks, long after the FDAA departed, front-end loaders filled with rubble plied the highway between Xenia and the quarry dump site at Fairborn. It was an extraordinary sight when you stopped to think about it—one truck after another filled with the fragments of a community—but nobody stopped to think about it. It was as ordinary as barges on the Ohio River. And in the same way—was it because they lacked the time or the inclination?—nobody thought much about the individual dramas filling those trucks. The hotel was just one of them.

Hal and Wink Black had known right away that it was severely damaged and that they would be lucky to save it. Still, there was room for hope. The first floor had received little damage, the stained-glass panels were (unbelievably) uncracked, and most of the old fixtures and furniture seemed fine. Wink crossed her fingers. Thursday morning she and Hal were back in Xenia. By then the inspection teams were combing the downtown streets, looking skeptically at the hotel; by Friday the Blacks knew they had lost. Hal signed the condemnation order without protest, but banked on the city's assurance that he would have a three-day notice before the thing was actually torn down.

He never got it. Moving the antiques out on the following Monday, amid heavy snow and rain which damaged some of them more than the tornado had, he began negotiating to sell his restaurant equipment. Because there was so much of it, he needed to find a supplier, and that took time. So he was angered and distressed when he returned later that week to find a salvage man taking out his restaurant fixtures. The city, it seemed, had given the Corps of Engineers the go-ahead, and the contractor was simply exercising his right of taking whatever was left before he tore the building down. Black went off to Stewart in a rage and demanded to know why he hadn't been given the three days' notice as promised. "Hal, I can't go around putting notices on every building in town," replied the harassed city manager. Black asked if he considered half a city block every building in town, to which Stewart re-

128

sponded, "Do you want us to tear it down or are you going to do it?" Black capitulated and the hotel was leveled.

It was the first commercial building to come down and the last that anybody wanted to see go. Buried in the basement were 1,500 pieces of old china that Wink Black never had a chance to rescue, and $6,000 worth of shoes from the adjoining store that the owner never got to. Buried in the dump was an ancient safe exhumed from the rubble; someone had tried to open it with a blowtorch and, failing, simply carted it away with the other wreckage.

The historical complex fared little better. Gutted and soaked, it sat pathetically until Monday, when a meeting of the Greene County Historical Society decided to save what it could. The rest would be torn down. Of the buildings, only the Galloway Cabin was salvageable—and that only by the most blithely optimistic stretch of the imagination. Its roof was destroyed, and so were the logs above its windows, but Xenia hung on anyway. Not so the Glossinger Center, with its romantic white columns and two-story front porches. Not so the Moorehead House, with its handsome Victorian features, nor the Snediker Museum. All were beyond hope.

"About 2 P.M. on Thursday I just took off and walked through King Street with my camera. It was pathetic," Cart Hill said later. For months prior to the storm he had been photographing Xenia block by block. Moving from south to north, he had just gotten as far as the old North End. Now he came for a final record. "I have a great love for history and architecture, so it came to me in a hurry. The area was absolutely devastated: the natural beauty was all gone, and we weren't going to see it again." He took his pictures and went away.

Interestingly, though, the wonders of technology made it possible to save more of the historical complex than met the eye. All its archives, its letters, manuscripts, and early journals were salvaged from the wreckage and rushed to a "deep freeze" in Dayton. They remained there, at temperatures from zero to ten degrees below, until they could be freeze-dried in one of several thermal vacuum chambers at the McDonnell Douglas Aircraft Company in St. Louis. The process involved transforming the moisture from a solid to a gaseous state and thus forestalling the mold, mildew, and general deterioration that traditionally plague water-damaged papers.

A third drama, notable because it did not end in the dump trucks headed for Fairborn, featured Mike Kuhbander. Mike was one of the few who didn't sign the release that would allow his property to be cleared. He resisted because he disliked the Corps of Engineers on principle. An outdoorsman, he was well aware of its two mangled dam projects just south of Xenia, one at Caesar's Creek and one at East Fork. "Some of the prettiest country around here," he would say, noting that each dam was half completed and both were hung up in court because the Corps had misrepresented their usefulness when they were first proposed. "It's an uncontrollable monster and I won't let it on my property," he said, and his handsome face—dark hair, innocent eyes—took on a stubborn set. But Mike was something of a loner anyway.

In all the tumult of the tornado, he took little help from any federal or philanthropic agency. He made one visit to the one-stop center, where he filled out a change of address form, and he accepted some groceries from the Red Cross. If he had his way, he would have left Xenia altogether and moved to Michigan, where the family had a cabin and where he would have better access to fishing and hunting. But Sheila put her foot down. She liked Arrowhead and Dayton was home. So Mike had vowed to rebuild where they were, salvaging as much of the house as possible. The living room, kitchen, and garage were gone, but the bedroom, he thought, might be saved. When the city inspector came by, almost two weeks after the storm, he told Mike it was a borderline case. The house was 50 percent destroyed, and anything over that was automatically condemned. Anything under was spared.

A week later Mike read in the *Gazette*'s listings that his house was condemned. He appealed the case and won (one of the few who did) and cleared away his own debris. He also elected to rebuild his own house instead of allowing the Arrowhead developers to do it—partly because he wanted to alter the basic Hiawatha pattern. To his way of thinking, Mid-Continent Properties was

130

unyielding when it came to making changes in its standard models. If Sheila wanted a different kind of floorboard, or a family room instead of a garage, she couldn't have it, he said.

In fact, the builders were going to some effort to rebuild the Arrowhead homes in accordance with the owners' wishes. They were adding garages, or converting garages to family rooms, and they even offered the new "family room addition" in their showroom for $2,400. They were using new, insulated materials in the reconstruction and had given one applicant a bid on a parquet floor. But all this took time: it took them at least two months to get organized, and Mike hadn't waited that long. Together with Don Markland, his pal from the night of the storm, he was rebuilding his house when the changes came through.

Unemployed at the time of the tornado, Mike had spent most of the weeks after the storm driving Kathy to school early in the morning (they were staying at his parents' house in Dayton) and then keeping vigil over his property during the day. Standing there, he had a lot of hours to observe one of the most despised and deplorable of the storm's aftereffects: looters.

They had, of course, come right away. That first night, Xenians couldn't believe how fast they cleaned out some of the stores downtown. Cart Hill saw three of them emerging from Hupman's Camera Shop (even before Jackie got there) almost as soon as he hit the street. Jack Jordan later noted that Hitchcock's Jewelers was stripped within five minutes. With windows smashed all over the business district, and virtually everyone concerned about his family in some other part of town, it was open house for the scavengers. "The overall looting was terrible; even with the army it was practically impossible to control it," said Chief of Police Ray Jordan. Shorn of his men, and preoccupied with rescue work, with no way to call additional help and no assurance they would come if he did, the chief could do nothing. Nine of his cruisers were unusable and his radio frequency was out. The frightened people crawling the streets made the distinction between shopowner and shoplifter almost impossible.

But the thing that amazed Kuhbander was their callous persistence in the suburbs. The looters he saw were virtually all white,

131

middle-class in appearance, with new or nearly new pickup trucks. Out to Buckskin Trail they would come, heading first for the copper piping, then the aluminum, then wood. They combed through the wreckage piled up on the streets, counting on their anonymity amid the confusion, but not hesitating to ask Mike's permission if they happened to see him. In the weeks just after the storm, he chased countless scavengers away, watching countless others like rats in the wreckage on lots farther down the street. "And by God, they weren't all from out of town either," Jack Jordan commented later. "My daughter went in to visit a friend in Arrowhead, walked in and saw three men rifling the kitchen. She knew one of them. They made some hasty excuses and left."

Their work was done in the daytime because of the curfew at night and it took many forms. It included lifting televisions, unscrewing cabinets, and towing automobiles. So many cars were crushed irreparably and left lying on the curbsides that it was an invitation for unscrupulous wreckers to come in, haul them away, and sell them for scrap (bringing about $90 a ton). When a Xenia patrolman apprehended one thief, he posted bond of $1,000 and forfeited it. There were reports of vigilante justice enacted upon some of the looters—groups of citizens would rough them up or pound in their cars—but as one policeman said, "None of 'em ever filed a complaint." By May 14 there were twenty-five arrests, and most of these were fined $100 and given thirty days in jail. After that, with most of the debris cleared, police felt it would have been inappropriate to call thievery looting, yet Mike Kuhbander continued to see those white, middle-class marauders stealing wood from construction piles well into the summer.

The community's special contempt for looters was modified only slightly when it came to sightseers (although Mike himself admitted that if the tables were turned he'd probably want to see the damage visited on another community). It took the form of signs on the slabs saying "SIGHTSEERS GO HOME" and "XENIA LIVES; SIGHTSEERS WON'T." And there was good cause for the outcries. No sooner did the National Guard lift its perimeter control, on April 22, than the city was inundated with autos from outlying counties and surrounding states. They came by the thousands, especially on weekends, causing monumental traffic tie-ups and preventing the Corps from doing any work because the glut of cars was so thick that their bulldozers and end-loaders couldn't move. Even while the Guard maintained its roadblocks on the main highways, tenacious motorists found the back roads and made their way in from the rear. Their remorselessness was one reason Stewart insisted on keeping the Guard as long as possible —long after the Guard thought it should leave—and it did not let up until all of the dramatic debris had been cleared, which took the Corps almost three months. Moon Mullins likes to recall a Saturday morning not long after the storm when he was working in City Hall and happened to look out the window to see Stewart stopped in traffic. "Sightseers go home!" Mullins yelled, and every head in every driver's seat on the road turned around except for the city manager's.

This animosity toward sightseers also reflected a spirit still building—the spirit that had surfaced first in the willingness of the wounded to let others be treated first. All over Xenia families fought to come back—they looked hard at their losses and figured how best to recoup. Fired by the editorials of a crusading Jack Jordan, they heeded his cry to charge forward together, as if to do less were to quit in the home stretch. It was a frenziedly defiant message that he proclaimed almost daily ("We're all in this boat together," etc.) yet it reached its mark. In little more than hours Xenia changed from a dazed and ruined city to a community of commitment. You could hear it in the hammers pounding, see it on the faces of friends, and taste it in the dust from bulldozed debris. It was in the bumper stickers that sprouted like wildflowers, saying "XENIA LIVES" or "XENIA, WHERE THE SPIRIT HAS JUST BEGUN," and it was echoed in the praise of disaster workers like Phil McIntire, who said, "I've never had an experience where the people were so willing to help. We'd ask for five volunteers and get ten housewives who brought in bean soup, sandwiches, and cookies. The result is that in less than a month the progress has been phenomenal."

And if most people could not do much, still they refused to do nothing. Start with a stick, one man said. A reporter from Detroit

133

had come to help his eighty-one-year-old grandmother in the midst of her horror, and he sketched his impressions vividly: the broken glass everywhere, the giant pieces of slate from the library roof which had sailed into her house and lodged in the walls; outside, two men boarding up windows and two others sawing into logs a giant fir tree that had stood in the front yard since 1935, and her car, once without a scratch, now with a hole the size of a man's torso in it. Wrote Paul Hendrickson, in the Detroit *Free Press*, "Crooked fingers around her hickory cane, Nonna clears her throat, pauses, then says with perfect seriousness, 'Honey, straighten that picture on the wall for me, will you?' "

12

EVERY DAY following Diane's funeral, Ricky Fallis went to the cemetery and spent some hours staring at her grave. Almost every day he would visit Diane's parents (he had always been close to her mother) and would talk about the past. "Why Diane?" or "Why couldn't it have been me instead of Diane?" he kept asking himself, torturing himself. "I'm lonely every day. I'll never love another girl as much as Diane." The very idea of seeing or dating another girl was repugnant to him, and in time his mother started to worry. "I guess it just takes some people longer than others . . ." she would say, and her voice would trail off. They lived in an old white farmhouse, eight miles west of Xenia, and now Ricky was spending most of his free time there, isolated as much by his emotions as by the vast, empty fields which surrounded him.

In Xenia he was known only as "the one who lost his fiancée." Because he lived so far away, had confined himself to Diane, had held two jobs and not attended the high school on a regular schedule, he had few friends to turn to, and indeed was a mystery to most of his contemporaries. "I wouldn't be surprised to see him do himself in," said one girl who knew Ricky casually, and, later sitting in the bunkroom of the barn (where he and his two brothers had been sleeping since a fire on the second floor of their home), Ricky admitted one sunny Sunday morning that he had thought of it.

135

Many a morning when Betty Marshall, the kindly manager of the root beer stand, opened her paper she too expected to see news of Ricky's suicide. The boy had come to her often in the months following the storm, always wanting to talk about Diane, wanting to know if her last words had been for him, wanting to know why she was dead and Betty was not. "He blamed everything on where she worked and said there could never be another root beer stand," Betty recalled. To Lela Dingus he was even more emphatic, vowing that if the root beer stand were rebuilt, he would blow it up. "Oh now, Ricky," she would say, "you don't mean that," and when Ricky insisted that he did, she would counter with, "Ricky, it's all over and done with—how can you be angry at a storm?"

But youth has resiliency and, in time, Ricky's served him well. By June he was out of the Hooven and Allison job he hated and working for the Morris Bean Company—the foundry that paid the best wages in the area. The work was still dirty: pouring metal to make the molds for aluminum castings, but at least it was something he had wanted and achieved for himself: he gave up the job at Dingus's in honor of it. Summer too was a help. June and July were beautiful that year, with shoots of green bringing life into the fields and blue chicory and field daisies brightening the roadsides. Ricky was sensitive to it—"You ought to see the place in summer," he had said shortly after the tornado. Almost in spite of himself he began to think about dating again.

Meanwhile, Juanita Hall was still under a doctor's care; she had been in the hospital once, the first of several sessions, and she was on tranquilizers. "I felt like when Diane died, half of me died with her," she said later. "I didn't know if I could go on without her." She then awoke in the night, sweating and screaming, from a dream that was to haunt her for months to come: a little girl, cradled in her arms, and Juanita dressing her in little pink bonnets, just as she had Diane. And she would think to herself in the dream, "I'll never let her go." Then the little girl would die, still in her arms. Juanita thought of calling other parents who had lost their children, but somehow lacked the nerve, fearing that they wouldn't want to talk about it. Indeed, those first few weeks after

136

the storm, her greatest comfort outside the family was Ricky. Just having him around, allowing him to stay in Diane's room if he wanted, was solace of a sort. He was a bridge to the past, a willing ear and a sympathetic heart. So it came as a shock when, on the Fourth of July, Juanita spied him with another girl—the girl from right across the street.

"It hurt me awful bad," she said. "He'd been coming over here, acting so broken up. Then—it was about midnight—we were at the fairgrounds watching the fireworks, and I saw him with this girl, one of Diane's good friends. The next day Ricky was over here, lying on the porch, and I told him he didn't look so good. He said his mother had given him a pill, and that's when I told him I saw him the night before." Very soon afterward, Ricky was calling to get his class ring back from Diane's mother; she asked for her daughter's in return. He refused at first, then finally relented. His convalescence had begun.

He dated several girls, at first talking too much to them about Diane, but soon that too subsided. Then in August unemployment came back to haunt him. Morris Bean operated two plants, one in Yellow Springs and one in Cedarville. The latter made molds for automobile tires, but in late summer, 1974, car sales were already beginning to slump and automakers weren't buying the tires they normally did. Ricky Fallis was one of the first casualties of Mr. Ford's WIN program.

At the urging of his mother, he went to Florida to visit his sister and then came home to start life anew. Thus began the long fall of looking for another job and the possibility of new romance.

It was not an easy time. For weeks and weeks, despite long days of searching in Dayton, Ricky was not able to find a job. And then there was Diane's mother. Seeing Ricky with new girls, she began chiding him for inconstancy: "I don't see how you can be going with somebody else, with the girl you were going to marry not dead five months," she would accuse him. And he would respond: "If that's what you think, that's the way it'll have to be. You might want to spend your life mourning for what's past, but I'm not going to."

By late fall he was seeing nothing of Diane's parents and quite a lot of a new girl friend. "I like her a lot . . . I love her, and I'll tell you, if anything ever happens to her, that's it. I'm never going to love another girl again." He had a new job at Hooven and Allison, this time as a string packer ("You put the string in a box, close it, and put it in another box . . .") and he was pleased with it. The company had just completed a long and costly strike when they hired him back, and Ricky was working two hours overtime every day. Since he worked from seven until five, and the girl worked from five until midnight, he saw little enough of her during the week, but made up for it on Saturdays. "We go everywhere—this Saturday I'm taking her to the steakhouse in Dayton for dinner. You name it, we do it. Trouble with me and Diane was, we never did anything 'cept go to her house or mine." In fact, said Ricky, the new relationship was all he could hope for. By the following August, if his job held out, he was planning to marry his new girl.

The effect of the storm on Gary Neff, Jackie Hupman's old friend, was less extreme but just as real. "Take my house," Gary was saying to her. "I don't need it—I'm working in Dayton anyway. I can get an apartment there." A thirty-two-year-old bachelor, Neff had recently become the happy owner of a cozy ranch-style in Amlin Heights. His house had been spared, and that was now his problem. "You feel guilty," Gary explained later. "I'm single; these other people had children. I could replace the things that were in my house, but they had things of sentimental value, like little toys the kids had made in grade school." He wasn't just talking about the Hupmans. He was talking about all the people in Xenia who had suffered the tornado and now had to try to pick up the pieces.

Gary had been downtown when the tornado hit, and worked until late that night helping people in the business district. He didn't know about his own place, but figured if it were gone there was nothing to be done anyway. Later when he saw it intact, he was grateful, "But the next day I started walking around and got sort of this guilty feeling, like, 'Why didn't it hit me and not somebody else?' " Gary asked for his two weeks' vacation immediately, and spent it working morning, noon, and night to help other Xenians. He offered his house to several of them, and was turned down, but he did sleep several strangers overnight, and he had his mother in cooking for countless people he'd never seen before. "People would want to pay, or give us things—furniture they'd pull out of their wreckage—but of course we wouldn't accept."

Much later, Gary was able to look back on his responses more objectively. He remembered that the guilt had been almost palpable, but in retrospect he was glad his own house hadn't been hit. "After working two weeks I was happy to have it, but I was very grateful to be able to help during that time. I continued to work on weekends after I went back, and if I'd had four weeks' vacation I would have taken all of them."

Ricky's and Gary's were two of a multitude of psychological effects that caught victims unaware but made doctors nod sagely because they had expected nothing less. "It has become increasingly clear that in a natural disaster no one escapes completely," said Ann S. Kliman, psychologist and disaster expert, in Xenia after the storm. "All are either direct or indirect victims. Direct victims usually respond by an increase in anxiety reactions such as fear of another disaster, feelings of being overwhelmed, feelings of depression, and rage and inability to cope or frenetic coping activity. Indirect victims often respond by feeling conscious guilt —guilt that they escaped while others didn't—and by an increase in guilt-related and stress-induced physical symptoms, such as accidents or explosive arguments at home, in school, and on the job."

What Ann Kliman was talking about was perhaps the ugliest consequence of the tornado. It surfaced in countless ways: a three-year-old reverting to diapers, an eight-year-old hysterical at the sound of a jet, a man breaking down while filling out insurance forms, a woman's acute guilt because her child was spared and her house untouched. You could sense it in the twitch around a victim's mouth as he talked about the storm, the schizophrenic stare of a homeless widow, the easy irritability of an anxious breadwinner. For some it surfaced sooner, and for some it came much later.

139

By the middle of November, Bill West, a locally recruited HUD worker, was saying, "Isn't it about time to start looking into the long-range effects of this thing? For example, I know two couples —old, dear friends of ours—who are going to get divorced, and there's not a doubt in my mind that it's the result of the tornado."

Few doctors would have disputed his observation. "In Xenia I think they'll have various neurotic and physical symptoms that they'll not relate to the tornado, but when you talk to them, it'll be quite obvious what caused them." The speaker was Dr. James L. Titchener, a senior staff psychiatrist with the University of Cincinnati, and something of an expert in disaster psychology. For almost a year he had been leading a team of specialists in probing the psychological effects of the 1972 Buffalo Creek dam-break tragedy. It was the first project of its kind ever undertaken (625 case studies were closely followed over an eighteen-month period), and it left Titchener in an enviable position for assessing the probable effects of the Xenia catastrophe, both short-term and long-term.

"People who have suffered a disaster have this tremendous need to see themselves as they were before," he explained. "It's their main drive. They'll admit all kinds of symptoms of change, maybe, but they'll insist: 'I'm still the same.' " His point is that they are not the same. They try to move forward and forget what has happened, particularly if the loss is grievous, but in so doing they repress the very feeling and emotions they should be ventilating. "The effects are covered up by defenses, particularly a denial of the anxiety that was suffered or the whole experience of coming that close to death and finding yourself that helpless. Take an automobile accident as an illustration of what I mean: there's a marked difference between the victim who will tell you he'll never forget the terror he felt as the car was spinning down the road out of control and the one who tries to block it all out. The first one recognizes what he's been through; he'll be all right." In short, Titchener learned at Buffalo Creek what Xenians were beginning to learn in the rubble of their yards: that the ruptured sense of control over one's own life was a lot harder to restore than damaged property.

The psychiatrist had gone to Buffalo Creek, West Virginia, at the behest of several Washington, D.C., lawyers who represented 650 of the Buffalo Creek disaster victims in a suit against the Pittston Coal Co., owners of the dam. Noting with concern the numb, zombielike behavior of many of their future clients, the lawyers felt it would be wise to have some qualified professionals look at them. The facts, as Titchener saw them: At approximately 8 A.M. on a Saturday morning in February, a slag-heap dam holding back a reservoir above the tiny valley of Buffalo Creek gave way and sent millions of gallons of cold water and black sludge coursing down upon the scattered settlements in the valley. Most people were at home when it happened, which was a blessing, but still 125 out of about 5,000 were killed. According to many of the disaster crews who worked on the case, it was particularly noxious because it was cold and wet and isolated and because, at any time of day or night, someone might dig another body out of the black ooze that covered the hamlets. (When it was all over, Titchener noted, the bodies of two children were never claimed.) In two years, people's psychological defenses against anxiety and depression had hardened considerably. And because these emotions were never properly aired, the repression was beginning to take its toll. "There was a change in their way of life," said Titchener euphemistically, "to what I call a more conservative approach: less ambition, less socializing, less interest in sex, fewer outside interests; more keeping the family close at hand, more drinking, smoking, and underlying depression—based on guilt, shame, and memory of helplessness."

In the days immediately following Xenia's tornado, health workers in the area mobilized to deal with the anticipated cases of guilt and depression. Dr. Oscar Cataldi, chief psychiatric consultant at Dayton Mental Health Center, devised a three-line system whereby disaster victims could first spill out their souls to paramedic volunteers who would simply listen. If a victim appeared to need more extensive counseling, he would then be referred to a second-stage center staffed by psychologists, mental-health technicians, and social workers. "Here we would let them talk with the idea of facilitating catharsis," Cataldi said. "We would say to them, 'This is your problem, what are you going to do about it?,' thus forcing them to think." With any luck, these professional counselors could help victims unload the guilt, shame, anger, or hostility they were feeling. "Depression," he said (shades of Dr. Titchener), "is really only introverted anger. Much better to let it out, express it, than to bottle it up." For victims who still needed help, the third and final stage of therapy would be admission to Greene Memorial, where tranquilizers and antidepressants could be administered and psychiatric therapy was available. "We were expecting to see hundreds of people," said Cataldi. "Right after the storm we made available a huge recreation center at Dayton Mental Health, and in Xenia I offered them enough people to cover for one week. During that time, Dr. Roberto Moronell, the DMHC clinical director, and I alternated morning and afternoon shifts at Greene Memorial." And during that time, Oscar Cataldi saw a total of three people.

What happened? Where was everybody? To this day, Cataldi simply turns his palms upward and shrugs. "They just didn't materialize. The whole thing calmed down, practically right away. We had eighteen people sitting there every day, all unused." What Cataldi, and many other doctors like him, expected to see was a reaction in three stages: first shock, then a feeling of being overwhelmed (particularly by the red tape) as the enormity of the tragedy set in, and, finally, depression. The shock was there—no one doubted that, and so was the sense of being overwhelmed— but the depression? Well, the best you could say was that it was like gasoline rationing: a bleak prospect that never came to pass. For weeks after the tornado people girded for the letdown. "Soon as the disaster crews leave and the TV boys pull up stakes and the hoopla dies down—then you'll see it," was a common prediction. Or, when that didn't happen, "Soon as the debris is all gone and they see what they're left with—then you'll see it." And when that proved false, "Soon as the summer's over, and the cold weather begins, and they're still not back in their houses and the government is still stalling—then you'll see it." The doomsayers ranged from sidewalk sages to trained analysts, and by and large, they all called it wrong.

Why? Were the townspeople too busy clearing out their houses and meeting insurance adjusters to feel depressed? Were they swept up in the spirit of Jack Jordan's editorials? Or were they unaware that emotional counseling was available? Any explanation was possible, and people in a position to know suggested all these and more. They pointed out that Xenia was swamped with aid from the start. That alone was substantial solace. Then, too, the hospital had continued to function, so that anyone badly hurt was immediately removed from sight. Xenians were spared what Dr. Titchener termed "the death imprint," or exposure to a mass of corpses which had been a source of severe psychological discomfort in other disasters. Xenia was close to Dayton and Cincinnati, and communications had been restored within twenty-four hours. In only the most general way did victims experience the isolation that was a fact of life in Buffalo Creek, for example. Besides that, it had its strong community spirit. Finally, it seemed to many of the doctors who visited the city that Xenia was helped a lot by its strong fundamentalist strain. The proliferation of signs like "GOD SAVED US" or "GOD SEES YOU IF YOU'RE STEALING" on the ruins of houses was an indication that many had turned to their faith for a resolution of their trauma.

Certainly David Graham had. "In the funeral home, the scriptures came to me," he said later. " 'Suffer the little children to come unto me.' The devil is the power of air. I believe God let it happen. The Bible says that in the last days God will pour his wrath down upon man unless he changes his ways and repents. What we've seen is nothing to what's going to happen—not necessarily a tornado, but we're living in our last days. Things are gonna get worse, not better."

Never much of a churchgoer before the storm, David became increasingly devout in the weeks after. His church, the Nazarene Church of God, taught that those who would be saved in this life must first repent of their sins. They must, in David's words, kneel before the Lord and say, "God save me." Prior to April 3, David had not repented. Was God therefore punishing him through the tornado? "No. He was waking me up maybe—He'll do anything to bring you right, make you realize His way. I went to church

143

one morning and I just felt the spirit of the Lord trying to draw me to the altar. So I went to the altar and confessed my sins and the minister prayed for me. It's mostly faith, you know. You gotta have faith to believe your prayers will be answered; otherwise it's all in vain." After the tornado, David Graham went to church twice on Sundays and sometimes on Wednesdays. He became head of the youth group the following summer. "God helped us afterward," he would say. "God Almighty. If it hadn't been for Him, we wouldn't have made it."

That he did make it had to be a testament to his endurance as well as faith. For in addition to losing three children, and his house, David lost his job and two fond indulgences: drinking and smoking. The job was gone because the foundry was gone. Caught by the side of the funnel, most of its back wall was destroyed and it was out of commission for the summer. David got food stamps from the Welfare office, but neglected to draw emergency unemployment because he didn't know about it. "I went to the bureau, but they didn't tell me," he insisted. Fortuitously, he had a modest insurance policy on his three dead children, and that is what got him through the summer. He used it to pay rent on the Fairborn apartment that HUD found for him, then to put a down payment and pay installments on a house in south Xenia, and to buy new furniture. "I don't know where it went, but it's gone now," he said in November. Sad enough if it were simply an isolated case, but many Xenians found themselves in similar straits.

The renunciation of alcohol and tobacco seemed almost divinely inspired. In his younger years, said David, he was not above a twenty-four-hour binge, and on Friday nights he liked nothing better than an evening in the local bar. Many times he had tried to give up liquor, usually to no avail. Then, about two months before the tornado, he had almost achieved it. In eight weeks, he drank only five or six beers altogether. With the storm, he stopped entirely. Any lingering desire simply vanished. Ditto the cigarettes. A four-pack-a-day man before April 3, he found the sight of a cigarette repugnant afterward. Not to mention that "our religion doesn't believe in smoking."

By October the foundry was in operation again, and David was

144

back on the job. But it was not the same. "I used to look forward to the end of the day when I'd go home to Sandy and the kids. Now I remember that they're not there." He started getting headaches, which he attributed to an old ear problem, but they increased in intensity until, at the end of October, he entered the hospital for tests. The result after one week: nerves. His ear was fine. In a bizarre and related incident, David recalled driving to his mother's one day in early summer, shortly after a rainstorm. Bobby was in the back seat, and somewhere en route, David turned to ask him if he wanted to climb in front. No answer. He asked again, and then Sandy turned around to look. Bobby was wrapped in a ball, clutching his heart and saying nothing. They pulled to the side of the road but as David approached him, the boy just screamed. They called the emergency squad, which came at once and took him in the same eerie state to Greene Memorial. With some sedatives, Bobby returned to normal, and the incident was closed, except that, very occasionally, he would burst into tears for no immediate reason.

Both David and Sandy missed the other children more than they could possibly articulate. On the wall, over the big color television in their new living room, were framed photos of the three: David, Billy, and Sherry. It was a simple enough room, with green shag rug, vinyl armchairs, and an aquarium, but somehow the pictures elevated it, as though a shrine had been added. David toyed with the idea of trying to undo his vasectomy, but he knew it was a complicated enterprise and uncertain at best. That aside, Sandy's diabetes was hardly improving—shortly after he went into the hospital, she began to feel sick at home: her blood sugar was out of balance. Their one hope was to take in some foster children, and by late fall they had signed up as candidates with the Greene County authorities. Coming home from church one Sunday morning they heard on the radio that Dayton needed emergency foster parents right away. Sandy was scarcely out of the car before she was on the phone, but the sponsors did not want these particular children taken out of Montgomery County. By Christmas, David had decided to leave Xenia entirely, maybe for Watertown, New York, where there was a paper factory, maybe "someplace out West." The point was to get out, preferably to someplace remote. "This town's always been bad luck to me," he said.

To Dr. Roy Miller, a psychiatric consultant from Columbus who volunteered his services to the town, it was significant that approximately 50 percent of the churchgoing population was fundamentalist, belonging to Nazarene, Pentecostal, or Church of Christ congregations. "It reduced the incidence of serious psychological problems, but it gave the ones which did occur a particular flavor. There was a lot of mystical interpretation, a lot of feeling that 'the hand of God' caused the thing." One woman went so far as to say that Xenia was a modern Sodom and Gomorrah, and that girls from Fairborn were not allowed to date boys from Xenia. The tornado was punishment.

Like other mental-health workers, Miller saw far fewer clients than he'd expected, but among those few he was struck by the number who talked about other tornadoes coming, maintaining that the first had been only a warning. A teenage boy, one of whose friends had been killed in the storm, took it as a sign of Divine Providence demanding restitution for some injury the friend had incurred. He told Miller that another tornado would visit the community soon, very likely on April 21—a widely circulated date.

"As I talked to them," said Miller, "it seemed in many of their minds to confirm their religious convictions and more or less to counteract the 'liberal' ideas of others. It was a kind of 'I-told-you-so' thing, almost a pride in disaster." Pointing out that fundamentalists subscribe to such "mystical" beliefs as faith healing and speaking in tongues, he said that the tornado was almost like a religious reenactment to some of them, like the great flood or the destruction of Babylon. "Symbolically, they believe, sinners are almost always warned first—thus the belief in the second tornado."

But, as history records, the second tornado did not come. Nor, strangely, did all the more publicly predicted results of the first. Traffic accidents did not rise, as had been anticipated, but actually fell. Crime was down too (though Police Chief Jordan had to

146

admit there were a lot fewer places to burglarize). The divorce rate was tougher to assess. Though Rich Heiland heard cocktail-party rumors of couples splitting up, and Jackie Hupman and Bill West could point to friends with sudden troubles, the records in the Greene County Courthouse as of November did not back them up. There were substantially fewer divorces filed in 1974 than in the year before. (However, the Courthouse records were fuzzed by their inclusion of several population centers outside Xenia. It is possible, given another six months, that divorces in Xenia itself would climb.) Alcoholism did increase, markedly, as psychologists had expected. By early November, Robert Mueller, supervisor of the alcoholism unit of the county health department, was estimating approximately double the number of cases he had had before the tornado. The problem surfaced for any number of reasons: uprooted lives, financial strains, unfulfilled promises of help. And though it was difficult to pinpoint how much of this was actually the result of the tornado, Mueller had two good indicators: his workers' caseloads had doubled since April 3 and the victims themselves made telling comments. Some reported drinking three times as much liquor after the storm as before, just to gain relief. Almost always, Mueller stressed, the tornado aggravated an already shaky situation. It did not turn teetotalers and social drinkers into drunks.

Some Xenians noted that a "live-for-today" attitude had taken hold of their community, and people who, on a Sunday, might normally have been cleaning out the garage or paying bills were spending the time with their children. Cart Hill had a German maid who, prior to the tornado, was frugality personified: each week she set aside a portion of her earnings for a trip back to Germany. Now she stopped saving, reasoning, "Better to take advantage of each day as it comes." People who had once been avid collectors now lost their taste for acquiring. Pack rats and connoisseurs both unloaded much of what they still owned after the storm.

Some men, like Bob Stewart and Jack Jordan, insisted that it hadn't altered them at all, and, to all outward appearances, it hadn't.

At the very least, Dr. Miller would say, the experience of a tornado would have to diminish one's normal arrogance and make him more compassionate. "We all have illusions we can *handle* anything. A lot of people go through their lives and never understand a feeling of helplessness. Now there's nobody in Xenia who doesn't understand that." Dr. Titchener would go further, and say that while he would have to see a given individual to make a valid assessment, he believed anyone who underwent a natural calamity could benefit from some kind of mild therapy. Indeed, psychologists and psychiatrists presented so many possibilities—depression from suffering too much, guilt from not suffering enough; immediate shock, delayed anxiety; hopelessness in the face of the devastation, despair at being relocated—that one wonders how anyone got off scot-free. Probably they reacted as Jackie Hupman did when a woman psychologist from Dayton advised her to seek some therapy—"I will when I have time!"

The advice had come unsolicited. Jackie was talking to the woman, a friend, some weeks after the storm, and her grief over the loss of her house must have been apparent. "People become aware of how attached they are to their possessions," the counselors were saying, "yet they can't grieve openly the way that a man who lost his daughter might. What comes to the fore is a very materialistic culture where you're attached to things but don't think you should be. You're in a double bind. So we give them permission to grieve."

But Jackie didn't need permission. The house was gone, and she was as sorry as she could be about it, and she didn't mind telling anybody who cared to listen. She did not, even when she had the time, seek therapy. Her immediate instincts were to make good the loss as quickly as possible, and to that end she began driving all over Greene County to try to find a house. When she saw a place she liked—usually an old farmhouse that promised a fine interior —she told her real estate agent, who then called the owner to see if he had any interest in selling. The search was fruitless. Then, toward the end of the summer, she became very excited about a house on North Galloway that was going up for auction. It had been appraised at $15,000, and though a lot had to be done with it, the basic frame was what she wanted. But the bidding stopped at $32,000, long after the Hupmans had to bow out. In desperation, she began poring through some old plan books of her father-in-law's—builders' texts from the early part of the century that showed several dozen standard models of the day. An Edwardian equivalent of Arrowhead, except that these houses were big and baroque, like "cottages" in Newport, and the most expensive of them could have been constructed, in 1910, for $6,000. In 1974 the cost was prohibitive.

Her salvation came quite by accident, while she was sitting one night with some friends in Amlin Heights. "Why don't you buy Bob Finlay's house and move it to your lot?" one of them asked. Finlay's was a chocolate-brown shingled affair on Market Street that had somehow been spared by the tornado but would not be spared by the urban-renewal projects being planned all around it. It would have to be razed, and Finlay had already bought a new place in Amlin Heights. "I just never thought of it," Jackie said later, but she sparked to the idea immediately, had Dick call Finlay the next morning, and call the city on Monday. No one had proposed anything like it, he was told, and he would probably have to deal with the contractors who would have salvage rights when it was torn down.

In that event, the city would buy the property from Finlay, and Dick would then buy it from the contractors. If all went well, he stood to get a substantial bargain, for salvage rights were seldom worth more than $4,000, and the cost of transplanting was only about $5,000. "Friends say it's fantastic inside, perfect, that it doesn't look like anyone's lived in it," said Jackie. "And it's got ten rooms; I don't know where they fit 'em all." One final touch that pleased her: Bob Finlay had grown up in her old house on King Street.

After the tornado, the Hupmans had lived for two or three weeks with a friend outside Xenia, then moved to a motel for a week. It was during this time that Gary Neff made his impulsive offer, which Jackie had refused. "I don't want your house, Gary," she said, but she was touched by his gesture. Then Dick's parents went to Michigan, making their house available for a month. In

"It made matchsticks out of them."

June, the family moved one last time, to Yellow Springs, to a five-room house with one bath. "Now I'm in a holding pattern," Jackie said in November. "The store's not definitely settled, the house is not definitely under way. Dick said to me not long ago, 'You're just getting super-hyper.' And I guess he's right, because I'm not getting anything done. I used to get up in the morning and make a list of what I had to do. By noon I'd be working on some project. Now it just doesn't happen. I guess it's because I'm not in my own home, or even my own town. It's like there's no incentive to get things done."

By the middle of November, however, Jackie had a whole new perspective on the loss that had weighed so heavily six months before. "It's like any loss; it's gradually going away. I have to stop and think now what it looked like. Much as I hated losing it, still, all it was was wood and concrete and plaster." In other ways, though, the tornado had left her unsettled and restless, different from her old self. For a long time she had nightmares in which she'd hear the roar, see things flying away, and feel herself floating on top of the wind. Then, sometime during the middle of the summer, she went through a period of resenting the children's presence. "I discussed it with Dick and he felt it too. I suppose it's just a rejection of responsibility, but sometimes he'd get home and after a while just say, 'All right, everyone to bed.' "

With November drawing to a close, Jackie was dreading the holiday season. Christmas was sure to be a letdown. She remembered the boxes of ornaments for the tree they'd had in the old house, one box for each child which was filled with the ornaments he or she had been given annually. She remembered the big round wooden table that had stood in the pantry, large enough to hold all the ingredients for the homemade candies and cookies she produced every year. Now it was stored in the basement. Last December she had made twenty pounds of peanut brittle, and who knew how much divinity and sour-cream fudge. This year, in a kitchen that wasn't much bigger than that round table, she wondered.

Yet despite the scarcity of people seeking psychological help, there were many greatly disturbed. And, of all the people affected by the tornado, perhaps Xenia's children were hardest hit. For weeks they had nightmares, or were afraid to leave their families, and some were physically sick. Psychologists emphasized that children would need special attention, because they might not have the opportunity adults had to "talk it out." They would have to be allowed to recall in full what had happened, and if, for a time, they seemed to have bizarre whims, these would have to be indulged. The storm left its mark on children of all ages (high schoolers became shaky in the tornado drills instituted that spring, and some, who had never tried drugs, tried them now), but on younger children its imprint was searing. Perhaps no one could testify to that better than Mrs. Gertrude Beam, lead teacher in the Nazarene Kiddie Kollege on West Second Street.

Mrs. Beam's "kollege"—really a day-care center for children between the ages of two and five—had been in session at the time of the tornado. The children had finished their naps, but there was still more than an hour before their mothers would pick them up. Mrs. Beam knew about the warnings but, like so many others, she paid no attention. A visitor that afternoon, the husband of one of her teachers, told her that if a funnel should be sighted, she should march the kids into the hall and tell them to lie down. At 4:30 he left the building, only to spot the approaching cloud, and he ran back in shouting. Mrs. Beam sounded the fire drill, in response to which the children lined up, and she took them to the basement. There she was met by more classes, under the care of a young teacher named Peggy Shaw, who thought she smelled smoke. Mrs. Beam had just time to tell her that it wasn't a fire, but a tornado, when the bricks started falling upstairs. A light fell down from the ceiling and a glass door shattered.

"What happened, teacher?" the children started to ask.

"It's the wind, a big wind like we've never had before," Mrs. Beam responded. "But you're all right. God's taking care of you." When it was over, she let them go upstairs and look around, but with the second warning they returned to the basement. There were between sixty and seventy-five in all, yet only a few cried in the dank, candlelit corridor. Because of the trouble parents had getting to them, some were there until ten o'clock that night.

When school reconvened, five days later, the children could talk about nothing else. Their drawings depicted ominous black funnels with chairs and cars strewn about the sky. Their only game was "tornado," a macabre performance in which one would listen to an imaginary radio and shout, "It's coming, it's coming," and the rest would hover in the corner. Then they would act out scenes of the wounded being lifted into ambulances and taken to the hospital. Psychologists said to let them play, but to teacher Ellen Allen, "It was so terrifying that I would look as long as I could, then break it up and say, 'Let's play something else.'" The sound of a bell, any bell, caused certain panic, and yet, because they had been relocated in a new building, fire drills were mandatory. Late in May, a Cincinnati photographer came to Xenia to shoot some pictures for a health magazine and the Kiddie Kollege held an impromptu drill for him. His pictures show five-year-olds cover-

152

ing their ears, clutching their teachers and sobbing.

Mrs. Beam, and most of the rest of the staff, were on tranquilizers. They too started at the sound of a bell—even in church—and Mrs. Beam alerted them whenever a fire drill was going to occur, contrary to state regulations, which required alarms to be sounded without prior warning. Somebody always stayed with Peggy Shaw during a drill, or even when the sky was threatening. For weeks these women dealt with youngsters who insisted on listening to weather reports in the morning, who forgot many of the things they had learned before April, and who shivered at every trek to the basement. The worst of it began to subside only as the weather outside improved, and their minds fastened onto other things. "Tornado" was played only on the darkest days and drawings portrayed happier scenes.

Yet some of it, thought Gertrude Beam, would never disappear. Her fear, their fear, of blackening skies, doors banging suddenly, and alarms ringing seemed permanently rooted. In July she took her five-year-old son, Scott, to shop in Shillito's, a large Cincinnati department store. In the middle of the first floor, surrounded by racks of pocketbooks and lingerie, with the mezzanine levels rising all around, she was suddenly afraid. It was too open, too vulnerable. What would she do if something happened? "Come on, Scott," she said. "Let's go to the basement. Things are cheaper there."

"Yes," agreed the child. "That'd be a good place to be if a tornado hit."

The reaction was not isolated and was not limited to women and children. Irrational dread haunted most Xenians who had experienced the tornado, and it would not loosen its grip even after months had passed. Let the skies cloud over, or the wind begin to rustle the treetops, and it was as though an electric current were rippling through the city. Jackie Hupman's heart started to pound and Bob Stewart glanced involuntarily out the window. No one talked much about it, and usually you couldn't see it, but it was there all the same.

To outsiders, never having experienced what Xenians had, this lingering dread was one of the most baffling—and conspicuous—

aspects of the disaster. They were a little bit humbled in the face of it. The psychiatrists expected it to last for a good long time, maybe as much as two years, but finally to fade. As Roy Miller said, "It's a decaying kind of fear because there is no reinforcing mechanism. Extraction takes place when the expected doesn't occur." Nonetheless, it was the most easily perceived and commonly shared of the tornado's psychological ravages. It was an early sign that people were going to need substantial help in coping with their own recoveries, and it was still a sign, eight months later, that the tornado was far from finished with them.

Robert Huck, pastor of the Xenia First United Presbyterian Church, had also anticipated the trauma. He was aware almost immediately that some sort of agency would have to emerge to deal with the physical, financial, and emotional problems of the townspeople on a *long-term* basis. The Red Cross would stop cooking food, the Mennonites would stop cleaning up, and HUD would stop paying rent, and then what would happen? Within days after the storm, he was receiving offers of help from other churches and donations from many sources, yet he had no place to channel any of them.

A week went by and he hardly had time to plan from one minute to the next. His own church, a white frame and stone structure on Market Street, one quarter of a block east of the tornado's path, had received only minimal damage, but nine other churches in town had been totally destroyed. One was the Second United Presbyterian, so that, among other things, Huck had to prepare to take in a second congregation. With Palm Sunday days away, and people more than ever in need of the comfort of worship, he was spending countless hours a day cleaning up, and he was doing double time on his job. "Our help is in the name of the Lord, who made the Heaven and Earth. Go forth into the world in peace, be of good courage, render to man good for evil," he told his listeners on Sunday. But sometime the next week, when he finally got a moment, he called a meeting of the Xenia Association of Churches, of which he was president, and proposed that together they try to do something for the future. It was a modest

154

gesture, but more than anything else yet tried, it launched the psychological recovery of the city.

"The tornado scattered everybody, but it brought them together in terms of spiritual identification," he said. "Its effect on the religious community was great as far as focusing on one goal irrespective of background: Baptists, Pentecostals, Episcopalians, Catholics, Lutherans, Presbyterians." (Xenia's Jewish families could be counted on the fingers of one hand.) Huck's meeting was intended to consist of Xenia clergymen only, but he saw to his dismay that it was quickly invaded by their counterparts in Dayton, the Metropolitan Churches United, and by a large contingent from the Dayton Mental Health Center, each of whom had his own ideas on how the disaster should be handled.

"You talk about emotional responses," Huck said later. "There were people tearing up the Red Cross, knocking the government, and telling us what to do. We were uptight because we very soon got the feeling that the Dayton people were trying to take over. They had the funding, the administrative structure, and the personnel." But that was the last thing Huck or any of the locals wanted. He caucused with three of his own people, came back, and asked all but the Xenia clergy to leave, and then began to plan in earnest. Out of those deliberations, the Xenia-area Inter-Faith Council was born.

Inter-Faith was an idea whose time had come at Wilkes-Barre. It was a collection of churches in that flood-ravaged community which combined to handle the physical and psychic needs of the townspeople and had been incorporated by the state so that it could legally distribute the cash donations that flowed in from all over the country. Now, with the assistance of Bob Hallett, director of Inter-Faith in Wilkes-Barre, the program was duplicated in Xenia. On Tuesday, April 16, Huck, Hallett, and a few other leading clergymen met with lawyers to draw up the articles of incorporation. Within four weeks—record time—the state had approved them, and the fledgling organization became official. Very quickly it vindicated the zeal of its promoters.

Inter-Faith picked up where other agencies left off and, perhaps surprisingly, helped in ways that some of the others couldn't. It went to bat for the girl who had lost her job at the hotel, the man who was injured and couldn't return to work, the family who was relocated, but suddenly had to pay $50 to $100 more rent per month than they had before. (HUD guidelines indicated that a person could use up to one-fourth of his net income for housing. Many families, especially large ones, had never used nearly that much.) Then, too, there were 1,400 families in Xenia who never sought help from HUD. "Some people didn't want to take help from the outside agencies," Huck explained later. "These were the independents, the kind who want to gut it out on their own and not ask for support." But they had to get help from somewhere. Inter-Faith was their safety valve.

The heart of the council was its "advocates," including trained social/church workers, former teachers, Dayton Junior Leaguers, and some hired recruits. Armed with lists of victims from HUD and Red Cross, they went out into the community looking for people to help (they even called apartment complexes where Xenians were relocated), or they interviewed whoever came to their headquarters in the basement of WGIC. For each new client advocates developed a "need card," detailing every kind of problem they could spot, and then set about resolving them. They would see mortgage companies for people who needed loan relief, delegate Mennonites to people unable to clean up their own yards, and find furniture for relocated families. Or, if the case seemed to warrant it, they would simply listen. Thus they became armchair experts on the psychological fallout of the April tornado.

"We learned very quickly that you can't talk to a person about his psychological needs until his physical needs are taken care of first," said advocate Maxine Scuba. "So many times a person would come in looking depressed—then we'd get them the refrigerator or whatever, and much of the problem would clear right up. The most visibly affected are men in their early or late fifties, approaching retirement. They put all their love into a home and family, then would look back and say 'What have I been doing?' I've seen it time and time again. This is November, and I know one man who has not been to work since the storm. A man goes through six months of getting his family back together and his way of collapsing is a heart attack. There have been so many heart attacks, accidents, and cases of diabetes since May, all supposedly nonrelated medical problems."

Over and over, Huck would encounter people so distraught by the magnitude of what had happened to them that they were unable to cope with the day-to-day trivia of living. "We find a lot of people who are incapacitated to the point where they find it difficult to call the phone company or Dayton Power and Light. They'd muddle through for three and four months without the service. So we'd do it for them." A college professor who had just moved his family to Xenia had lost a son and seen three other family members hospitalized: the man couldn't even think about getting new clothes. So Inter-Faith thought for him.

Much later, Robert Huck reflected that it was this ability of Inter-Faith to offer physical as well as emotional solace that was the key to its success. The doctors who came to Xenia immediately after the tornado offered only emotional counseling. But even if that's what a victim needed, it was not what was uppermost in his mind. "We discovered that by giving assistance in a financial and physical way, we were also helping in an emotional way," said Huck. "Everyone was so busy picking up the garbage in his yard that he didn't have time to straighten out the garbage in his mind." Inter-Faith became the repository for much of that excess.

By the middle of November, the Council had processed 3,500 need cards. It had collected $110,000 from the Tornado Relief Fund started by two local banks and a former mayor of Xenia. It picked up $600,000 from the Greene County Disaster Relief Fund, started by certain Dayton banks and churches. Of this, it had already distributed $350,000, usually in the form of cash grants. Requests went from advocates to the Inter-Faith staff to three board members who met twice a week, and were empowered to release up to $1,000 to a given individual. "The terrible process of distributing money," Huck called it. Yet it had to be worth it. The pastor's modest gesture had turned into a vehicle as important to the recovery of the city as HUD or the Corps of Engineers.

Easter Sunday came and went in windowless churches with

patches on the roofs. In a drizzly sunrise service at Randolph Park, nearly a hundred people crowded beneath an outdoor shelter, gazing at the preacher standing on the picnic table. The following Wednesday, April 17, the one-stop at Shawnee moved to the YMCA to make way for the reopening of school. Students from the damaged elementary schools doubled up with classes in the unharmed buildings. Junior High was transferred to schools in Fairborn, to attend classes from 3:00 to 8:00 P.M. (which meant that the *Gazette* had to start coming out in the early afternoon to maintain home delivery). Xenia Senior High met at the same odd hours, at the headquarters of its arch rival, Beavercreek, but there were signs all over the building to welcome them.

13

LONG AFTER the storm was over, and people's minds began to sort out all that had happened, the memories of the help they received remained vivid. Almost everyone had a favorite story. Ray Higgins liked to tell of the Saturday afternoon, three days after the twister, when he was heading uptown on foot and Janice asked him to get a loaf of bread. He trudged to the corner of Second and Detroit, and entered a converted storefront where the Salvation Army had set up headquarters.

"Have you got a loaf of bread I could have?" asked Ray.

"Sure do," replied the volunteer, pulling one out from his stacks of provisions.

"How much?" Ray asked.

"You don't have to pay me a thing," the man said. "Just go to church tomorrow and thank the Lord for it."

"I'd be more than willing, if only I could find a church to go to," Ray countered, chuckling at his own wit.

The story stuck, partly because it was evidence of Xenia's devastation, but mostly because it showed how ready, willing, and able most volunteer agencies were. Xenians simply could not believe how fast they arrived, how tirelessly they worked, and how well trained they were. Just the food they brought was a godsend. The tornado had knocked out almost every grocery store and restaurant in the city, as well as all the fast-food franchises—a loss most

159

urban planners would be happy to sustain, but hamburgers were conspicuously hard to come by in the months that followed. Then the aid poured in, and people talked endlessly about "how wonderful those Mennonites were," or how "I couldn't have made it without HUD." More than anything, they talked about the Red Cross: what it did right, what it did wrong, or what it didn't do at all. When all the returns were in, the consensus was that the Red Cross did a fine job indeed, but not without creating substantial resentments. The reasons were complex.

The Red Cross is America's largest charity, with an annual budget approaching $206 million, met entirely by voluntary contributions. From the government it takes not a cent, but it does operate under federal fiat, which sometimes leads to confusion.

The American Red Cross (modeled after the international organization of the same name) was founded in 1881 by Clara Barton as a relief agency for soldiers in battle. Twenty-four years later it was assigned two responsibilities by Congressional charter: to provide emergency relief and postemergency financial rehabilitation to victims of disaster (anything from a two-alarm fire to an earthquake), and to render special services to men in the armed forces. Among the latter would be the arrangement of military furloughs, social services to military families, and contacts with prisoners of war. Obviously, without government funding, the Red Cross was not legally obligated to abide by the charter. But it did, and does, simply because the charter conferred an official sanction that it would not otherwise have. It gives the Red Cross clout. And in Xenia, on the afternoon of the great tornado, clout was its greatest asset.

As Don Redenbo, director of disaster services for the Dayton chapter, put it, "In Xenia, both the Governor of Ohio and the Congressional Charter said that the Red Cross was the chief disaster agency. These things, combined with the experience of our volunteers, give us the confidence to do a good job. We're accused of throwing our weight around sometimes, and it's probably true. But I do think that's a matter of egotism and experience, of knowing what to do. In a flood, for example, our volunteers are trained to tell you not just that the water's high, but that you can see rooftops two hundred yards away. When they say it's bad, we know it's bad. In Xenia, we had volunteers who worked for forty-eight hours without stopping."

Almost literally from the moment of touchdown, the Red Cross was moving in fourth gear, organizing shelters, sending in food, tending to the wounded. Indeed, according to the mythology of disasters, it was doing everything it was supposed to do so fast and effectively that no one could say precisely what set it all in motion. The Dayton disaster canteen, equipped with a stove, sink, refrigerator, and enough food to feed a thousand people, was on its way to Xenia in minutes. Simultaneously, volunteers were phoned, blankets and cots requisitioned, food sources tapped. Within hours, the Red Cross had dozens of nurses, medics, and two-way radio teams—many of them the ones Dickson Burrows used—all struggling through the traffic and past the police barricades into Xenia. Five more mobile feeding vans, from Akron, Toledo, and Columbus, rolled in, and cafeterias were established in Cox, Shawnee, and the YMCA. By nightfall, approximately 2,400 were sheltered and food was available for anyone who cared to eat it.

And almost as quickly, friction erupted. People at the YMCA became irritated when a local Red Cross volunteer began ordering people around, insisting that his training be respected and his procedures adopted. His voice grew louder as his courtesy toward some of the Y's regular employees dimmed. Later, as other Red Cross employees saw what was happening, they agreed it was intolerable and the fellow was relieved. But the incident pointed up several things: he was only a volunteer; he was probably faced with more stress than he could handle, and he had suffered severe property losses of his own. The combination had proved too much. Under different circumstances, it would have been entirely forgivable. As it was, he was the lone local Red Cross representative and he left a sour taste in many mouths.

Afterward, Red Cross spokesmen pointed out that he might have tarnished their image, but he did nothing to slow the delivery of aid to the victims. And this was the paramount concern. Quarrels there might be . . . misunderstandings and even outbursts of temper. But the needs of the victims always came first. If only because the Red Cross is so big, with no rival in its ability to respond to all persons' immediate needs, it is vulnerable to more internal dissent and more outside criticism and guilty of more visible oversights than any other agency. But when the issues surfaced, they were always softened by the question: are the needs of the victims being met? The answer was always yes.

It was a madhouse, that first night, of radio communiqués, sandwiches in process, and people under pressure. Not for sixty-one years, since the Dayton flood of 1913, had the chapter handled a calamity of this scope. There had been smaller tornadoes, it is true, and plane crashes and explosions, but not even a dress rehearsal for a performance like this. Allen Johnson, thirty-eight years old and director of the Dayton Red Cross, had been through many crises, and he knew that first reports were either garbled or exaggerated or both. Accordingly, he was reluctant to believe what he was hearing about Xenia. He was up to his ears in administrative chores, none of his seasoned volunteers had reported back to him yet, and Redenbo was gone. Gone of all things, to a Red Cross disaster-directors' conference in Battle Creek to be brought up to date on new provisions in Public Law 91–606—the Disaster Relief Act of 1970. When Redenbo heard the news on his car radio, he spun 180 degrees and fairly flew back in the opposite direction through the dark, wet night to Dayton.

"I arrived at one thirty in the morning, saw that the place was in turmoil but doing what it was supposed to do, and I went directly to Johnson for a briefing. Since he hadn't been out of the office yet, he sent me at once to Xenia to look at the damage. I drove right out, not encountering too much traffic by then, but also I couldn't see much. Arrowhead was off to the right, blocked from view. So I came into town, and I was thinking that it wasn't too bad, and then I saw what had happened to Kroehler's, and on down West Main Street, and when I got to the railroad tracks, I . . . well, I put my head down on the steering wheel and started to cry." That's when the Red Cross first knew how bad it was.

Oddly, though, Redenbo had a difficult time transmitting his findings to chapter headquarters. It was not so much that Johnson wouldn't listen to him as that he had no way of grasping the enormity of what he was hearing. For three days at least, the chapter director did not leave his Dayton headquarters; hence he had no firsthand knowledge. As Red Cross workers from other parts of the state, and then the country, began to come in, they sensed this lack. "You could almost picture the Dayton staff in shock themselves," said one. "They had laid out lousy programs, contrary to national policy—like replacing unauthorized items—and they made the rest of our work very difficult for a couple of weeks. For some of the national people, it was frustrating as hell."

There was more to it than that, however. There was, in Dayton, the strong sense that local people were trying to keep this a local operation—almost as if that would be good for the chapter's prestige. The vibrations were subtle but inescapable. Dayton's head caseworker was detailed to Xenia, and Allen Johnson saw no reason why she wouldn't be adequate. The Dayton chapter appointed all workers with any directorial responsibility and made no effort to supplement them with more experienced national personnel. On the surface it was all as it should have been—the needs of the victims were being met. But still there was an edge.

Speaking about the experience several months later, Allen Johnson said, "In the past, when a disaster of this magnitude occurred, national experts would step in on the assumption that those of us who live here can't handle so much. This last time, however, I was literally in charge. And I think in the future they'll give authority to the local chapter. Most of our major and minor decisions were bounced off local figures—we tried to get the administration of the disaster in line with what the community wanted. Overall, I think the community was very satisfied." In many ways he spoke true. No doubt the community *was* very satisfied with the Red Cross's performance. And local officials indicate that their positive experience in Xenia has meant that in future disasters the Red Cross will place far more responsibility on its local chapters. But total local control is not likely, especially in light of what ultimately happened in Xenia.

By the Friday after the tornado, the Dayton chapter realized that the situation was worse than it had thought and asked that an "advisor" be sent in from national headquarters. On Saturday

Don Hannah arrived, and he assessed the situation brusquely: "There was a lack of awareness of just how technically involved a disaster operation is. If you're used to dealing with fires, and you're suddenly faced with five thousand homeless, it's just tougher. There are legal problems, long-range problems . . . you need technical people who have had a lot of experience with major disasters. Those first forty-eight hours we were meeting needs without having the kind of controls we normally exercise. Red Cross groups sometimes met needs as they saw them rather than going by the guidelines."

Hannah wasn't blaming anybody. He only knew that the Dayton chapter was swamped, unsure of how to handle some problems and unequipped to handle others. Instead of following Red Cross guidelines, some volunteers were granting more than they should—too much food and too many furnishings. It was a sympathetic reaction, but contrary to procedure and one of the first things Hannah set straight. At the same time, he sat down with Allen Johnson to explain the variety of problems facing them. In short order, Hannah brought in a national food man (to arrange provisions and oversee the distribution of meals), a national accountant (to coordinate records and supervise prompt payment of vouchers), a national supply man (to handle the hundreds of thousands of pounds of donations that had to be warehoused and distributed), and a national caseworker (to oversee the hundreds of varying situations that would inevitably arise). By Sunday P.M., the local operation had taken on a national flavor; by Tuesday he and Johnson were meeting with the Red Cross vice-president, Joseph Foley; the area manager, Truman Solverud; and the national director of disaster services, Enzo Bighinatti. There it was decided that Hannah would become a full-fledged director, with decision-making authority of his own. Though the Dayton chapter remained officially in charge, there were few illusions that it was doing the job alone.

As director, Hannah was to the Red Cross what Stewart was to the city—the final word on dozens of decisions that had to be made daily. When it was necessary to negotiate for continued use of the Y as Red Cross headquarters, Hannah was the man who did it. When two hundred policemen from all over Ohio suddenly arrived to help, Hannah arranged for a kitchen to feed them—in the county jail. When Red Cross volunteers were working too long and too hard, or staff people weren't getting paid, or shelter teams operated without support, Hannah set it straight. He could innovate, as he did when he designated volunteer psychologist Steve Wilson to help out with the emotional difficulties of caseworkers as well as victims. And he could irritate. At the fairgrounds, where the Red Cross was supplying a feeding station operated by some unaffiliated volunteers, Hannah told them it was going to lose those supplies if Red Cross identification were not properly displayed. Predictably, the volunteers were incensed, and refused. After some haggling, the station continued to operate and the Red Cross continued to support it, but it was one more instance of bad feelings all around.

Hannah's duties were as unglamorous as they were essential. All day he would move from shelter to shelter, if only to see that they were meeting government health standards, or go from Dayton headquarters to Xenia's City Hall, to iron out administrative hangups. He thrived on it, but at night he was exhausted. Back to Dayton he would go, to the Holiday Inn and its cocktail lounge, and there, until nearly midnight, he would swap stories about the day and about other disasters with the steady stream of fellow workers who straggled in. He would talk about the Truk Trust territories, in the South Pacific, where he had once gone to drop supplies to a native chieftain, but learned too late that the mailboat which had brought him there docked only once every six weeks. He talked about Vietnam, where soldiers had died in his lap, or Bangladesh, where he had seen stacked up the bodies of those who had died of starvation, and sometimes there were tears in his eyes, because he had seen so much.

In any disaster, the Red Cross program is designed to restore people, as nearly and as quickly as possible, to some sense of their former selves and dignity. Its primary concern is taking care of all emergency needs, including food, clothing, shelter, and medical care. It will provide a victim with groceries if they are available,

165

food vouchers if they are not. It will give him money for new clothes—$80 for garments, $15 for shoes—to be spent anywhere he wishes. It will supply basic furniture to all and special items to people with special needs. (In Xenia, one lady asked for two men's shirts size 16½ and an electric can opener. Reason: the day after the storm she had tripped on a branch and broken her arm. She needed the shirts to fit over the cast and the can opener because she was "tired of eating cookies and bananas." It seemed that two days after the storm a truck loaded with seven hundred cases of bananas came into town, and finding no place to unload, turned them over to the Red Cross. For days people were eating bananas. Now this lady wanted to open some canned food and she didn't have two hands to do it. The request was granted.) The Red Cross will not, however, supply rugs, color televisions, and the like, despite the strongest importunings of its clients. So steadfast is this rule that in the Deep South, in areas that flood often, some residents remove first those belongings that the Red Cross will not replace.

Finally, the Red Cross is empowered to find temporary lodging and pay rent for one month for all people whose homes are destroyed. This provision is vital in smaller disasters; in Xenia, where a national emergency was instantly declared, it became relatively less significant. Reason: HUD was on the spot almost immediately to find housing for the homeless. It would pay for temporary quarters for up to one year, and during that time, would assist them in making a permanent relocation.

Indeed, in the case of Xenia, the total impact of the Red Cross was substantially diminished because of the federal government's prompt response. In minor disasters, the Red Cross is the only large service organization present; even in most major disasters, it takes several days for the President to declare a national emergency. And unless and until he does, the Red Cross continues to be the primary dispenser of relief. In Xenia, with the government on the spot so quickly, there was some inevitable duplication of services. For example, the Department of Agriculture was offering food stamps while the Red Cross gave out food vouchers. Similarly, there were people who would have preferred one month's rent right away; instead, they had to make an application to HUD. "This way you see some people become completely dependent and some others completely independent," commented Bill Lentz, disaster director for the Cleveland chapter. Ultimately, for the immediate emergency services—the lost dentures, the shirtless child, the families without food—the Red Cross was as helpful in Xenia as it always is in a disaster. But for the long-term concerns —the casework and housing—the Red Cross saw its load lightened considerably. The government took over.

As any volunteer could attest, none of this work was easy. It involved a delicacy and dedication unsuspected by the layman, perhaps described best by Jean Blair, the national casework supervisor Don Hannah brought in from Pittsburgh: "If you're true Red Cross, you always have your bag packed. I arrived in Xenia the morning of the fifth and surveyed the damage by myself. The chapter had done exactly as the training manuals state with the shelters at Cox and the Y. I was trying to determine where family service would be. It requires a huge amount of space to house this center—a gym or auditorium. We like to keep our records together, and we need space for workers to interview victims in private. They may feel embarrassed, have various reactions to what has happened. Interviewing in a noisy room is extremely hard. They can't say what they feel if they're shouting; they must be comfortable. To do this work, you have to be very mature. You have to have a lot of intuition to understand what the needs of the community are, and most of all, what people individually need."

Not knowing any of this, but still eager to help in any way they can, most laymen respond to the emergency by traipsing to their attics. The result is a perennial headache for the Red Cross, vividly described by Frank Stipkala, the national public relations man brought in from Cleveland: "If there is one thing I would like to tell people sometimes, it is not to send us their second-hand clothes. We get so many offers of clothing really not fit to be used . . . when people suffer and are humiliated, they need their dignity restored. A guy who likes conservative clothes shouldn't have to wear somebody's two-year-old plaids. That's why we give people the money to buy what they want. If you really want to be helpful, take your four best suits out of the closet, or send money."

It was a point the Red Cross tried to make over and over in a subtle way, and always without success. Not only were the used clothes inappropriate to the needs of the victims, they had to be cleaned, sorted, sized, and stored. All of which took time and people. Some donors even asked the post office to verify the arrival of their package! But just let one letter appear in the local papers (as one letter did) suggesting that no more clothes were needed, and a thousand condemnations would come down: "The Red Cross doesn't want our help. The Red Cross doesn't need support." The same held for used appliances. One day Stipkala got a shipment of sixteen damaged washing machines, all donated. "Not one you could have used," he said. "People feel there's some wand you wave and these things come together." They were nothing but trouble. The same philosophy even applied to people, to the dozens of wide-eyed ingenues who walked in the Red Cross doors and asked what they could do. "Where were they when we were training volunteers?" cried an exasperated Redenbo. "What *can* they do?" In fact, the Red Cross trained numerous people on the job, for casework, for clerking, for aid in the shelters. But there were many more jobs that first-timers could not handle. The level of their commitment would have to be tested during the next recruitment campaign.

At the height of its Xenia operations, the Red Cross was serving some fourteen thousand meals a day—as many as three thousand in a given shelter—and was utilizing over three thousand volunteers. Food was good; the typical breakfast included bread, butter and jelly, sausages, scrambled eggs, and half a grapefruit. Entertainers from Dayton provided diversion; nurses were available to watch children while parents were occupied; on Easter, the Red Cross organized an Easter Egg hunt (lightly attended due to a tornado alert) and for weeks afterward was distributing the jelly beans and baskets of chocolate eggs it had solicited from all over the state. Inevitably, there were some victims who didn't want to leave the shelters at all (a fact in any disaster), but the day had to come, as it did on Tuesday, April 16, when the last three

168

families left Cox School. It had been, in Frank Stipkala's estimation, an extraordinarily successful program; maybe the classic example of seeing that the needs of the victims were being met. As PR man, Frank had spent the better part of two weeks recording interviews with refugees in shelters. He noted what they were eating, commented on their physical appearance, and talked to the staffs that served them. Later, he transcribed the tapes for news releases or handed them over directly to the radio stations. Innocent enough on the surface, but it irritated a lot of Xenians.

To them, it sometimes seemed that the Red Cross was at least as interested in promoting itself as it was in helping them. Besides Stipkala, they watched Red Cross workers all over the city attach Red Cross flags to every available window space, the halls of every shelter, telephone poles, and (as the Dayton chapter's final report said) "anything else left standing." As one businessman said anonymously, "The Red Cross was under tremendous criticism because they have the world's worst PR. The day after the tornado the Salvation Army came in and the Red Cross man at the YMCA said 'Get out—this disaster belongs to the Red Cross.' It seemed to me they go out of their way to create a bad image of themselves. They spend their life patting themselves on the back and play down the efforts of other people. The Red Cross did a fantastic job, but so did everyone else. You read the Red Cross releases and you wouldn't know anyone else was in town."

Why do it at all? If the PR efforts offend so many people, why keep them up? According to Bill Lentz, the answer is twofold. First, people respond to the symbol—they see the Red Cross and know there is help inside. That alone is a good reason. The second is more subtle. The Red Cross exists primarily upon what its fund raisers can drum up every fall. If people aren't strongly reminded of the good works it has been doing, said Lentz, they're inclined to say, "Why give?" The Stipkalian techniques and the identification ad nauseam are their answers. Even so, it's unlikely that everything would come up roses for the Red Cross under any circumstances. The plain fact is a lot of people just don't like it.

Either they still bear a grudge from World War II days, when the Red Cross charged them for coffee and donuts (not by choice;

the government asked it to), or they are put off by the alleged pushiness of the Red Cross in a disaster area. The trouble at the Y and Hannah's insistence at the fairgrounds were two good examples. By the same token, the organization suffers the potshots of smaller agencies who resent its federal mandate. These are not the agencies, Lentz stresses, like the Mennonites and the Salvation Army, who are fully skilled and stand on their own, but the fly-by-nighters who rise up and raise money, all in the name of helping their fellowman, then wither almost as fast. "There's money in disaster work," Lentz says with a pause. Then he cites the incident, in Xenia, of one group handing out $10 bills on the street. The media covered it thoroughly, and it was Lentz's educated guess that the agency in question did nothing but hand out those $10 bills, and that 90 percent of its expenses were administrative. It irked him that those were the people who got the coverage. At least Frank Stipkala would interview representatives of other service organizations to paint a complete picture of the disaster. He wondered if they would be as honest.

The last straw was Harry Reasoner's report for ABC television. It was an hour-long special aired in May, and Stipkala had bent over backward to be helpful to the camera crews. He had gotten them into shelters, arranged interviews, all "to give them what we thought would be a fair approach to the storm. So about halfway through the program he shows one little lady muttering imprecations about the Red Cross. And that was all. He never identified her, and left the whole impression of the Red Cross not doing a particularly good job. All based on what one person said." Stipkala felt it was particularly demoralizing for the volunteers who had taken two to three weeks off from work to help in Xenia. Why, for God's sake, did they always have to pick on the Red Cross?

14

AT SIXTY-TWO, with white hair, a youthful face, and eyes that flash behind dark-rimmed glasses, Eli Nissley is a fascinating figure. He can pound a hammer as effectively as he can organize men, and in Xenia he did both. Short and plainly dressed, sitting in a makeshift office under the grandstand of the Greene County Fairgrounds, he wasted little time on things unrelated to the matter at hand. Yet it was hard to say he was a typical Mennonite.

Of all the odd and impromptu groups that come into a disaster, the Mennonites may be the most disparate. In the United States there are between fifty and seventy thousand of them. They come in about twenty-five different "flavors," as Nissley likes to say, ranging from the dour Amish in their black broad-brimmed hats and zipperless overalls to modern chaps who look just like everybody else. But they're all fired by one purpose, to help their suffering fellowman, and that Nissley expresses best: "My whole life I've tried to pattern myself after Jesus Christ. Our motivation is for a testing; we are concerned, we are told very plainly in the Bible that he who doesn't love doesn't know God. I've found this to be a very true experience. If a man sees another man in need, and 'shutteth up the bowels of compassion'; how can the love of God dwell in a man like this?" Under these guidelines the Mennonite Disaster Service (MDS) was organized in 1950, to aid recovery from a tornado in Kansas. Mennonites are present in almost any disaster setting, and inevitably, they are the most cherished volunteers there. They seek no publicity and work tirelessly until their job is done. "Just a Mennonite's word is worth more than a contract with anybody else," said one Xenia official.

When the Xenia tornado struck, Nelson Hostetter, chairman of MDS in Akron, Pennsylvania, called Leo Yoder, his coordinator for Western Ohio, and asked him to go to Xenia to see what could be done. Yoder left the next day, with other leaders of the Western Ohio division, to survey the damage. Friday he called Nissley.

"Eli, can you come to Xenia and help us out?"

"Leo, I want to. But first I must ask my son; I have promised to help him on his farm for two months."

As Nissley explained later, a promise is a promise, whether to one's son or one's God. Before he could agree to anything—even rescue work in Xenia—he had to secure a release from that promise. It was readily given, and that afternoon he drove south to meet with Yoder.

They set up at Cox School, committed themselves for a minimum of six weeks, and decided to direct all their initial efforts toward cleanup. Woodlawn Cemetery, Xenia's largest burying ground, was waist deep in upended trees and branches—so much so that many of the gravesites were indistinguishable. The Mennonites made this their first target, then turned to the scores of homesites where, for one reason or another, individuals were unable to cope. (The Red Cross had no reserves for manual labor, and the Corps of Engineers was removing only the debris that endangered public safety.)

Traditionally, however, Mennonites confine themselves to specific kinds of victims: the uninsured, the underinsured, and those unable to help themselves—the aged, for example. They find their clients by combing the damaged areas, or by referrals, or by word of mouth. In Xenia, they no sooner set up shop than they were besieged with requests, many of which they had to turn down. "You have to weed out," cautioned Leo Yoder, "because even people who are well to do will ask for the free help. You have to ask a lot of frank questions. Do you have insurance? What is your financial status? Do you have a job? Social Security?" Many was

172

the time, said Yoder, when he would interview a prospective client and watch him squirm at the interrogation. Once, he was confronted by a lady with a broken front stoop. The house was well out of the tornado's path and the damage was on the northeast side, but she insisted it was storm-induced. Yoder respectfully declined the job.

As it happens, a substantial number of Mennonites are carpenters, or at least skilled with their hands. A substantial number also live in small towns or rural townships, consistent with the simple life their people have pursued ever since an ideological split with the Anabaptists at the time of the Protestant Reformation. Each evening, at the close of work, Nissley would review the upcoming jobs, then get on the telephone to Leo Yoder, who had returned to his own home in Archbold, Ohio, just outside Toledo. Yoder would hear him out, then, from 6 P.M. to 11 P.M., call these small towns all over Ohio for volunteers to help Nissley the next day. He was never refused. His people left their jobs willingly, and they offered money just as readily. "You make a plea in the church and it just pours in," said Yoder. "It's a matter of seeing your brother in need. When we wanted to buy a trailer and truck with a two-way radio, we made a plea in the churches and raised ten thousand dollars in only a few weeks."

Under this system, Nissley had a different crew almost every day, numbering between twenty-five and fifty. At first it was difficult to disperse them, with no street signs and no addresses, but they became a common sight—particularly the Amish, with their long beards and distinctive dress. "It's an application of nonconformity to the world," Nissley would explain. "The Bible says, 'Be not conformed to the world but transformed by the renewing of your mind.' " The Amish women, in their close-fitting white bonnets and long, plain dresses, reinforced the image. Xenia was the first disaster where Mennonite women had been involved to any degree, but they were needed in the shelter cafeterias and at the hospital, and Nissley thought they were a great addition. They helped too with the distribution of food and clothing. Nissley tells the story of one such worker who was alone in an upstairs room when those below her suddenly heard a series of shrieks, a distinct cry of "A finger, a finger!," then silence. Rushing upstairs, they found their comrade fainted on the floor and sure enough, lodged somewhere in the woodwork, a human finger blown in with the wind.

The Mennonites were everywhere, and stories of their good works abounded. For one farmer, they cleaned a sixty-acre field in a day; the job would have taken him weeks. For one divorcée, they rebuilt a house. "I'd gotten to the point where I was going to give up," she said. "When you called, it was like a wave sent out of heaven." For Rosemary Ray, a black widowed lady on North Columbus, they rebuilt a home and business in one. Rosemary ran a day-care center and she had only enough insurance to buy the materials.

The Mennonites, in sum, did the jobs no other agency was equipped and/or willing to do. They eased the anguish of countless victims who had no other support and, more than likely, they kept some homeowners in Xenia who might not have stayed otherwise. Consider Clara Swartz, a seventy-four-year-old widow whose house sustained major roof and structural damage. In the aftermath of the storm, she hired a "contractor" from West Virginia to do the work. He started, then said he would need money to continue. Since she had her insurance, she gave it to him. The work progressed, but Mrs. Swartz noticed that it was exceedingly shoddy. Complaining to the foreman, she elicited another request for money in order to set things right. When she refused, he quit the job and left town, which confirmed a growing suspicion that he was one of the many fraudulent builders who descend on stricken towns like Xenia, grab off some cash, and run. But Mrs. Swartz called the Inter-Faith Council, and they called the Mennonites. In October, Leo Yoder was back in Xenia repairing her house.

The largest part of their work was finished much sooner, however. The Mennonites worked six days a week, and most effectively on Saturday because their children joined them. But never on Sunday. At night, they either returned to their farms, or, if they were staying over, they went to the Kennedy Avenue Methodist

Church in Dayton and slept on cots. It was a grueling and gratifying experience, sustained until well into the summer when most of the calls proved to be petty and they felt truly released from their promise to Xenia.

15

FOR HUD it would take longer. Maybe as long as two years. HUD was the big one, the agency in charge of housing approximately five thousand homeless people, and, as Phil McIntire said, "It's godawful complicated. . . . This is the operation that will make or break the success of the disaster program." But big operations were nothing new for HUD. Founded in 1965, after a five-year effort to push it through on the parts of Presidents Kennedy and Johnson, to provide safe and sanitary housing for every American, HUD became the eleventh U.S. executive department. Since then, it has been responsible for any number of urban renewal, rehabilitation, and community development programs, including public housing, subsidized housing, and subsidized leasing. Especially through its FHA-insured loans to individuals unable to obtain financing without insurance, it has made homeowners of low- and middle-income families who formerly had no hope of ownership. In the process, it has also left some sections of America's inner cities rotting and abandoned, primarily because the residents were not able to maintain the dwellings it rehabilitated. In this regard, some critics might say that HUD has created more than a few urban disasters all by itself. Nevertheless, among its recondite responsibilities is the handling of all housing for federally declared disaster areas, and in that it has succeeded quite handsomely. Certainly it did in Xenia.

176

"The system was perfect from the beginning," said Charlie Betterton in retrospect. "It was the first time a disaster office has ever gotten into operation that fast, but our people were ready for the victims and they knocked 'em out like clockwork. The first day we housed thirty-six families and by the fourth we had built up to a hundred."

Like everyone else in Xenia, Betterton was working under intense pressure, and that meant juggling superiors, subordinates, and disaster victims all at once. Arriving at 9 A.M. on the Saturday after the tornado, he pored over aerial maps of the damage and promptly realized he would need four to five times as many personnel as had been allocated—no easy chore on the federal payroll. He was allowed to hire all the local recruits he wanted (HUD retains no volunteers), but no more experienced HUD personnel. So Betterton did the only thing he could. He called a number of his former colleagues in St. Louis and Kansas City—"everybody I ever worked with," in fact—and asked them to come to Xenia to help out. Once there, he could take them on as local recruits, in accordance with departmental policy. And, as he suspected, the ploy was successful. Betterton was able to convince a total of sixteen experienced workers to come to Xenia—enough to double his original staff. He then used them to train the real locals.

All of whom he needed badly: "On Sunday morning, myself and twenty others arrived at the assistance center at Shawnee School. Such a massive volume of people I've never seen. There must have been two hundred and fifty of them, all done with the other booths and waiting to see HUD. So I gave 'em numbers, told 'em to line up, and we all began taking applications." It looked like a busy bakery on a Saturday morning, except that it lasted for three days. Not only did it take up Betterton's time, it sopped up his "damage survey" and "existing resource" people—all of whom should have been out verifying damage claims and scouting potential housing. "When I wasn't helping out with the victims, I was on the phone arranging personnel, equipment, and vehicles," he recalled. "It used to be that GSA cars were retired after sixty to seventy thousand miles; now they drive 'em until they fall apart. It seems we were getting a lot of the ones that were falling apart."

By Tuesday night, six days after the tornado, Betterton had enough reports of existing housing to feel he could begin processing applications. But he had no phones to call the victims, and his placement was not geared up. No matter. The wunderkind declared that the HUD center would open on Thursday, come what may, and he set about arranging it. He drew up a release for the local media saying that if you had made application to HUD on Sunday or Monday, you should come in for placement on Thursday. Meanwhile, he got back to Ohio Bell, who had promised him thirty phone lines by Wednesday. So far he had only six. A quick plea to Steinlauf, and by the following Monday he had all thirty. His government furniture hadn't arrived yet so he set up tables. He didn't have enough GSA vehicles so he rented what he needed. All day Wednesday he worked to develop the traffic flow in HUD's spacious new center. It had to be able to move like a rapids, because he had projected to his superiors that he would have 250 families housed by Sunday. They had laughed.

As it happened, Betterton fell thirty families short of his projection, but even so the achievement was unparalleled. At the peak of its operations, the HUD office employed 104 people and continued to house several dozen families a day. Sitting in a small office in the rear of the main room, surrounded by graphs showing weeks elapsed and families processed, Betterton was like the distant captain of a large ocean vessel. Outside, the atmosphere was electric. Phones ringing, people jumping up and down, a sign that said "HOUZ 'EM," lines of gray desks with pallid victims talking earnestly across them.

Most of the housing advisors were young, as though drawn from a campus rally, and they were idealistic. Like Peter Stillwell, an ersatz songwriter from upstate New York who had seen films of Xenia on television, put his wife in the car, and driven out. Or Ellen Hart, a late-night waitress at Nick's Lounge on North Detroit. Tired of her routine, she had gone to the Red Cross to help, and raised her hand quickly when a voice asked, "Does anybody want to work long, hard hours?" She didn't even know what the job was.

Indeed the hours were long and hard. Said Ellen: "I'd get here at seven-fifteen A.M. and wouldn't get home until ten one night, twelve the next. It was mass confusion. But you'd watch people come in the door, see tears, hugs, everybody telling stories, and you really didn't realize how hard the hours were till you woke up and it hit you." Said Peter: "There is a terrific mental strain dealing with people who have been through a traumatic experience. They have to talk, talk, talk. The result is, it's taxing; but we eat it up. They even had a counseling room for employees where you could go to talk if you were down and depressed. No one used it."

The filing process was essentially the same for all victims. In they would come, to the one-stop or HUD headquarters, and make preliminary application. With that, a site inspector would go out to their former home, to make sure they were telling it like it was. At the same time, HUD's housing inspectors were out scouring Greene and Montgomery counties for temporary places to relocate their clients, which sometimes took a little hustling. "Look," they would have to say, "Xenia is a disaster area, and these people need housing now." Even under crisis circumstances, some landlords reserved their right to be skeptical. Once the applicants were okayed and the apartments located, HUD housing advisors like Stillwell and Hart started to match them up. They were authorized to pay the victim's rent up to three months (assuming he had no insurance) and, after that, on a month-to-month basis up to one year. During that time, HUD would help the victim relocate permanently.

Ken Shields was one of the hundreds who lined up at HUD those first weeks. He filed first at the one-stop center, then came back the next day to the new HUD headquarters. "Where would you like to relocate temporarily?" he was asked. "If you want Xenia, you'll have to wait a while because there isn't much. If you want to go out and look on your own, call us and we'll inspect whatever you find." Ken did just that, and within a day or two he'd located the Dayton Victory Housing apartments on Shroyer Road, in Kettering. Built during the Second World War, they offered the closets and cupboards that newer apartments with swimming pools often lacked—and three bedrooms besides. All for $185 a month.

He called HUD; a man came out the next day and signed him up. Less than fifteen days after the tornado he was relocated. Three months later he had found a new house in Kettering, similar to the one he'd had in Windsor Park but older, and called the HUD people back to say he was going to move. They were surprised—usually people didn't find permanent housing so fast—but Ken was near the Shroyer Road Baptist Church, which he loved, and this was what he wanted. Even in Xenia he had talked about moving to Kettering. So the papers were processed, the bags were packed, and once more the Shields family picked up and moved. When it was all over, Ken and Pam felt they were particularly lucky. Not only were they located where they had always wanted to be, they were more secure than they had ever been.

From the Red Cross they had received $430 in clothing vouchers, which had afforded them a very happy day at the Dayton Mall. They had received several bags of groceries as well as $78 worth of food vouchers, which they asked permission to use for meat only . . . because the Department of Agriculture had given them free food stamps for a month. They received $250 in wages for the days he was kept away from work, from Ken's employer, the Hobart Manufacturing Co., and $300 from a collection contributed by fellow employees. From her relatives, Pam Shields received enough used furniture to get the new house under way. From the ladies' auxiliary at Shroyer Road Baptist she received bedding, brooms, and kitchen utensils, many of the same things, in fact, that she got in the HUD "living kit" that was distributed to all disaster victims. For her new appliances she took advantage of the deal Frigidaire was offering to all tornado victims. From the insurance company they received a check for $22,000—a year previously Ken had increased his coverage to the full value of the house; he had bought it for $18,500. They also received $4,000 for the sale of their land in Windsor Park—meaning a net profit of $7,500. The Shieldses had boxes of extra bedding on their second floor and money in the bank. They had never been better off.

The Shieldses' own foresight, plus the generosity of those

The wreckage of the new McDonald's on West Main Street

around them, left them in good shape. But there were those who tried to take illicit advantage of federal largesse, and that's why Dave Meade was in Xenia. As he put it, "Disasters are the best time in the world for rip-off artists to rip off the government. If a person isn't sharp enough to do that, he ought to be locked in a mental institution. When you're taking two hundred and fifty applications a day, you can't check each one thoroughly. And I would like to make one further comment: It wasn't blacks, it was whites."

Meade was a specialist in trouble—people who tried to cheat HUD or were having unusual difficulty getting their needs met. He knew all the underhanded techniques used to get larger apartments than people were entitled to, or smaller ones so that they could keep the difference in rent, or to double up and split the extra payment, or to get HUD to pick up some of their rent prior to the disaster. One woman in Xenia rented a furnished apartment, then learned that in HUD's "furniture kits" she could get furniture from the government. She therefore asked the landlord to remove his things and put in a request for the HUD kit. ("It was very rude of her," said Peter Stillwell.) Meade was also irked with the teenagers who tried to use the storm as a means of getting away from their parents: "These kids under eighteen slip in with their applications on top of their folks'," he would say. "They think it's a good way to get a place of their own. Like I just caught a little punk tonight. He was in Texas when the tornado struck and he came in here after his parents to get himself a house. Well, he's gonna be unhoused."

A conservative dresser, with heavy glasses and close-cropped hair that is gray around the edges, Meade looks like an advertising executive—except that when he smiles he reveals a sizable gap between his two front teeth, which destroys the whole image. And he smiles often. "Sometimes it seems that half the people in Xenia are shacked up," he said mirthfully one afternoon. "But we'll house 'em together if they make application together." He explained that an inordinate number of unattached couples seemed to be coming in. Meade would ask them if they were living together—"and they made no bones about it." It was just as well: in the HUD furniture kits double beds were the only beds available. As one official said, "The government doesn't recognize that people might sleep separately."

In fact, shack-ups were a common feature of any disaster, and they provided Meade with some diversion from the generally grim business at hand. One of his favorite stories involved a young man and woman in the northern Ohio floods of 1972. The two had not been living together before the storm, but now, confronting new and strange quarters, they decided to give it a try. "Two weeks later the gal came snorting into our office and wanted a place of her own," Meade recalls. "She said she couldn't live with him." Did HUD comply? "Nah, I conned her into going back and trying it over again. She stayed too!"

In Xenia, matchmaker Meade didn't always fare so well. The incident that stuck in his mind involved a white girl who had been living with the black manager of an apartment project in a small town close to the storm path. Two weeks before the tornado, the couple had quarreled, and she had moved out, to a dormitory at Central State University. She was there on a temporary basis, she explained, to avoid harassment from her boyfriend. Then the tornado struck and, as luck would have it, hers was the one badly damaged dorm. She was again looking for a home. Applying to HUD, she was refused on the grounds that her CSU housing was temporary and HUD was only prepared to make good the loss of permanent homes. She was furious. She accused Meade and HUD of discrimination and threatened to take her case to higher authorities. Meade gave her the addresses. Then he recommended a metropolitan housing project in Dayton and, as he expected, that is where she wound up.

But for every rip-off or every Shields, Betterton would point out, there were probably twenty more whose houses were either uninsured, or could not be insured for anything like their replacement value. In this latter category Xenia's older citizens were especially vulnerable. They lived on Trumbull Street, or Allison, or West Second, in big old frame houses that had been built around the turn of the century and paid for long ago. To duplicate them anywhere else would have been prohibitive, yet because they were located in declining neighborhoods their market value was very low. When the wind took them, the inhabitants were literally left out in the cold.

Mildred Carter, a favorite of Ellen Hart's, might have been one of these, but her house, fortunately, was repairable. When Robert Chessman, head of damage assessment for HUD, told her it could be saved, she declared, "For one minute I could just hug and kiss you for that." And she did. Most of her peers fared less happily. They would receive their $8,000 to $12,000 settlement—whatever their limited insurance yielded—and then have to live in an apartment with no hope of leaving it for anything like what they had before. And because they now had $8,000 to $12,000 in the bank, the government expected them to pay their own way—not only for the new housing, but for all the public-assistance benefits they had hitherto received automatically: food stamps, Medicaid, and Supplemental Security Income. They were expected to pay until their equity ran out, and then they could return to the public rolls. Death or destitution, whichever came first. It was one of the great injustices, Betterton thought, and he hoped to make someone in HUD realize it before he left the department.

Indeed, there were quite a few things Betterton would have liked to make the department realize, and he brooded about them often. To wit: why couldn't HUD develop full-time disaster-response cadres that would stand ready to react to situations like Xenia? At the time of Hurricane Agnes there were only five HUD employees specializing in disaster work, and they were all in Washington. Since then, the department had allocated five more, and had distributed one each to its ten regional offices. There, theoretically, they were training other HUD people with different responsibilities as standby disaster crews. Which meant, said Betterton, that you might or might not get them should the need arise. Any decent analysis, he insisted, would show HUD spent more money training new people for crises than it would cost to keep a permanent crew on standby. To aggravate the situation, though Betterton would never complain about it, people like himself were left in a kind of departmental limbo. Not being one of the ten allocated to an official disaster slot, he remained a sort of "permanently temporary" disaster employee. Hired as a "local" in Mississippi, he had never really lost that status, even though he'd risen within the ranks and become one of HUD's most valued workers. As a result, he was not eligible for the government pension that people in permanent positions would receive.

With his kind of track record, of course, Betterton had received many permanent career offers from both within and without the government. But he stuck with disaster work because he was committed to its improvement. Specifically, he wanted three things. He was convinced that the FDAA should be pulled out of HUD and returned to the Executive Office of the President, as it had been under the Office of Emergency Preparedness. "It's such a highly specialized field that it doesn't need to be part of HUD," he would say to anyone who would listen. "When problems arise

184

with other national agencies, FDAA has to go from one Secretary to another. That shouldn't be." Second, he wanted HUD's disaster-response unit to report to its own department head within HUD, and not to the assistant secretary for housing management, as currently was required. Disaster work, he continued, was so important that those involved with it should have a clear channel to the top. Originally they had had one, but when George Romney was Secretary of HUD, he felt there were too many people reporting directly to him. Thus his rerouting of the organizational flow. Finally, Betterton wondered why the new Flood Disaster Protection Act of 1973 included no provisions for temporary living expenses for victims of a flood. It provided comprehensive insurance for their property, but nothing for the interim period when they were without resources. A little like the shoe without the sock, Betterton thought.

By the end of April, HUD had relocated 928 families in temporary housing and still had 237 to go. By the middle of May, all applicants had found temporary quarters and the search for permanent homes was well begun. How long the office would remain in Xenia was still unknowable, but the speed of the operation made it look as though a year might not be too optimistic. HUD officials were proud that they had been able to relocate 50 percent of the families in Greene County and 30 percent in Xenia.

They were also aware that they had begun to integrate the city in an unprecedented way. The tornado's destruction of Wilberforce, virtually an all-black community three miles to the east of Xenia, had seen to that. It had sent dozens of black families to HUD, which in turn had placed them with white families in whatever temporary housing became available. For many Xenians, it was something of a new experience.

16

THE TORNADO came thundering down on Central State University as if it had been saving up for some hideous grand finale. It skinned all the land between town and the school, leveling the open-air farm that Central State maintained just east of campus, crumpling the car in which student Laura Lee Hull was on her way to see her mother, and killing Laura Lee. It picked up the truck that Ralph Smith, a Central State maintenance man, was driving, killed him too, then knocked off most of the houses on Clifton Wilberforce Road, including some which black professionals had built when they weren't allowed in the newer neighborhoods of Xenia. It deposited hunks of metal in wooded gulleys that might never be cleaned up, and it dropped tons of waste in country creeks that had to be bulldozed so they wouldn't back up and flood.

From the highway, Central State was unarresting—the kind of place you'd pass without blinking if business didn't deter you. One of two small campuses that comprised the community of Wilberforce, it spread in a modest panorama of brick and stone at the intersection of Brush Row Road. Still, it was a campus much loved by students and faculty alike—"the yard," they called it.

Now all that was wiped out. The tornado came screeching across Scarborough House, traditional home of the president of Central State, and left the president's wife standing in the back hall while it brought the house down on top of her. It toppled the post office two blocks away, and buried Oscar Robinson, a long-time postal worker, in the downpour of bricks. As it had in Xenia, it hit the loveliest area head-on, wrecking all of Arnett Drive with its stately trees and turn-of-the-century façades before moving on to the more ordinary buildings that filled out "the yard." Galloway Tower, the school's dominant landmark, met the wind with clock face, bells, and a cornice set squarely atop it, like a mortarboard without the tassel. When the storm had passed, the mortarboard was gone.

The tornado bore down on a track meet in progress behind the stadium, reminding the competitors ruefully that just two days before, Coach Don Balloon had said the only thing that could stop a track meet was a hurricane. In fact, it so frightened CSU's star runner, Tony Egwunyewga—a Nigerian who had never heard of a tornado—that six weeks later he froze in place when a tornado watch was posted at another track meet, on the final leg of a qualifying heat for the mile relay divisional championship. As a result, CSU failed to qualify.

The storm saved plenty of punch for Wilberforce University, CSU's neighbor, knocking down four buildings there, including Shorter Hall, the oldest on campus and once a part of the Underground Railroad. It destroyed in short order Central State's credit union, killing its director, Evelyn Rockhold, in her car behind the building. It crunched the campus medical center beneath the upended water tower. It uprooted or clipped in midsection virtually every tree before it, finishing by ripping down a rare forest of virgin beech trees behind Banneker Hall, on the north edge of campus. (Rare because, whereas beech is usually associated with maple, these grew next to oak, tulip, and black cherry trees.) Only days before, plans had been made to proclaim the woods a Natural Area, thus preventing any commercial exploitation. Now, feared biologist David Rubin, the state wouldn't want it. He couldn't have been more wrong. Now, for the first time on record, the state had a "climax community" of beech destroyed by a natural disaster. How would the woods rebound, they wanted to know. They were more interested in preserving it than ever. When the funnel had passed, sixteen buildings had been wrecked completely and lesser damage was visible on all the others.

It happened so fast that no one had time to think about it until they went out to look at the evidence, and then they were struck dumb. ("My finger's cut," someone said to Walter Bowie, the assistant dean of students, but when Bowie looked, he saw the top had been severed.) Whereas in Xenia it had seemed initially as though only a few streets or a single neighborhood had been leveled, here there was no such illusion. Survivors could see in a glance that virtually all their university was gone. Still worse, the devastation only invited the grimmest speculation about what man would do next. Would the state rebuild the school? Would the surrounding community come promptly to its aid? Recent events, and a history of strained relations with Xenia, made Central Staters pessimistic.

Since its beginning, Central State had been predominantly black. Founded in 1887 as the normal department, or teachers' college, of the much older Wilberforce University, it was for many years the wellspring of black teachers for black public schools throughout Ohio. (It was also the butt of young white boys' jokes: "You keep gettin' grades like that and you'll end up at Central State Teachers College.") In 1947 the school became an independent university, but soon thereafter, with the breakdown of segregated education, it shifted its focus to the underachiever. It took students of average or less-than-average attainment and, by offering remedial courses and one-to-one instruction, equipped them with the same basic skills as other undergraduates.

Sometime during the mid-sixties, the school began to suffer from declining enrollments, due in part to a sour image acquired during some campus disturbances, (the National Guard had to be called in briefly), and in part to lagging admissions nationwide. And, since 1961, when its great mentor Charles H. Wesley retired, it had undergone two administrative turnovers, involving two permanent and three acting presidents. Worse, the number of state-supported universities in Ohio had now proliferated to twelve, and Central had far and away the highest cost per student

188

($1,375 vs. an average $1,026). Ominous questions arose. Was there still a need for an all-black school? And, looking ahead, would it be possible to attract the white students who would be essential if enrollment were to increase and the cost per capita decrease? Rumor had it that the state was considering closing CSU altogether. The Board of Regents had never come right out and said so, but the vibrations seemed unmistakable.

And they scared a lot of people. People who believed, along with Dr. Lionel Newsom, Central State's president for two years, that the option of a black university for black students was essential: "I don't think black students, who have been the adopted children in American society, would ever feel natural if they're always going to be in the minority. They need this as a part of their growing up; it gives them the confidence that they can go it alone and operate as individuals." To that end, he had created on campus an open, friendly atmosphere where blacks were, for once, a thriving majority. In return, students and faculty were deeply grateful for the sense of self and school. Now, just seconds after Newsom felt his administration building come crashing down, he could not suppress his fear: "I thought to myself, 'The state is in a position to unload an institution it has wanted to unload for a long, long time. How do you convince them to keep it?' Everything we had worked to build, all the progress we had made in recent years, all the sympathy we were beginning to garner around the state, I saw all that vanishing with the tornado."

But the first hurdle was survival for the night, and Central State did not mean to fail at that. Dr. Newsom ran across Brush Row Road, to his roofless house with its rafters sticking into the air, to find his wife. Bowie was left in charge of the campus. Grabbing a whistle from his car, the dean blew for all he was worth, gathered the students by the administration building—what was left of it —and organized them in groups to search the campus, moving from the outer perimeter to the center. Fortunately, the place was small, say a half-mile square, and this could be done fast and efficiently. (When it was over, Bowie, an ex-career man with the army, could not resist comparing himself favorably with his war-

189

time hero: "When I saw the destruction, I felt like Patton," he said. "Did you ever see the movie of Patton where George C. Scott walks to the graveyard and says, 'I've been here before'? Well, that's the way I felt—I'd been there." Narcissistically or not, he felt he was the only man on campus fully able to cope.)

"Someone's hurt in Jenkins Hall," he heard a voice cry, but it was too late to do anything. Evelyn Rockhold's body had been uncovered. She was laid out on top of the rubble and, like Oscar Robinson shortly thereafter, left alone for several hours because there was not one other thing that could be done for her. So frantically were the students searching for more bodies that one recalled threshing through the library ruins for twenty minutes and never seeing a single book. He was too absorbed in looking for people. Bowie turned from the flurry around the credit union to see Win Jackson, the school's federal funds coordinator, with blood covering his arm, carrying a young girl from the registrar's office out of Bundy Hall. He was white and she was black, and badly cut up. "By then I knew we had a real calamity," Bowie recalled.

Within the hour Dr. Newsom returned and set up headquarters in Dabney Cafeteria, where Dorothy Chapman, director of CSU's food services, was already gearing up to feed the refugees. She still had gas to fuel the stoves, though she didn't know for how long, and she had plenty of fried chicken, hamburger, milk, and ice cream that "had to be used right away." She worked until 3 A.M., feeding anyone who wasn't too frightened to venture from his dormitory basement, and later won accolades from the entire campus. "Dorothy Chapman was a rock," said one official. "She is one of three or four people at most who kept this place alive that night."

The storm had demolished the medical center, but nurses and doctors were safe, and they too set up a first-aid station in the cafeteria. Just as promptly, the campus ambulance began inching its way through the debris, picking up the wounded. Once filled, it headed out Route 42 for Greene Memorial and almost at once headed back. The road, of course, was impassable. Where cars and trucks weren't battling for space, gigantic trees and huge chunks of houses made progress impossible. Reporting these conditions to Bowie, the driver then headed off in the other direction, for the hospital in Springfield. And Bowie knew they were trapped.

It was the beginning of a long ordeal. Students huddled in basements, afraid of further tornadoes. Faculty members left, most of them, to see about their own families. There was no electricity and thus no light. No water and no plumbing. And, save the Cedarville Canteen, which returned quickly to Central State, no sign of the help that was cascading into Xenia. The university was isolated, physically and spiritually. But what made it all so much worse than it needed to have been was the general apprehension, felt by most Central Staters, that their isolation was deliberate.

For years, relations between Central State and Xenia had been uneasy. University old-timers could remember well the fight to integrate Xenia's movie theater in the late 1940s, and the resentment that surrounded the opening of the golf club, and the segregated restaurants that lingered into the fifties. Forever, the city's resident black population had been safely sequestered in the East End (barely touched by the tornado), and Wilberforce was another community entirely, separated by miles of cornfield and decades of estrangement that not even the enlightenment of the sixties could totally abate.

In recent years, housing patterns had begun to change. History professor Joe Lewis and Walter Bowie were both living in Pinecrest, not perhaps to the entire delight of their neighbors, but it was a step. Central State officials felt that the community was learning to live with, and not just next to, its blacks. Xenia had a black former mayor and blacks were represented on the City Commission and the school board, and a black occupied the director's chair at the local Red Cross.

What resentment remained seemed targeted primarily at the students. Over and over CSU undergraduates would point out that they spent a small fortune annually in Xenia, yet received almost nothing in return by way of ads in their sports programs or their newspapers, or donations for their fund-raising projects. They didn't even get the sense that the community appreciated their

191

business. It angered them that the only coverage the school seemed to receive in the local media was negative (i.e., trouble on campus or a change in administration) and that their sports were given short shrift or skipped altogether. "If we win big, we get a small writeup in back and that's it," they would say.

Now the memory of these hurts played into their fears. As Joe Lewis recalled, "We felt insufficient, cut off. It was like the tornado only reinforced the attitudes a lot of us already held. We felt the way we were handled was a lot less efficient, say, than if the storm had happened to Cedarville or Wright State. In fact, as soon as the thing had passed over, I looked out and said, 'Man, this is it.' My paranoia suggested to me that there were a lot of people who would like to see us go right on down."

He was wrong. In Xenia, most people didn't realize for hours that the school had been hit. Bob Stewart didn't learn until midnight or later; Dickson Burrows didn't find out until 3 A.M. Radio and television stations were also slow in learning the truth, as Jackie Hupman's mother so innocently revealed. Yet even if they had known sooner, it probably would not have brought aid to Central State any faster. So choked were the roads, and so dark and rainy the skies, that it took a unit from Wright-Patterson almost until midnight to clear a path to Central State. From that time on the influx of aid was steady: first military and Red Cross caravans, then shipments of water and food, and finally the National Guard. By morning Central State was on its way back.

The suspicion of prejudice persisted, however. The Red Cross was accused by some of being "a white man's organization"; the feeling persisted that the media was not always fair. In October, when the NBC special was aired, and only a minute or two was devoted to Central State, a petition was drawn up to protest the slight. Worse still, all the media consistently failed to mention Wilberforce University, which had lost almost one-fifth of its total campus. The sad fact was, however, that Wilberforce was a private institution and its future was never in doubt. For every story it could tell, Central State could tell one better, always with the shadow of its endangered existence to add to the drama.

But Thursday brought Governor Gilligan. Compassionate and

192

reassuring, he told a morning audience of as many CSU affiliates as could be assembled, "I just came here to say stay cool and that Central State is going to live and serve Ohio for a long, long time to come." The sighs of relief were almost audible.

Dr. Newsom placed one man in charge of the academic problems of recovery, another in charge of students, a third in charge of buildings. He sent the students home. Result: by Thursday afternoon the campus was a ghost town, full of broken buildings and Guardsmen in uniform. There was a perimeter control around Central State, and none but authorized personnel were allowed inside.

The next few days the atmosphere was tense, with faculty members picking through their offices, damage survey teams writing off one building after another, and no one certain if or what to plan for the future. Rumors abounded that Central State had been closed for the rest of the year. In fact, the students had been told to leave a number where they could be reached once things were brought under control, and Newsom's one goal, in the midst of so much chaos, was to bring them back as soon as possible. Tentatively, he penciled in April 16, a week from the following Monday, as the day to bring back the graduating seniors. The deans heard his plan, and agreed, with one amendment: he should bring back *all* the students a week from Monday.

At first it seemed absurd. The place was devastated—at least 75 percent destroyed. And yet . . . the more Dr. Newsom listened, the more he liked it. Except for one, the dormitories were still intact as were the cafeteria and a couple of smaller office buildings. Maybe it would work. Trailers could be brought in. Classrooms borrowed from Wilberforce. It might be the one bold stroke that would save Central State.

And, as it turned out, that's exactly what happened. The decision to bring all the students back a week from Monday, ten days after the disaster, galvanized the university. Instead of allowing people to turn their backs, it threw everyone—students, faculty, administration, politicians, and the Ohio Board of Regents—into the fray at once, forcing them to realize that this tiny campus was struggling for its life, and that it did not mean to fail.

The decision came not a moment too soon either, for on Monday Governor Gilligan did an about-face, and threw the entire Central State community into an uproar: "A predominantly black institution such as Central State University has a role to play in our state system," he told an unsuspecting press conference that morning, "but it is too soon to say if the money—$75 million and maybe even $100 million—can be found." Stressing that the ultimate decision on rebuilding would belong to the Board of Regents and members of the Ohio General Assembly, he said they would have to consider "not one institution, but the entire system of higher education in Ohio."

Could this be the same person who, only days before, had told them to stay cool, that Central State was going to "live and serve Ohio for a long, long time to come"? Gilligan went on to say that the legislators would have to establish a "balance" among claims on funds devoted to higher education. For example, medical schools in both northeastern and southwestern Ohio were asking for money. "I don't envision it as coming down to a choice between Central State and the medical schools," said the Governor, "but there are conflicting claims on the limited resources of higher education. I am satisfied that there is a role for such an institution, but it could be the end of it if, in its collective wisdom, the General Assembly decides not to rebuild."

Newsom's rebuttal was swift: "Either pay the cost now as an investment or pay it later in destruction." For Dr. Newsom, a gentle man, the words were unusually strong. And there was more to follow: "We subsidize railroads, airplanes, every damn thing in the United States, and when we talk about a few more dollars to subsidize a black person, it's not realistic. Central State is the only institution in Ohio that black people control and where they are free to be models of leadership. Read Marx and some of the other revolutionaries and then find out how important it is for the U.S. to provide an opportunity to get blacks out of the ghetto."

He won his point. The very next day Nixon came to Xenia with his promise to cut the red tape and make good all losses. He gave

194

Gilligan full assurance that he would receive the funds to rebuild Central State.

Said HUD Secretary James T. Lynn: "The funds will come from an as yet undetermined source to finance the project."

Said Henry L. Whitcomb, official of the Ohio Board of Regents: "Federal funds will cover what the state and CSU cannot afford in a rebuilding program."

Said James A. Norton, chairman of the Board of Regents: "Federal law provides for replacement costs, so there will be no extraordinary state costs."

Said Governor Gilligan: "Now I am more optimistic than ever that Central State will live and continue to be a valuable link in Ohio's higher education system."

When all the shouting was over, it was conceded that Gilligan's timing had been poor and his information inaccurate. If nothing else, his damage estimates had been way off base. Instead of $75 to $100 million, the final estimate of actual tornado loss was $18 million. The Gilligan gaffe was put quietly to rest. "Have you ever blown one?" one of his aides asked the newsmen.

Xenia and CSU followed similar scenarios, but with some start-ling differences in the denouements. The Red Cross, for example, noted some irrefutable instances of student dishonesty at Central State, but chose to overlook them rather than raise the specter of a "black-white" shouting match. The volunteers sensed nothing unusual until twelve days after the storm, when, as Dr. Newsom had planned, the students returned to campus. Finding the Red Cross there, and learning that it was prepared to make good certain of their emergency losses, they began to file claims. "They wanted hi-fis, stereos, and tape decks replaced," Bill Lentz said later. "Presumably, in that amount of time, their emergency needs had been taken care of, but now they were telling us that their cars were still loaded from spring vacation, and smashed in the storm, or that their rooms were damaged." Much of this was false, he knew, and he demanded verification from the school. But much of it he let go, explaining, "I believe that for those who really needed it, it was best to give them the benefit of the doubt." When Dr. Newsom confirmed the likelihood of some foul play, Lentz was mollified. "We wanted him to know we'd made some concessions."

He made more concessions on the Red Cross clothes vouchers that were normally provided. Suddenly finding that the whole voucher went for one pair of shoes or one pair of pants, he explained his leniency: "To the black male, clothes are very important psychologically. Thus you couldn't hassle them on why they wanted to go to a particular store. I knew why they wanted it, had to have it."

Thomas Kelley was less philosophical. His experience was with looters, a different breed from those Xenians had seen, and he was bitter. Kelley was the university's purchasing agent, operating out of an office in the basement of Bundy Hall, and he took cover there when the tornado hit. "Not a paper was ruffled," he said later, recalling that he went outside to help others and much later that evening came back to lock up, carrying the contents of the trunk of his car, including his bowling ball, which he secured in the closet. By Friday, the National Guard was on campus and the office, he thought, was safe.

On Monday, when he returned to work, it was a wreck. Windows were broken that hadn't been, the door frames were jimmied, and every desk had been rifled, drawer by drawer. Missing were: his naval clock, five Coca-Cola lighters that he had collected, a Sony tape recorder, and a plaster-of-paris Buddha which a jeweler friend had given him many years before. The closet was sacked, except for the bowling ball. His conclusion was regrettable but inescapable: the National Guard had looted the building.

"Let me just ask you who else it might have been?" he said later. "There was no one else on this campus, the students had gone." He could point to a filing cabinet which was crumpled only near the lock, and one of his employees had watched Guardsmen moving heavy office machinery into their trucks. Said Kelley, "When he asked what they were doing, they said they had to get in to move the office equipment. So I went over to the commander's office and registered a complaint. He just said, 'We have people from all walks of life, and it's just one of those things.' "

How Central State pulled itself together enough to reopen on April 15 is still a mystery. Certainly part of the impetus was fear of what might happen if it didn't. Part too was help from the immediate community—the ubiquitous Mennonites, and the hundreds of alumni and church group volunteers who poured in to clean up. And part of it was the speed with which various state agencies came to the rescue. The day after the tornado, the Chancellor of the Board of Regents was on the scene. The state architect's office was coordinating the cleanup, helped by the Department of Public Works, the Department of Natural Resources, and the National Guard. In ten days they had the debris cleared, a handful of basic buildings ready, and the dormitories generally repaired. Students attended classes in mobile units, dormitory lounges, and, occasionally, off campus. Wilberforce University, itself pressed for space, lent classrooms where it could.

For all the heroism and hasty reorganization, however, there was little to relieve the starkness. Said William Pruitt, a junior, "It hurt me very badly that Central State was destroyed; I felt a deep-down, emotional hurt. Because it's like anyplace you've been for a while and like; subconsciously you fall in love with it; it's like a small diamond." Sensing this, Dr. Newsom was concerned that many students simply wouldn't return. That spring, only 1,300 out of a total 2,150 did; the next fall, all but 41 were back. "Now we have a standard," he said, explaining what he thought they all felt. "This is my turf, me, my school. Let's make it live."

In fact, it was difficult to say what the students did feel as they resumed campus life. "The tornado built a stronger bond between the administration and students," said one sophomore unequivocally. "Before, we didn't feel totally close to them, or the teachers, but now there's an awareness that we're all here together." In interview after interview with a suddenly hungry press, students and faculty alike talked of a renewed unity and spirit, and the need to build together.

Yet Dean Wilson Jefferson, Jr., in the May 16 issue of the campus newspaper, sounded a sour note: "Persons from outside the university have come to aid us in cleaning up our university;

197

yet we were hard pressed to find members of our family to do the same work even with pay, not to mention that some of us have already managed to replace the litter and glass and trash that others had worked hard to clean up. . . ." His comments, in a column called "Dean's Corner," seem to suggest that not even a monster tornado will alter many people's basic personalities for very long. While it is true that most Central Staters suddenly felt closer to their school than they ever had before, it is probably not true, as the platitudes to the press would indicate, that they spent every waking moment thereafter thinking "unity, family, togetherness." And given a disaster's potential for uprooting all things familiar, it is somehow comforting to know that soon enough and despite it all, undergraduates were goofing off again.

In the same vein, speculation about the changed nature of town-gown relations seesawed between definite improvement and no improvement at all. Dr. Newsom was optimistic that the cooperation necessitated by the storm could be sustained in the future, and cited as a step in the right direction "Community Appreciation Day"—a football Saturday in September when a number of Xenia's VIP's were invited to CSU for lunch and the game. Bowie was more emphatic: "Town relations have changed for the better; I talk to city officials more, and this fall I'm to be installed in the Kiwanis." Like Joe Lewis, he lost no time making plans to rebuild in Pinecrest. Joe's return was made particularly gratifying by his election in the fall to the Greene County Central Commission—a committee that publicized local campaigns. He had run against a white in the fifth ward, which was mostly his own neighborhood, and won. On the campus itself, the significant logo "CSU–XENIA LIVES" was painted on a large construction wall, illustrated by some campus buildings, a dove of peace, a swirling funnel cloud, and a parody of Michelangelo's God touching it into being.

Sometime during the summer, toward the beginning of July, Yvonne Stewart drove onto campus for the first time since she had left it the previous January. A part-time worker in the data-processing division, she had substituted for someone else the past winter, and now she was being asked to fill in again. She was appalled by what she saw. Wrecked buildings still unrazed. Twisted girders and broken cement strewn across the yard. "It was depressing, barren," she said later. "It seemed like the cleanup went so fast in Xenia, and here, it was like nothing had been accomplished at all."

In a sense, nothing had. The initial work at Central State, tree clearance and campus litter, had gone very fast. But the big things —the lecture halls and office buildings—were forever in limbo for the very frustrating reason that the government could not decide what to do. It could not decide how much property loss had been sustained, or what portion of that loss it should make good. For, despite the assurances of Nixon et al., it very quickly became apparent that the federal government was not going to pay for all the damage done to Central State University. Some, but not all.

The HEW and FDAA survey teams that had swarmed across the campus immediately after the tornado, slide rules and blueprints in hand, were there to ascertain the extent of damage. Before any building could be razed, let alone any new construction begun, they had to decide exactly how much the original structure was worth (its depreciated value), and, on that basis, determine how much they could allocate the university. Then, with the federal figure in hand, the state had to decide whether it wanted to use that money to repair the damaged structure or tear it down and build a new one entirely.

For reasons no one could accurately explain, all this took about twice as much time as usual because the federal government decided to send in a second wave of survey teams shortly after the first had completed its job. This second group was substantially more finicky—"picayunish," Dr. Newsom said—in its findings, and questioned a number of the conclusions of the first teams. For example, the school might have put in a claim for a battered typewriter in the list of damages already submitted to the feds. Now, the second teams wanted to *see* that typewriter before they would allow it. In a hundred similar ways, the federal teams slowed the momentum of Central's renewal.

"We had our difficulties and disagreements," said Dr. Faud Suleiman, the university's vice-president for financial planning.

Graduation day at Central State, under the ravaged Galloway Tower

"For instance, one of the teams estimated the roof of Bundy Hall, at the time it was destroyed, to be worth only $3,500. Can you imagine?! But deep down, we knew we'd get some money from the feds, and deep down they knew they'd give us some. It was just a matter of how much."

To confuse the issue even further, Central had chosen an offbeat plan for reimbursement. Going in, it had two choices: it could accept "categorical grants," which would provide 100 percent refunding on the condition that specifically damaged buildings be repaired or replaced, or it could get "flexible funding," a brand-new program which would provide 90 percent refunding to be used to repair or replace any building with a direct relation to the campus. Central State chose the latter. It wanted the option to forgo some buildings that had outlived their usefulness and the freedom to erect new ones which would better serve its purposes.

All of which was fine, except that the government had had no experience with flexible funding, and now it was uncertain how to implement it. Again the delays were endless.

By the middle of November, however, Suleiman was beginning to see his way out of the dark. "Our losses from the tornado totaled approximately $18 million," he said. "But we had other needs prior to that, so the total we're looking for is $32 million. Of that, we now figure to get about $8 million from the feds. We're getting another half million from insurance.* And we're asking the state for $18 million. The rest we'll have to raise ourselves, from foundations, fund drives, and private sources. So we're talking about several million dollars—far more than we've ever raised before. I'm hopeful that we can do it in three or four years," then laughingly, "and that I can keep my job." He rustled uncomfortably in his seat.

Was he angry that the feds had reneged, after so many sweeping assurances at the time of Nixon's visit? Oddly, no. "It was a matter of whether you want half a loaf or no loaf at all. I think Nixon's statement gave us new hope for keeping the university open and it did yield us a good portion of the cost of rebuilding. I don't believe universities are a federal obligation. They belong to the state and are state responsibilities."

Outside his window, beneath a gray November sky, the tornado's ravages were still much in evidence. Bundy Hall was down to its basement floor, where the university telephone system was encased in cement. Most of the other buildings were gone, but some, like the once sprawling Banneker, survived like amputees after a war. Galloway Tower stood firm without its mortarboard and shorn of the auditorium that once surrounded its base. Now the two lower stories were naked and exposed, showing plaster walls and the outline of staircases where rooms had been ripped away.

The university had done what it could. Using nearly $6 million

*If this sounds low, it should be pointed out that state institutions are not insured—it would be too expensive. However, on a campus like Central State, buildings like the student union or the dormitories, which are built with revenue from bond levies, are insured to protect the bondholders. Thus the $500,000.

originally allocated from the state for a performing arts center, it had cleaned up and made its emergency repairs. A new administration building was already under way on the foundation of the old library, and plans for a new library were in the works. Its funding requests had been presented to the state; its expectations from the government were understood. Its quest for private support was Faud Suleiman's challenge. Now all anybody could do was wait.

17

WITH THE ADVANCE of spring, bluer skies and fringes of green softened the destruction. Here and there a daffodil poked through the rubble. Emergency workers stopped running quite so hard, and took time to say "hello" and "good morning" and to open doors for one another. Just before Don Hannah left the city, he drove by a ruined house whose owner was out front, weeding the yard. "That lady had faced the fact that her roof was gone, but she was taking care of the place anyway," he said. "It was a sign that Xenia was on its way back."

In less symbolic ways, Xenia had been on its way back almost from the moment the tornado left town. On Friday, April 5, City Manager Stewart had recommended to the commissioners that they retain the services of the Miami Valley Regional Planning Commission to draw up a plan for the orderly rebuilding of the city. Much had been wrong with Xenia before the tornado—it was, after all, a hodgepodge of narrow streets and nonsensical zoning left over from horse-and-buggy days. Now a "golden opportunity" existed to rectify those mistakes, and Stewart urged that it not be allowed to slip by. MVRPC had worked with the city fathers before, on sewer lines and transportation routes; now it was willing to make Xenia a priority, and push all other work aside to develop a land-use proposal for the future.

For most Xenians, however, the primary concerns had been

more immediate. How to get the house rebuilt as quickly as possible. How to get the kids back in school. And how to get back in business. They felt pressured by the city to sign releases so the Corps of Engineers could tear down their houses and thwarted by the city when they were denied permits to rebuild at once. As Bud Schmidt, a businessman who seemed to own every other piece of property downtown, put it: "How the hell can a guy run a business if he has to run around and ask somebody every time he wants to do something? We got some floating city manager who hasn't been here three years, and some kid building inspector, and you gotta ask them. Hell, they should be asking me. I own the buildings. I'm just gonna go ahead and fix 'em."

On Thursday, April 18, the city made official what it had been doing in fact ever since the tornado. It put a moratorium until June 1 on reconstruction permits for the core area. This meant, in effect, that no one in the central business district, the area around Kennedy Korners, or the old North End could lift a finger for at least six weeks. They could, if they wanted, apply for the permit in the hope that their particular building would not conflict with the city's overall plans . . . but since no one yet knew what those plans might be, the possibility of success was remote. Only residents of Pinecrest and Arrowhead were exempt. Because their areas showed "adequate planning during original construction," they were free to repair or rebuild at will. As might be expected, the response to this dictum was not always generous.

"I think the city officials are being overtechnical in some of their rulings," said Nicholas Carrera, Greene County prosecutor. "In my view, a town is composed of its people and not its buildings and I take exception to holding people back from fixing their property. I have told people to go back to their buildings." As good as his word, Carrera set about repairing his own law offices near the Courthouse and refused to stop even when Stewart and Fister ordered him to. Contending that a building permit obtained more than one year previously made his position legally correct, Carrera never stopped hammering throughout the considerable flap surrounding him. And he got away with it because Building Inspector Fister lacked the manpower to stop him.

Jack Jordan, however, took him to task: "Xenia, in the wake of a devastating act of God, finds its inhabitants daily wrestling with the conscience of self and/or community, a horrendous decision for many. It is horrifying, therefore, to this editor that we should find within two weeks that the prosecutor of this county should set an example of defiance of emergency authority. Proceeding to repair his office building without sanction of municipal authority in such a time is a challenge that cannot go untested. Emotions run high, but it is no time for Nick Carrera, the prosecutor, to place himself above the laws applicable to all, setting a precedent that could lead others into reckless acts ending in death or injury." Strong stuff, but moderation was in short supply all over town.

Ever since the rebuilding controversy had begun, Jack Jordan had watched with a strange mixture of apprehension and excitement. He was afraid of what might happen if someone didn't take charge and guide the redevelopment systematically, and he was excited because he knew—believed? dared hope?—that here at last was a real opportunity to make Xenia a showplace city. The German cities that were bombed during World War II and then rebuilt exactly as they had been soon decayed. But the cities that waited and drew up forward-looking plans had grown and prospered. So Jordan took up the gauntlet.

"Our values have changed," he wrote one week after the tornado. "If permanently, our dead will not have died in vain; our injured who survived may live to see a better day. We have the opportunity to establish a master plan few communities can match —from industrial development, shopping areas, cultural centers, public schools, residential developments and far beyond. Our limits, in a sense, are what we make of them." And five days later: "Do we want to build a New Xenia or simply put the old one back together again? Bluntly, there are those willing to jump right in, patch up and call it quits because their own little kingdom again seems secure. Who's kidding who?"

To some it seemed that Jordan was using his editorial power to chart the course of "my town," as he called it, and to denounce any who disagreed with him. To others he was providing the rallying cry the city needed. Jordan himself denied either role, saying only that he wanted Xenians to take advantage of the emergency aid offered them and to support the city officials as much as possible.

And there was more to Jack than his editorials, as the city soon learned. Two days after the storm, he began to pick up vibrations that alarmed him: businessmen jockeying for a fast comeback, realtors rubbing their hands over the possibilities, city officials operating in a vacuum. Jordan began making phone calls to a few select people: Jim Cox, perhaps the most powerful lawyer in town; Bill Eichman, the appliance king and past city commissioner and mayor; Doe Hawthorne, president of Xenia National Bank; Joe Kennedy, of Kennedy Korners, and others. "Could you hold yourselves in abeyance?" he asked them. "Could you resist making any definite commitment to any group or concept until we can get something organized that will benefit us all?"

The project he had in mind was a citizens' task force, composed of the community's business and professional leaders, to serve as official go-betweens for the city administration and the townspeople. The committee would coordinate rebuilding efforts in the best traditions of New England democracy: it would listen to all the inflammatory rhetoric of disaffected homeowners, then report quietly back to the commissioners what the people wanted. The city commissioners liked the idea and appointed Stewart, Jordan, and Eichman to choose the committee. By Wednesday, April 24, they had finished their deliberations and nominated seventeen people (including Eichman and Jordan) for the job. Thursday the new group met for the first time and agreed that displaced residents and businessmen should be its first and biggest concern. It had also decided on a name for itself: the "Spirit of Seventy-Four."

It was vitally needed. For years, as most Xenians knew only too well, there had been no real citizen leadership in their city. The Chamber of Commerce, a leftover of Rotarian yesteryears, was for all intents and purposes moribund. Certainly there were powerful individuals, like Cox and Kennedy and Eichman, but for the most part they went their separate ways, leaving the running of the city to the hired officials. Most of these were young, and relatively new, and the businessmen felt anything but comfortable in dealing with

206

them. As Eichman put it, "We don't much like to get involved." Then, one month before the tornado, a little thing called the Topics Plan polarized them absolutely.

Topics, simply put, was a proposal from the state of Ohio that Xenia widen the north side of Main Street (Route 35) and the west side of Detroit (Route 68) in return for funds for a new traffic signal system which it badly needed. It seemed almost a perfect trade-off to the city officials, but it made businessmen see red. "You're on the outside," cried one. "We just hired you—why don't you put your money where your mouth is?" Others concurred. "They were going to take six feet of sidewalk, which was costing us several thousand dollars. We just got a committee and said to the city, 'You're not going to do this.'"

And the city didn't. It settled for a compromise plan which called for new lane striping and the elimination of parking spaces at certain intersections. Xenia got the money for its new traffic signals anyway. This confirmed a number of businessmen's original suspicions that they did not have to approve the plan to get the traffic lights, but it did settle the dispute amicably. And it did stimulate the development of the Downtown Businessmen's Association, the "committee" which had told the city "No!"

With Topics put to rest, the DBA had turned its attention to something no one liked to talk about, but everyone knew was a fact: the slow death of the central city. To realize it, all you had to do was look around. Except for Main and Detroit, the streets were little more than one-way alleys breeding traffic snarls. Parking was the impossible dream. The stores—ranging from a pawnshop to a Penney's to a Kresge's—were drab and uninviting, housed in ancient buildings with sleazy modern façades. They were fast losing business to the malls and shopping centers outside the city. If a customer wanted staples—baby powder or underwear —Xenia was fine. But for anything more exotic—even clothes for the kids—he went to Dayton. Some progressive Xenians had even hired a consulting firm from Cincinnati to give them ideas on how the area might be improved. Their proposals had included a minimall, more trees, and better use of the city's period architecture. People had listened attentively, and had then tabled the findings

207

for further consideration. The DBA was just getting around to them again when the tornado struck.

Now the downtown was in turmoil. At a glance, it looked almost as easy to do away with the whole area as to try to preserve any of it. For several weeks, thanks either to debris along the curbs or demolition, walking was hazardous, and the city asked businessmen not to advertise, so as to reduce foot traffic as much as possible. Stores announced their reopenings via small, black-bordered notices in the *Gazette*. Everyone—shopkeepers and onlookers alike—agreed that the time was ideal for a facelifting, but they knew too that the health of the community depended on the fast resumption of trade. It was a tough dilemma, and the first impulse was to get the cash registers ringing.

Then several things happened. The city lifted its ban on repairs, permitting people who had suffered minor damage to call their contractors and make plans. Tuffy Snider prepared to go back to the Corner Pharmacy from the uptown trailer where he had been operating temporarily, and Bud Schmidt was able to put a roof on Penney's. Merchants who had to relocate did so with such alacrity that by the end of April all but a handful were seeing customers somewhere. Cox and Brandabur, the city's largest law firm, was operating out of the dining room at the Xenia Golf Club, and Dumbault portrait photographers were snapping pictures at the Blue Moon Dance Hall. As the debris was cleared and the wrecked buildings carted away, it gradually became clear that the damage was not so all-encompassing as had originally been feared. Cherry's was gone, for example, but that did not mean the People's Savings and Loan on the same block had to be torn down too. McDorman's was gone, but several buildings next to it were not. Was there really any reasonable alternative to letting the proprietors rebuild? The panic of the first ten days surrendered slowly to a wait-and-see attitude.

And all the time, the Spirit of Seventy-Four was preaching patience. Jim Cox, who had been president of the DBA, was now secretary of the newly created committee on rebuilding, and he urged the merchants to look past the next week's payroll. "A plan is coming," he promised them, "a plan that will turn around our

208

downtown to the point where it will be healthy not for just five or ten years, but for forty or fifty. We have to look ahead; we have to say, 'All right, we'll put up with some temporary inconveniences in the short run for a better deal in the future.' " His calm, authoritative tone, backed by the commitment of Bill Eichman and Joe Kennedy, both heavy losers in the tornado, reassured the storekeepers. The spirit was beginning to work as Jack Jordan had intended.

For one thing, it was confirmation that Xenians themselves and not "some damn group of outsiders" would guide the course of redevelopment. Every day of the week, and usually on Saturdays, committee members picked the brains of their fellow citizens. "What do you want for Xenia? What do you want for your neighborhood? We want your input for incorporation into the final land-use plan." (Bill Eichman got so sick of the word "input" that he thought he might pass out if he heard it once more.) They talked with people in every section of the city and from every interest group, then split up into subcommittees to synthesize their findings. The hours and energies they expended were not to be counted—the future of their community was at stake.

Throughout Xenia, the concept of "The Plan" hung heavy in the warming air, touted by the community leaders, prophesied in the columns of the *Gazette,* and speculated about at business luncheons. What would be the outcome? And was the whole thing right anyway? People questioned seriously the propriety of forbidding a man to use his property as he saw fit, either before or after any plan was submitted. If the Plan called for radical changes in the previous layout of Xenia, they wondered how that would affect landowners. They knew that some people were going to be hurt.

Take Dick Hupman. Forever, his camera shop had been in a prime location, one half block west of the Main and Detroit intersection. Office girls would drop off rolls of film at lunchtime; traveling salesmen would wander in between appointments, and maybe buy an Instamatic or a camera case. Cart Hill, perhaps the most avid and prolific shutterbug in town, was two blocks away, symbolic of Dick's close proximity to a lucrative clientele. Now Dick was doing business in a trailer on a used-car lot, one mile north of town. The only way people could reach him was by automobile; the only customers who would know he was there were old and steady ones. His space for inventory was severely limited, allowing only for a few good cameras and lenses. Slide storage boxes, for example, had to be ordered by the gross. Dick didn't have the room for them, so he didn't carry them. If a patron wanted anything unusual, it had to be ordered, and by that time the patron had probably gone elsewhere.

At an early meeting of local businessmen with Small Business Administration (SBA) officials, Dick learned that he needed to file earnings records, tax forms, past records of annual volume, and a projection of his next year's business in order to qualify for a loan. "How can I project my business?" he asked. "I've never been through a tornado. I know what my business was on April 2, but since April 3 I don't know how many people have moved away, how many people have started shopping elsewhere. How do I project?" The answer was succinct and unsatisfying: "You know your business. You will have to project it." To Dick it was an insult. "I thought, since they'd had so much disaster experience, they might have some idea of what to tell me. Instead, they implied that I didn't know how to run my own business." But it was just one in a long line of frustrations.

Dick became a regular at the Spirit of Seventy-Four meetings that affected either his home or his business, and he became known as one of the more outspoken "younger businessmen" (he was forty) in town. "I just want to know when I can rebuild, how much it will cost me to rebuild, and how long it will take to sign a lease on temporary units," he cried out at a meeting in May. But of course there were no answers. Although the Plan was not slated for unveiling until June 1, word had already leaked that a spiffy new mall might rise on the block where Dick's camera shop had been. If so, there was no telling what kind of location relative to his former one Dick might procure—there was not even the assurance that he would be able to afford space in the mall. He was learning rapidly that his business in the trailer was about 50 percent of what it had been downtown, and he wondered now

210

whether enough business remained in Xenia to buoy him to his former level even if he did return.

"People walk in all the time and say, 'When they gonna let you rebuild?' or, 'If they'd a just let you alone you'd a been back by now,' and it's frustrating because how can you answer them?" he said one day. "After all, they're on your side." Sitting in the back of the trailer, in flowered shirt and blue jeans, his feet up on his desk, Dick tried to mask his concern. "What alternatives do I have?" he said, smiling. "I have nothing to base decisions on—I don't know whether the mall will cost two dollars or eight dollars per square foot. Yet I have to be for the renewal. I know what business was like before. The whole downtown was going down, losing business to the suburbs. It was just a matter of time before the bottom fell out."

Every day that Dick remained in the trailer he suffered a little more, yet he was willing to do it for the sake of a better Xenia. The image of what he wanted was not precise in his mind—he was no urban planner—but both personally and professionally he yearned for something significant to come out of the mess that nature had bequeathed him.

If the tornado had left a hole in the heart of Xenia, it had also left its citizens with a thousand suggestions for filling it: put garden apartments in the old West End, make the North End a historical district with brick streets and gas lanterns. Get rid of those tacky fast-food chains on Route 35. Remove the foundry from West Street. Put in a green belt around Shawnee Creek. Widen Second Street. Eliminate Green Street. Everyone sensed that great things were impending. Signs went up. "THINK BUY BUILD XENIA!"

Cart Hill knew it wasn't going to happen overnight. For ten years, during the 1960s, he had sat in his office in the First National Bank of Cincinnati and watched the long, slow process of urban renewal unfold. First the plans and discussions, then the personality conflicts and the struggle to find a suitable developer, and finally the beginning: a renovated central plaza that poured new life into the city, but was a Pandora's box from which emerged new questions of how the next block should be developed, and the next and the next. Now Xenia was trying to do the same thing in a few months. Hill read with dismay a headline in the May 2 *Gazette,* "Old North End to Be Restored." If there was anything that wouldn't be restored, he knew, it was the old North End. The rambling brick houses, the leafy trees—they could not be duplicated. Yet here was a speaker from the Spirit of Seventy-Four telling the residents, "Be patient, be understanding, take time to plan, and be optimistic about the old North End. We can rebuild it."

If it weren't so pathetic, Hill might have laughed. But all around him he noted a desperate edge to the discussions, as if Xenians were clinging frantically to anything that reminded them of the past. When you got right down to it, what could have been more impractical than the old North End with brick streets and gaslights but without its old houses? If anyone had stopped to think for one minute, they would have realized there would not even be money enough to peel the blacktop off the brick. But it was not a time for logic; it was a time to ache for the things they never knew they had. In his view, the same emotionalism had been responsible for much needless razing of tornado-damaged buildings. "The city was so eager to get the feds to pay for the removal that they pressured the people into signing those releases before they had a chance to evaluate their property properly. I know; I make appraisals all the time in this business, and a lot of those houses on King Street could have been saved." To back up his argument, the bank president displayed numerous slides of damaged buildings before they were torn down and of others that had been allowed to stand. Alas, there was frequently little difference between them.

A newcomer to local business practice, Hill was astonished at the city's apparent lack of interest in private money. "There were a lot of people who wanted to get in here right after the storm," he said, "but no one would listen to them. I and several others made many suggestions to the commission for outside funding, but they didn't want it. 'It's too soon,' they would say. 'We're not ready for it yet.' In situations like that, you can either go for the federal dollars or private. Xenia had been promised the first, and was afraid that if it accepted commercial developers, its position with the feds would be compromised." Even before April was out, the city was applying to HUD for funding in the neighborhood of $50 to $75 million in damage losses. No one really knew what the proper appraisals should be, and worse, no one really knew how the feds might respond or with what. They only knew that they had been promised and deserved help for having suffered so grievously. To Hill, who had worked in a bigger bank in a bigger city, and who had seen what private money could do, they were mistaken. "They didn't need a Galbraith," he said, referring to the powerful Columbus developer who had molded Cincinnati's Fountain Square, "but a Koetzle or a Hallenstein, the kind who have done malls or condominium developments on a smaller scale around the state—they might have been able to do something here." One afternoon in May, Cart walked out of his office to greet a developer from Indianapolis who wanted to talk private investment. He hadn't made any headway anyplace else in town, so he thought he'd try Hill. "It was too bad," Cart said later, "but I had to turn him away. I told him the interest just wasn't there."

Yet there was more to it than that. For all its national attention and heroic recovery, Xenia was still a small town. Its dominant opinion-makers were either businessmen unused to big-time transactions or economically unsophisticated professionals. When in early May Jack Jordan became temporarily vexed at the government's delay in sending money, he ran an editorial that listed some of the uses assigned to federal funds. Among them: $60,000 to study Polish bisexual frogs and $12,600 to investigate the chromosomal makeup of chipmunks. "Lest we feel a little guilty at accepting Washington doles," he concluded, "consider how much better uses could be made of those funds here." It was a clever ruse which no doubt hit the mark with many Xenians, but it was a long way from calling for alternative sources of funding. Like most small towns, Xenia was suspicious of new ideas and new people. The federal funding was safe. Cart Hill's idea was new and so, for that matter, was he.

Almost as soon as he arrived in town, Cart had started urging

213

the other financial institutions to hire a consultant to study ways of updating the central city. The result had been the proposals which had been tabled just three months before the tornado. Cart had also hazarded the opinion that it would be nice if one could buy a pair of conservative shoes in the city, had expressed his regret at the lack of good restaurants, had joined two civic boards, and had built the Citizens' National Bank into an aggressive enterprise that was taking business from its rivals. "Cart has moved very fast . . . ," Jack Jordan would say, and his voice trailed off to leave you with the impression that in Xenia, maybe, the race was not always to the swift.

In any event, Hill was not asked to sit on the Spirit of Seventy-Four, despite his proven dedication to the well-being of Xenia, and when a corporation for the redevelopment of the downtown was finally established, Hill had nothing to do with it, although he was the only one around who had had any experience in setting up corporations. "I didn't have the proper fear," he explained. "Jordan couldn't stand that. Once you've been nailed, you're supposed to shut up. I didn't do that." The *Gazette* would later publish Hill's criticism of the corporation and the *Gazette*'s response thereto.

Cart was, on the other hand, asked to sit on a downtown redevelopment subcommittee of the Spirit, and on a "reforestation" delegation ("That's how much they thought of me; I think we distributed 13,000 pounds of grass seed"). Together with Keith Maynor, president of the Xenia National Bank, and Mayor William Wilson, he backed the Xenia "Tornado Relief Fund," a vehicle for all those who wanted to donate money to the city, but, for reasons of their own, preferred not to do it through the Red Cross. Hill's and Maynor's banks held the funds and distributed them throughout the city, notably to the Inter-Faith Council. Beyond that, his recovery activities were almost totally banking-oriented.

He first slapped a moratorium on all mortgages and virtually all loan payments to prevent a run on deposits. He talked with customers giddy with insurance money and families hysterical with loss. He addressed luncheon clubs whose members normally

214

found it challenging to balance their checkbooks and to government officials whose responsibility it was to refinance the city. Like Dick Hupman, he was at the mercy of uncertainty and could make no plans to rebuild the branch until The Plan was determined. But also like Hupman, he was very much in favor of any improvements that might be negotiated and more than willing to wait. Happily, his premonitions of pressure on the bank's reserves never were confirmed; just the opposite happened. "People had nothing to buy and all the food was free," he explained. "Besides that, they continued to take their mortgages and loan obligations very seriously. At first they worried whether the bank and all their records were still here, but after that our biggest problem was what to do with all the insurance money that came flooding in."

18

INDEED, if any facet of the Xenia tornado was a story with a happy ending, insurance was it. Almost as soon as the storm system moved in over Ohio, switchboards were blinking and telephones buzzing as branch offices alerted regional headquarters that an emergency was at hand. Jack Jackson, a claims representative in the Centerville, Ohio, office of Allstate, recalled sardonically that he was on the phone to Cleveland when hailstones the size of baseballs began drowning out the sound and he went to the window to see what was happening. "Just a minute, John," he said, "it seems like we're gonna have a little windstorm," and they both chuckled because in the insurance industry a "little windstorm" is not all bad. It triggers scores of small claims—damage to a workshed roof, a broken window here and there—and thus lowers the average cost per claim when, at the end of the year, total money paid out is divided by the total claims filed. But this time Jackson didn't laugh long. Centerville is a suburb of Dayton only fifteen miles east of Xenia, and that afternoon it was a box seat for observing the monstrous funnel headed northeast.

Allstate was one of dozens of companies that kept their switchboards open late that night. As Jackson put it, "We'd anticipated a lot of hail damage, and we called all the employees we could get in touch with for the sake of reporting claims that night. As word of the severity of the tornado damages filtered through, we called

216

our regional facility at Hudson, Ohio, and advised them of a catastrophe loss [the big apple]. That set the gears in motion." Of course it took a long time for a true picture of the Xenia scenario to emerge. With telephone lines gone, people in shock, and a police perimeter around the city, it was difficult for agents to get in or for victims to get word out. By midnight, the Centerville office of Allstate had handled fewer than seventy claims, mostly of the nickel-and-dime variety.

By Thursday morning, however, enough agents were seeping through the roadblocks to comprise a subculture of their own. They were ubiquitous, faces grim amid the rubble, Polaroids snapping, sympathetic to the victims they met, but clearly on a business trip. They had to decide how many extra claims representatives they would need, how many adjusters, and how much it would all cost. These preliminary reports were then cross-checked with company files on past disasters. Said Jackson, "The home office can tell in minutes how many houses are gone or partially damaged, how much in living expenses we will have to pay, how many cars rented, motel rooms, etc." Within days, trailers were set up to house emergency delegations from some of the larger companies, potentates from New York flew in to survey the scene, and insurance representatives sat at the FDAA one-stop center. "In this kind of situation," commented one agent, "you don't have time to count the hours. You just know you're going to be working from daylight to dark in the field, locating and helping people, and then you're going to go home or whatever place you can and unsnarl paperwork."

The dedication paid off. When it was all over, the vast majority of homeowners had little but praise for the manner in which their claims had been handled. There were numerous stories of insurance adjusters writing out checks in front of a devastated lot, and many more of an initial payment for living expenses soon followed by the whole compensation. Dick Hupman went looking for his agent, a local man, the Friday after the tornado, and was told that he was picking through the rubble of his office. Walking to the spot, Dick found him with a check in his pocket already made out to Richard Hupman. "That's living expenses," he was told. "Find

217

yourself a hotel or a motel, and when that runs out, come back and see me."

For many of the businessmen, however, life was not so simple. Jim Kennedy, the young heir to Kennedy Korners, waited months for his full payment. Because the various buildings in his shopping complex were insured by five different companies, and the contents were insured by seven, Kennedy dealt with one man from the General Adjustment Bureau who represented them all. He got some money right away, primarily for content loss; then the battle began. "The city inspected us and said the place had to come down," he said. "Then we had two engineers of our own look at it and they said it had to come down. Next came a state building inspector and he agreed with the rest of 'em. So then the adjuster sends in his people and they say it can be repaired." A heated exchange ensued, with Kennedy threatening to go to court and pressure applied from all sides to make the adjuster come to heel. "You can either jawbone your way through it or sue," Kennedy said. "Fortunately for us, jawboning worked. But it was frustrating as hell. You pay your premiums on time year after year and you expect to get your money without a hassle. Well, it was a hassle." Jim was not fully paid off even by Christmas, and he noted that several of his business peers, particularly the powerful Kroehler's, had been put through the same kind of wringer. "And oddly enough, a lot of it was blue-chip companies," he added. "The little ones, the ones you don't hear about so much, they paid right up."

Months later, the Ohio Insurance Institute and the American Insurance Association dubbed the April tornadoes "Catastrophe No. 74" and conservatively estimated the total losses at more than $430 million, of which fully $75 million occurred in Xenia. Inevitably, some companies suffered severe losses, and for one, a proposed rate reduction on homeowners' policies in Ohio was delayed. Industry-wide, the consensus was that reserves had been adequate to handle the disaster. But if another of similar magnitude occurred any time soon, rates would have to rise sharply.

Nonetheless, insurance was the lubricant which greased Xenia's comeback. It provided the surest and fastest infusion of cash the city was to receive and made it possible for most people to rebuild

218

long before the commissioners approved their doing so. It gave them a confidence no amount of bureaucratic promises could match, and it even deterred some of them from seeking federal aid as fast as they might have. Said Jack Look, the Small Business Administration attorney who arrived in Xenia almost three weeks after the tornado, "This town actually has more cash than it's ever had in its life. Usually reality shocks people into asking for help. Here, the influx of so much money already has permitted people the luxury of shock and inaction. It gives them a lot more time to get going."

Look was frustrated, partly because people were not acting wisely in their own behalf, and partly because the SBA was in a bit of a pickle. The problem arose from a misunderstanding. In the first week to ten days after the storm, SBA representatives, it seems, had advised disaster victims to use insurance money to pay off their old mortgages and then to take out an SBA loan at 5 percent for the purpose of rebuilding their homes. The prospect was too good to be true. Here was a chance to replace 7 or 8 percent mortgages with 5 percent loans, all at the government's expense. In their distress, Xenians never doubted what they were hearing, but did eagerly what they were told. Then the boom was lowered. It wasn't true after all. The SBA officials had been misinformed. They were permitted to make such a deal only in the case of floods. In floods, victims usually had no insurance because flood insurance was difficult or impossible to obtain; in floods, SBA officials were empowered to pick up a first mortgage and combine it with an SBA loan so that, in effect, the first mortgage was paid off. But not in Xenia. Here, where most people had insurance, the best the SBA could do was to pay off the uninsured portion of their losses.

It was just the kind of thing to spoil a federal agency's good name. "They screwed us," people started saying. "They told me to pay off my mortgage and now I can't get it back and how am I going to be able to rebuild? I've been ripped off by the feds." Indeed, when the rumors started flying that SBA loans would not be made for previously insured losses, a minor panic ensued. It subsided very slowly, and with the aid of a great deal of patient explanation on the part of Look and his colleague, Wayne Luders, disaster project director for Ohio.

"Some of you will have some bad things to say about us. Go ahead, there will be no holds barred," Luders told a group of businessmen in one of his first meetings. "I won't say that we can help everyone in this situation across the board, but we are urging anyone who feels he's been misled to come in and see us. Each case is different and I would like people to meet with us in a one-on-one to have it explained." Luders had an affable, golfing-buddy approach that Xenians immediately warmed to. He looked honest and talked straight and he continued to urge, over and over, that everyone with any kind of loss come in and see him. But they had to come and discuss it individually.

It later developed that the SBA did in some instances make good an entire loan at 5 percent. First, of course, it tried to get the bank or lending institution to reinstate the canceled mortgage. But when that failed, as it did in one out of ten cases, the SBA picked up the loss on its terms. (By disaster law, it had to stay with 5 percent for all disaster loans.) And this was so fortunate for a few people that there was reason to fear it might touch off a whole new wave of resentment if it became generally known. One man, for example, had taken the original SBA advice to heart and paid off the loan for his Pinecrest home. "I was told financing would be available," he said, "and then nothing happened. I began hearing rumors, so I checked into it and went back to the mortgage company to ask them to reinstate the loan. No dice. So then I go back to SBA with the form they had given me, tell 'em the story, and they made me the loan for the whole thing." This man had always wanted a new house, one where "the wood smelled fresh," and now, after twenty years and raising a large family, in an economy that had pushed interest rates almost to 11 percent, he was getting it at 5 percent, as originally promised.

During the two months Wayne Luders was in Ohio, he uncovered almost three hundred mortgages paid off prematurely because of bad SBA advice. One way or another, he renegotiated every one at terms that were comfortable for the client and, in so doing, reaffirmed the SBA's reputation as an organization of hon-

220

orable men. Yet for some people that was not enough. Possibly because they believed the government did not have the right to make a mistake, and possibly because they needed a scapegoat for their misery, they continued to take offense at the memory. Like the stale odor of a red tide, it clung to Xenia for months.

It was impossible to say when the emergency phase was over. Some charted it from the time the National Guard left the city, on April 22, and they could get a drink at the Hofbrau Haus again. Others felt it coincided with the closing of the Red Cross operations at the Y, one week later, when teenagers could again play pool and senior citizens could sit in sewing circles without stumbling over caseworkers filling out forms. By then, certainly, in the opinion of the experts, most emergency needs had been met.

All over town people stopped fussing over the comparative effectiveness of the Red Cross and the Salvation Army, and began to make peace with whatever place HUD had found to house them. They used the yellow port-o-johns less and less, as they found fewer reasons to return to their lots, or even to Xenia. At Wright-Patterson, Norm Steinlauf wangled more evenings in Cincinnati, where he had a choice of three gourmet restaurants to rebuild his strength, and Phil McIntire and Mike Chavinski grew increasingly annoyed at being saluted every time they entered the base. By the end of April they had done everything that an emergency operation required: the one-stop was shut down, the damage assessments were completed, and the other federal agencies, coughing and sputtering though they might be, were doing as Steinlauf directed. FDAA headquarters in the airplane hangar had all the exuberance of a county fair one week after closing, and its three principals looked forward gloomily to the months of paperwork Xenia would require. By the end of the first week in May they had all returned, gratefully, to Manhattan.

Even the media began to withdraw. Grudgingly, they had to admit that Xenia had been almost done to death by now, and that if they kept it up there would be nothing left for the "three months later" or "six months later" stories that would inevitably follow. Tourists, though, had no intention of leaving the community to itself. As long as there was debris to be viewed or misery to be contemplated, they would continue to flock there, leaving Bob Stewart frustrated almost to the point of knots in his stomach, but helpless. "If we reinstate the emergency status and call in the Guard, that means reimposing the curfew and again banning sales of liquor," he said. "We're better off gutting it out." So they waited, as day after day truckload after truckload, hauling off the rubble, stripped away the tourist attractions and bared Xenia to the bone.

It was tough to watch. Jim Houchins, director of the Corps of Engineers operations, had warned that the town was going to look unexpectedly stark once his men had finished. And day by day his prediction seemed to be coming true. Houchins estimated that 800,000 cubic yards of debris were removed all told—most of it to an abandoned quarry on Route 235 that belonged to the Southwest Portland Cement Company. It took two weeks to clear away Kroehler's (the last to go because of the insurance war), and ten days to level the Steele Building (which some people said went only because Doe Hawthorne, president of the Home Federal Savings and Loan next door, wanted to get rid of it).

Ray Higgins watched the progress in a doleful spirit; he remembered most of the landmarks that were disappearing, and he knew he would not live to see the eventual reconstruction. "I'm seventy-seven now," he said with finality. "The Xenia I knew is gone." Deciding that it would be foolish to write about anything else, he laid aside three columns he had backlogged, and began to create his own remembrance of the past. "The workmen who built the Steele Building in 1895," he reported, "complained that the iron was not properly prepared, but the workmen who tore it down in the wake of the tornado treated those old beams as precious metal." Or, of the hotel: "It contained registrations of baseball teams that came to play here and remained overnight and should show the name of Charles Dickens, the British author, who reported an uncomfortable trip to America at the height of his fame."

Higgins knew that the Steele Building had been built by a Belgian architect who couldn't make up his mind what it should

222

look like, and that the Courthouse had been built in part by his own father, a stonemason. All of it was set down in the "Cracker Barrel" column and people responded gratefully. "I didn't know that, Ray," or "Funny, I'd forgotten those things," he would hear on the street, and he smiled his thanks. Then his eyes would narrow and he would say in mock jest, "This younger generation thinks that anything that happened before World War II is ancient history. I hope they're reading it too!"

On Tuesday, May 21, HUD announced that it was reserving a $3 million federal grant for redevelopment in Xenia. The money, taken from reserves earmarked for HUD urban renewal projects all over the country, represented the last funds available under fiscal 1973–74 allocations, but immediately raised the hope that more would become available when the 1974–75 allocations were made. The announcement was greeted with much fanfare in Xenia —banner headlines in the *Gazette* and a renewed excitement at the Spirit of Seventy-Four meetings—and it came not a moment too soon. Depressed at the emerging nakedness of their town, and weary with waiting for the moratorium to be lifted, Xenians were impatient with what they perceived as a lack of federal empathy.

Simultaneous with their discouragement, however, were the ongoing hopes for the Plan, now nearing presentation date. Besides protracted chatter about its righting past wrongs, there was considerable speculation that it would include pre-tornado dreams. To wit, the bypass completed around town, a high rise for the elderly, two sewer trunk lines leading out of Xenia, and a much needed industrial park south of the city. "Xenia today is well known for its disaster," Senator Howard Metzenbaum told them soon after the storm. "But it won't be so well known in three months; in a year it'll be even less so." The implication was that they should plug hard immediately if they wanted results. So they began by reaching for the moon.

19

THE PLAN was unveiled on Saturday afternoon, June 1, exactly as scheduled, at a well—but not too well—attended meeting at the OSSO Home. Packaged in a ring binder, its 185 pages filled with maps of pre-tornado zoning, recommended land uses, and alternative concepts, it was a carefully conceived, laboriously detailed document, aptly entitled "Xenia Rebuilds." No one could argue with its major precepts. The Plan called for an end to the helter-skelter development, with houses and factories and stores all on top of one another, that had characterized much of Xenia in the past. It proposed a mall in the downtown business district, a green belt around Shawnee Creek, and a neat isolation of industry in the southwest quadrant of town. It urged the widening of several principal streets, and it noted, without emotion, that while the flavor of the North End was gone forever, "a distinguished atmosphere can reappear if proper design controls are followed." Indeed, looking at the proposed land-use map, with its graceful interweaving of dots and lines and heavy dark squares, was like looking at a handsome patchwork quilt.

"We have the capability and the duty to come up with a better quality of life not only for ourselves, but for our grandchildren," said lawyer Jim Cox in support of the Plan. "It is our duty to those who died and suffered serious injury to come up with something better. Do not reject all planning because

224

you personally disagree with one or two things. These planners are professionals and you can see it in what they've come up with here." All over town, leaders like Cox were talking up the Plan, imploring fellow Xenians to read it, criticize it, and then make suggestions. The point of the whole thing, they kept saying, was that here was a signpost, a set of guidelines for future growth. It was designed to be flexible and to give the city a number of options in charting its future. As Jack Jordan put it, "It's our ball game to win or lose."

The city—meaning Stewart, the commissioners, and the Spirit of Seventy-Four—had targeted July 1 as the date for some kind of decision on how the renewal should proceed, and they were all eager to get going. Stewart had already won permission to set up an office of community development, and had hired twenty-nine-year-old William Korte, of HUD's Cincinnati office, to run it. ("I want somebody who runs, not walks," he said when he announced the appointment.) Korte was to oversee all land acquisitions for the city and to coordinate the actual implementation of the downtown plan. Meanwhile, the moratorium on rebuilding in the central business district was extended through June 28, and the task of seeking citizen input was begun in earnest. All along, of course, there had been dialogue between the city fathers and the townspeople about how Xenia should be rebuilt—but always in the shadow of the unknown Plan. Now the Plan was in hand, and it was vital to learn what the general reaction was.

At first it was hard to determine. Gordon Shepard, a member of the Xenia city-planning commission, raised his voice in protest only five days after the unveiling, arguing that many business areas would be rezoned as residential and that businessmen had better approach the proposal warily. Shepard was also indignant because the planning commission per se had never been consulted during the development of the Plan, and charged that the City Commission was ignoring it. "We are only a recommending body and we have no power," he said. "There has not been good rapport between us and the commission, and the commission can do what it wants. They may already have their minds made up." He was, of course, instantly and icily rebutted in the pages of the *Gazette*, by both Moon Mullins, president of the commission, and by Jack Jordan.

Most businessmen, however, and indeed most residents, were far less critical—at the outset. They wanted to know how a particular aspect of the Plan was going to affect their own situation and, possibly, the surrounding neighborhood; the rest they would leave for someone else to worry about. What about a return to single-family homes along West Second Street? What about single-family and professional office units, as before, along North Detroit? This was the kind of question most often asked; and for a time, it was enough to hear someone official-looking reply that nothing was definite yet. When a group of downtown merchants expressed their concern about the same issues Gordon Shepard had raised, Jim Cox assured them that no zoning changes were certain, and that until the city adopted a plan, nothing could be predicted. That was all they wanted to hear.

Indeed, as the weeks slipped by, public-spirited Xenians began to sense a growing apathy among the citizenry at large. On Wednesday, June 19, fewer than 250 residents showed up for a city-wide meeting at the OSSO Home to hear representatives of both the city commission and the planning commission. And of those 250, it was apparent to reporter Rich Heiland that few had bothered to read or try to understand the Plan. "They were mostly just there to attack specific individuals or groups," he said later. "One woman launched a scathing attack on Jack Jordan, claiming that he failed to publish letters by her in the 'Saturday Forum,' then . . . charged that the Spirit of Seventy-Four was not to be trusted with conveying citizen feelings to the city. . . ."

She said a lot of other things too, but more than likely she was articulating what a lot of Xenians were feeling. Asking only when they could return to their city, their answer was a 185-page tome that most of them had neither the inclination, nor the ability, to read. It was all well and good to explain patiently that the West End really wasn't suited to residential housing, but how do you convey that to a seventy-five-year-old railroad pensioner who has lived happily between Kroehler's and Kennedy Korners for the

226

last twenty years? How do you tell him that the house he has thrived in—a four-room, one-story shack—is impractical if not impossible to rebuild?

David Lyon was the man in the middle. "The thing people don't want to talk about is change," he theorized at the time of the controversy. "Every time the subject comes up there's a great silence. Well, you've got to change some things." Lyon, thirty-one years old and fresh from a job as coordinator of Dayton's community renewal program, had come to Xenia a year earlier, hired by the city after a grandstand effort on the part of planning commission chairman Al Klose to convince his peers that a planner and staff were needed.

"I saw three problems right away," Lyon recalled, "cluttered zoning, lack of land for industrial development, and a paucity of either multifamily housing or any decent housing at all in the thirty-thousand-dollar range." The city was like an old house that no one had redecorated; Lyon had to make it habitable for a modern, bustling family. Then, in one fell swoop, the tornado made zoning distinctions moot, rendered important industries homeless, and eradicated much of the city's low-income housing. (Xenians were surprised to read, in the small type of the Plan, that 47.9 percent of the disaster victims had incomes of less than $10,000, while 16.7 percent had incomes under $6,000.) "We have now a magnificent opportunity for implementation of a complete urban strategy," Lyon said shortly after the storm. "But just changing the face of the buildings is not going to cut it. We must change the land use, develop architectural themes, get rid of shoddy, sloppy development."

Could he be blamed for thinking big? His opportunity was indeed a planner's dream: to have a city stripped naked and quivering to be rebuilt. But there was a hitch. It had to be done exactly right, for it was going to be around a long, long time. Lyon realized that: "Before, with a program, if you failed you still had what you had before. If we fail now, it could kill the city." And then the line he hesitated to say, "A whore with plastic surgery is still a whore."

227

Believing as he did, Lyon pumped hard for adoption of the Plan. He spoke to embittered businessmen who wanted James' Market to return to its former location instead of the government center being proposed in its place. He met with North Enders who wanted single-family houses all the way to Church Street instead of the apartments suggested by the Plan, and he pleaded with West Enders to be reasonable: "You might have had a gas station in your neighborhood that stayed open until midnight and kept you awake, or maybe your street is too small. We all know of areas that should be improved, and now we have the chance." When all else failed, Lyon would try the ultimate tactic, "You've got to think of the good of the overall community." But all too often that merely sent angry homeowners storming out of the room.

What finally happened in the waning days of June is anybody's guess. It was increasingly clear that the bulk of the townspeople, when they troubled to study the Plan, had grave reservations about it. They wanted "Xenia back the way it was," and no amount of logical argument could dissuade them. Their minds were made up.

Increasingly, too, the majority of the city leaders and decision-makers seemed to have *their* minds made up: they wanted the Plan. Lyon looked to it for salvation, Spirit of Seventy-Four leaders pushed it as the shortest (and surest) route to a bigger and better Xenia, Jordan plugged it in the *Gazette*. "*Xenia Rebuilds* is a thoughtful publication that too few people have examined," he wrote. "If approached with an open mind, the book may be both exciting and stimulating—it could open vistas of local suggestions that otherwise never would be tapped."

On June 27, the Plan was adopted. Announced by a banner headline in the *Gazette*, it was modified somewhat before final approval by the commission and it thereafter became known as the "overlay zoning plan." This meant, in common terms, that Xenia's previously scattered zoning scheme was now to be "overlaid" with the proposals set forth in the *Xenia Rebuilds* document. It meant that the city fathers, for the most part, liked what the MVRPC had come up with, and intended to implement it as far as possible. It meant that Gordon Shepard may not have been all

228

wrong when he suggested, earlier in the month, that some people had their minds made up from the start.

July was hot. It was marked, in Xenia, by sunny days and the sounds of rebuilding everywhere. In Arrowhead and Pinecrest the houses were reappearing so fast that it was beginning to be difficult to tell what had happened—from the elevated level of the bypass, the roofscape looked to be unbroken again. The West End and the North End were bleaker, with vast sections of open space to haunt the eye, but there, too, the reconstruction was under way. Kennedy's was operating an open-air market on its old lot, selling fruits, vegetables, and a profusion of hanging plants. On King Street, the three *casas grandes* belonging to Bud Schmidt, Delmar Bone, and Jessie Chew were well on their way back. Most other lots lay empty, or were still disfigured by a battered shell, but a few showed foundations poured and a first story rising. Downtown, the library, the Courthouse, and City Hall had been sandblasted. Older homes had been painted a gleaming white, and geraniums were growing in front gardens. Cart Hill's bank had had the ugly black scar removed from its façade. The net effect was cleanliness and pride, a desire to make the most of what little remained, and, in that way, take heart for the great deal that was left to do.

On July 6, the antiques from the Xenia Hotel were auctioned off. The event—and it was an event, covered by news media from Dayton and Cincinnati—took place at the gargantuan Montgomery County Fairgrounds coliseum. Hal and Wink Black had lured between two and three thousand spectators, some from as far away as Texas, by advertising in newspapers throughout the tristate area and in antique trade journals nationwide. Bidding started at 10 A.M., with the antique glassware going up first. There were dozens of pieces, representing every variety of cut glass and crystal, and the auctioneer held each one over his head. Still some spectators couldn't see, and they started to yell, "What's he got? How can I tell what I'm bidding on?" It took several hours to unload all the glass, but when the receipts were totaled, they amounted to more than $11,000.

Next on the block was the furniture, and this too was difficult to display. The auctioneer moved from article to article, assuming that the bidders had examined everything beforehand but finding all too often that they hadn't. People pushed and shoved for a better look, shouted to be heard, sweated in the glare of the television lights. But they bought. The highest price paid was $1,000 for a four-poster cannonball bed of solid cherry—Wink considered it a museum piece. The same purchaser bought a matching dresser with marble top for $500. A Regina disc music box went for $850, an eighteenth-century blunderbuss for $200. The McKinley bed, however, came in below Wink's expectations, for a paltry $675. What surprised everybody were the relatively large prices paid for hotel memorabilia: stationery, postcards, silverware, lamps, faded pictures, and worn fixtures. "They wanted some souvenir of their town's history," Wink said in retrospect. "It's like a lot of locals wanted hotel bricks to put on their terraces. One lady picked up a few because she'd spent her honeymoon there."

The auction lasted until 7 P.M., and, all in all, the Blacks were extremely pleased with the results. The take came to more than $20,000, and if some things hadn't done as well as the owners expected, many others did far better. At the end, Wink Black was exhausted—physically, not emotionally. "Nothing is emotional after a tornado," she said.

From his semidetached position, Cart Hill watched the renewal progress of his adopted city. Partly because of his differences with Jordan, and partly because it was a time when voices were best kept low, he worked behind the scene deliberately, quietly visiting Stewart or the city commissioners whenever he had something to say. Urging them to sustain the moratorium as long as need be, and not to bow to pressure groups, he impressed on them his concern that no action be taken too quickly, lest it not be in effect too long. Privately he shuddered when the Plan was adopted so quickly. It had all gone so fast, he speculated, that the rumblings of discontent had been artificially repressed. Undoubtedly they would surface.

The only time Cart raised his voice publicly—thus invoking public criticism—was to question the procedures surrounding the formation of the Xenia Community Urban Development Corporation. "XCURC," as it came to be known, was the hasty creation of several city officials and civic leaders who were suddenly told that they must have a private development corporation in order to oversee the disbursement of the $3.5 million urban renewal funds (an extra half million had been added) the feds had pledged. As Jim Cox put it, "We were told one morning that this corporation had to be set up, and we were told to have a board of directors by that afternoon. We didn't make that deadline, but the board was named the next day." The purpose of the corporation, simply put, was to coordinate the process of renewal in all its particulars: land acquisition, clearance, planning, and project construction.

Cart's gripe was that Jordan was heavily involved here too. "Is it true that Spirit of Seventy-Four president Jack Jordan is heading up the corporation, or was at least instrumental in setting it up?" he asked in a DBA meeting in August. The question was pointed, but not out of line, for there were many present who felt XCURC was not broadly enough based and who wanted assurance that it was going to be handled correctly. Not only was it deciding the fate of the businessmen's environment, but it was a profit-making venture whose shares were for sale. Cox replied that Jordan was in no way involved with the corporation—the editor considered it would constitute a conflict of interest—but many other Spirit of Seventy-Four members were involved. The naming of the board "was arbitrary," Cox confessed, "but given the problem it was the only way we could do it."

Predictably, Cart was rhetorically spanked in the *Gazette* for his outburst. "A Thursday meeting of the DBA . . . prompted Cart Hill, Citizens' Bank head, to question my heavy-handed involvement. Why? I don't know. I'm not involved," complained Jordan. But this was one case where the hunter was under the gun as surely as his quarry. Throughout August, the feeling grew that Jack Jordan had gone too far with his editorials, had talked about "my town" once too often, and had criticized one person too many. This mood surfaced at the end of the month in a sign reading "JORDANVILLE" that was left outside Dick Hupman's trailer. There was a flurry of speculation about who had done it, but Jordan just laughed. "I don't think it's so bad," he mused.

Besides, there were more important things to think about. July 1 had come and gone, with no word of any new federal funding beyond the $3.5 million grant announced in May. In fact, the urban-renewal program from which it sprang had been terminated by President Nixon, and there was a question when or if Xenia would qualify for any of the "community grant" money replacing it. Here and there the government had sprinkled a little more cash —$100,000 from HUD for planning, $50,000 from the Economic Development Administration to help with economic recovery— but nothing like the $30 million locals were forecasting as the sum needed to implement the Plan. Also on the minus side: Kroehler's had committed itself (after a long and difficult round of negotiations) to staying in Xenia, but had not inspired a lot of other industries to follow suit. School Superintendent Carl Adkins had arranged for temporary modules to be used for classrooms in September, but he was having a hellish hard time convincing the feds to give him the right kind of modules: the Cadillacs and not the Pintos. He knew his constituents were liable to be in them for some time to come.

Worst of all perhaps, the Plan was not working.

Parts of it, alas, had been impractical all along. The suggestion that the Xenia Foundry violated the residential character of the North End, and might therefore be moved, was hopelessly quixotic. The foundry was vital to Xenia's immediate economic recovery, and was one of the first things repaired. The suggestion of a green belt along Shawnee Creek fell flat. Shawnee Creek babbled through some of Xenia's prime industrial real estate, and the notion that such land could be purchased by the city and then be given over to greenery soon proved preposterous. Even in the West End, where planners had made a point of overcoming past zoning foulups by proposing a clustering of townhouses, apartments, etc., all was for naught. Who was going to pay for them?

In late August, the cries of anguish were heard once again: businessmen groaning because they couldn't rebuild: property-

232

holders insisting they were being cheated; homeowners clamoring to have their old neighborhood back. All familiar themes, but now the city fathers began to take them seriously. "If we keep on like this, the present administration isn't going to be around much longer," said City Commissioner Charles Cook. For the first time, they admitted they might have moved too fast.

North Detroit Street was a case in point. For years it had been flanked on the West by sturdy old houses with front porches and shady trees, on the East by Shawnee Park. Then, more recently, with the influx of traffic that a state highway brought, many of the homes had been converted to offices for doctors, dentists, and the like. The zoning was altered accordingly. Now, under the overlay zoning plan, North Detroit was switched back to residential—specifically, medium-density residential, meaning apartments, townhouses, whatever. Many people who owned land there, and had bought it specifically for office use, now found that they were prohibited from doing what they'd planned and, to boot, that their property was worth less as residential land. It seemed that people didn't want to live on a heavily trafficked street like North Detroit. If the dilemma was not solved, realtors insisted, the land would lie vacant. Other areas suffered similar woes.

On Thursday, August 22, Dave Lyon gave the city commissioners a confidential list of proposed changes in the overlay strategy. The move represented a capitulation on two counts: it was Lyon's admission that he had been wrong in holding out for too much change too fast, and it was the commission's admission that a "bigger and better Xenia" might not be synonymous with a reasonable and realistic Xenia. Said Lyon, some months later, "It was a question of money and how far a city can legally go to prevent people from using their land as they want. Take West Main, where the Mobile Station and the Goodyear Tire Center are. They were zoned residential after the tornado, but who's going to make it go? Or look at King Street. It's fine to talk about an historical concept, but who's going to develop the controls? How do you build an historic house? Again, reality. The benefits would accrue to the people already living there, and the cost would go to the person who was trying to rebuild. So this became a low-priority item. The most important objective was to get back to a permanent situation as quickly as possible; we felt that putting up additional road-blocks would have encouraged people to leave the city. Cities are like individuals. Our dreams don't always come about. So do we hold out for the dream, and let everything else stand idle, or do we get the city rebuilt?"

It was a sobering, and in many ways sad, realization, a surrender to the facts. Commending the action, Jack Jordan could not help editorially commending Lyon too: "Last, but by no means least, this step marked the maturing of City Planner David Lyon. Lyon had, since the tornado, often been accused of not communicating with the public, and with not being able to get his ideas across in understandable fashion. This week, in the work session, Lyon was every bit the planner with concise and well-studied reasons for his suggestions. If some had doubts about the abilities of Xenia's planner in the past, his actions in past weeks are a cause for re-evaluation. Lyon obviously is listening to the community and trying to respond."

It took a little over a month from the time Lyon presented his changes to the commission until they were adopted into law. By then it was the end of September and Xenia could see rather accurately where it was going. Much of the original Plan had been scrapped. Street improvements had been temporarily shelved, and traffic was flowing as fitfully as ever. West Main and North King had been opened to construction—the Burger Chef was back in business on the one, and two-story pillboxes were rising on the other. "FOR SALE" signs littered the West End and North Detroit; the foundry was humming once more.

Only downtown in the eight-block area bounded by Main, Mechanic, Church and Detroit was there no sign of activity, no work crews digging, no glass walls rising. This was the "urban-renewal zone," or as it came to be known, the "superblock" reserved for downtown renovation. Here, the city fathers promised, would stand the one important feature of the original plan that had not been scrapped: the mall. It would infuse new life into the decaying central city and, perhaps more important, provide Xenians with real evidence that some good had come from the tornado. Already they were talking excitedly about it: "It will bring shoppers in from miles around." "It will make Xenia a beautiful small city." Sometime in September, or thereabouts, a subtle shift occurred in the local vernacular. Instead of talking about "the Plan," people started talking about "the Mall."

20

FALL CAME early that year. Normally a golden time when sunny afternoons soften the loss of summer and the leaves ease slowly from the trees, it struck with a killing frost the first week in September. It ruined a patch of green beans that the Mallows were ready to pick and hastened the maturing of the acorn squash they sold alongside their pumpkins. But for the farmers, the early cold was just one more in a lengthening list of meteorological annoyances.

The summer had been marked by drought—a long, waterless interlude that lasted from early July until well into August, forcing them to irrigate daily. "Sometimes that's good," Ralph said. "We water the fields while the people with the gardens forget to. Then their plants dry up and they gotta come to us to buy." But this year the Mallows' roadside trade had been off about 30 percent. The customers weren't there. During the summer, they had changed the tires on their tractor no fewer than eighteen times: the glass and metal left from the tornado kept puncturing them. They had been unable to spray what few apple trees remained, first because debris precluded access to them and then because their water mains were shut off for eleven weeks.

By the time the frost hit them, both brothers were resigned. They salvaged what tomatoes they could, picked the end of the corn, and got ready for the long winter of refurbishing their imple-

236

ments. Their greenhouses were at last under construction, and their mother's new home, a white, L-shaped bungalow of no particular style, was virtually complete. It was a far cry from the farm scene they had inhabited six months before, but they spoke with the confidence of modest ambition: "It'll come back . . . next year has to be better . . . besides, there aren't that many truck farmers left around here . . . the demand for this stuff's bigger than ever." Come Halloween, their home-grown pumpkins, the big, round orange ones that urbanites spend hours searching for, would sell for seventy-five cents apiece. Slightly smaller ones were slightly less.

For Rich Heiland, the advent of autumn was melancholy. The gathering cold, slipping through the cracks of the unheated farmhouse where he was staying, was an uncomfortable reminder of how long he had been away. He watched the gray skies hanging over still green fields and felt the blast of a wintry wind, and knew instinctively that the world was different. The sagging corn was a signal that the growing season was over. The ruddy complexion of his neighbor, Mr. Murphy, was the result of chill, not sunburn. The sputtering tractor, which had seemed to laugh in the summer, coughed and wheezed in the cold. Rich still wasn't back in his house, and now he described himself as displaced—a cold word that he hadn't wanted to use. "This morning," he wrote one day in September, "sitting at the kitchen table with a cup of steaming coffee and watching Mr. Murphy's tractor disappear up the muddy road, I realized it has been winter longer than I thought, and I want to come home. We all do."

He spoke for many. Still not back in their homes, or offices, people were hearing one thing from their contractors, another from the city officials, and a third from their neighbors. It all added up to a grim helplessness they were powerless to express. Rich also touched, in a subliminal way, the nagging sense that more and more were experiencing—the hunch that maybe, despite all the guts they had shown and their willingness to work, it just wasn't going to get much better. The mall was their one bright light.

As conceived by MVRPC, the mall was to be contemporary in

design and slow in evolution. It was to start with a few shops, and steadily expand as the need for more space became apparent. It could stop growing whenever Xenia wanted, but was envisioned as covering the whole four-block area bounded by Main, Detroit, Church, and Galloway. Market Street would be closed. (An alternate plan called for a mall only half that large, leaving Market Street open.) This was seen as the most practical way to restore office space to retailers, to bring suburban shoppers downtown, and to arrest the decay of the whole central business district by significantly upgrading a part of it. "All downtown businessmen must work together if the CBD is to be successfully reconstructed," the Plan warned. "The result will be an exciting, unique area if local businessmen have the creative vision for developing an area which possesses some of the historic qualities of the old Xenia while providing a stimulating new environment too."

The city had sparked to the idea. Delegations from Richmond, Indiana, came to talk about their mall, built in the aftermath of a cataclysmic explosion several years earlier. Delegations from Xenia went to Richmond, and to Columbus, Indiana, and to Kalamazoo, Michigan, where other "model" malls had been created. As June wore into July, Bill Korte's office of community development focused more and more on the northwest quadrant of Main and Detroit, where widespread damage made a mall ideal, and gradually the urban-renewal zone took shape. The HUD grant of $3.5 million was seen as seed money for this area, and was designated as such when the city made its formal request for the funds in August. It would enable Xenia to buy the land, pay relocation benefits, make site improvements, and plan for its future use. Then XCURC could receive the property, and either sell it to a developer or develop it itself.

Korte was excited. Stewart was excited. (Indeed, only Ray Higgins seemed not very excited. "A mall," he sputtered. "I'm going to tell you something: I've never seen a mall and I don't know anything about it. All I know is what I read in the *Gazette.*" The explanation for this remarkable cultural deficiency is that Higgins didn't drive a car—he never had. He seldom left Xenia, and when he did, it was not to visit malls. He wasn't curious.) Korte was so wound up, in fact, that when he arrived in Xenia in June he predicted to Stewart that ground would be broken by September. "Hold on, friend," the city manager had replied. "I like your enthusiasm, but you're in for a hell of a letdown if you think urban renewal works that fast." Stewart thought it would be at least a year before there was even a hint of construction.

The vision Xenians were now entertaining called for all four blocks to be built up at once, with a major department store from Dayton or Cincinnati anchoring the project. (The rest of the renewal zone would go to apartments and low-cost housing.) So strong was the image that it inspired Rich Heiland to write about Xenia gaining the admiration of the nation, "when television crews come to town to film shoppers lolling about an open air shopping area, sniffing flowers, listening to concerts, buying goods that before they had to go to Dayton to get."

As often happened, however, Stewart's prediction was correct. The HUD money was released to Xenia the last day of August, and Korte began the long process of appraisals the first day of September. It was rough going. To insure that each property-holder was offered a fair price for his land, two independent appraisers evaluated every lot. When they were finished, a third came in to insure accuracy. The result was progress at a snail's pace and a thick file on each parcel. By the end of November, only a few deals were completed, and there was already resentment.

"There's no pattern of consistency in the way they're buying," Hal Black charged. "They hop from one lot to another, pay a lot of money here and a little money there, and they haven't enough to buy all the land unless people settle for the prices offered." If the accusation was more bitter than accurate, it was entirely un-derstandable in the light of Black's position. Not only did he own the hotel property along Detroit Street, he also held two lots on Market Street—all situated well within the proposed mall. To his way of thinking, all such lots should be of equal value. After all, the mall was to be inward facing, covering four blocks equally. Why should a lot on the corner of Main and Galloway be worth more than a lot on the corner of Market and Detroit? Just because it was closer to the center of town? Black thought not. He thought

239

the city should pay all property-owners equal dollars, and he was prepared to go to court to make his case.

What touched him off was the announcement that Bill Eichman's lot, the site of the old appliance store on the corner of Main and Galloway, had gone for $53,000. ("I thought it was very fair," Eichman said.) "Fifty-three thousand dollars!" screamed Black. "When all he had was forty-nine feet of frontage! My two lots together on Market Street have eighty-four feet of frontage and they've only offered us forty-three thousand for the both of them. You call that fair appraising?"

Korte did. His defense was that property purchased for urban renewal—all across the country—was evaluated according to its former, not future, use. Thus Eichman's plot, at the center of town, was deemed the most valuable in the whole renewal zone —far more so than the hotel plot one block away. "In fact," said Korte, "when XCURC, or whoever, eventually sells this land, they'll sell it for less than we bought it for. It's simple economics: The prices we're paying are, in many instances, more than any merchant in some future mall could pay and still make a profit. Remember, we're buying vacant land for forty-five thousand dollars or better. If we sold it based on its future value, the owners would get less."

Like all touchy municipal issues, there was probably much to be said on both sides. There were rumors that Eichman was treated favorably because he had once been mayor of Xenia, and more rumors that the city fathers were "screwing the people on Market Street for the good of the people on Main."

Hal Black complained to Korte about not receiving an appraisal for his hotel. Over and over he would hear, "Oh, Hal, they were promised for this week: I just don't know where they are."

What was all too clear was that the city had been very reluctant to make public the prices paid Eichman and the few other property-holders first dealt with on West Main. Only when Pete Fusco, a much resented reporter for the Dayton *Daily News,* came in and blew the lid off did Stewart and his associates change their strategy. What was also very clear was that, right or wrong, Black was going to fight it to the finish. By the end of November he had

240

banded together most of the Market Street property-holders, and they had hired the best land-acquisition lawyer in the state, Hugh E. Kirkwood from Columbus. Kirkwood assured them that win or lose, they would get at least the amount the city had originally offered them.

To Korte it was all part of the game: "I think people should be satisfied; if it were my property I'd seek legal advice too; they have every right to do this." No doubt the city would get the land in the end, but meanwhile the groundbreaking was cruelly postponed. Korte maintained his optimism, and told Stewart that his biggest trouble the following spring would be complaints about the mud in the streets and the traffic snarls as a result of the construction. To which Stewart would always reply, "Remember what you said about September, Bill?"

For the city manager, it had been a long eight months. He was pleased with the work he had done to date, particularly the hiring of people like Korte and MVRPC, and with his success in keeping the various interest groups from one another's throats. Stewart was the ultimate administrator, able to choose men, pick brains, and ask questions without expecting glowing reports for answers. Said Korte in November, "More than any other person, he's held this city together for the last six months. Without him, I wouldn't be here." Still, Stewart was frustrated.

On a personal level he was considering building a new house to take the place of the rental his family had occupied since May, but he questioned whether 1975, with five commissioners coming up for re-election, was the time to do it. He knew these men, liked working with them, yet feared for their safe return to office. Reason: economics. Since the tornado, Xenia had been operating on revenues it had taken in during the previous year. But come 1975, with 40 percent of the tax base destroyed, Stewart knew he would not have the money needed to keep the city going at its present clip. Barring a grant from the state, which he had applied for but doubted he'd ever receive, the only alternative was to raise taxes. And in an environment where most citizens were still recovering from personal losses, and had in November voted a sizable new school levy, he wondered how a proposed tax increase would be greeted. More than likely, an opposition group would spring up on a platform of no new taxes, and then what would happen? "As long as the city maintains its momentum, I want to be part of it," he stated. "We've learned as much in eight months as it normally takes ten years to find out. But if they get a group in charge who doesn't want to keep that going, I don't know how much good I can do."

He was confronting the frustrations that many influential Xenians were facing. The frustration of trying to rebuild on a grand scale with limited resources. The frustration of changing, and disappearing, federal programs that in another day might have made all the difference. The frustration of an inflated economy where developers were reluctant to undertake new construction and where the normal growth processes were stunted. He was frustrated because many Xenians, even the most well-intentioned among them, were still too provincial to see beyond their own immediate interests.

"The other day," he said one afternoon in December, "I said to Jim Cox, president of the Downtown Businessmen's Association and of XCURC, 'Why not go after Penney's hard to take a place in the mall?' Cox said we couldn't because Bud Schmidt owns the building Penney's now rents. If Penney's moves out, what does he do?" To Stewart, it was short-sightedness, pure and simple. If Penney's came into the mall, he surmised, and the mall were a huge success, it would very quickly make the rest of downtown more appealing to other merchants, and Schmidt's building would be rented in no time. "Keep in mind," he said, "that the urban-renewal quadrant is only one area of redevelopment. We're saying that's only one sector. But it might kick off things across the street and all over town."

It was simply hard to be dispassionate when one's own business interests were involved. Doe Hawthorne, president of Home Federal, was all for the renewal zone—unless it affected the drive-in facility adjoining his building. If it did, Home Federal would be forced to move from town, he said. Hill too was for the renewal; he was the first to make a definite commit-

242

ment to move his business into the mall. But, when mention was made of a competing bank coming in also, he became cautious. "I had to give Stewart a little lesson in Economics I," he euphemized. "I had to tell him that there's just so much money available in Greene County. . . ." To Stewart, these concerns were understandable; what was regrettable was the inability to see that a better Xenia might benefit all of them in the long run.

By December, the prospects for the mall were anything but certain. Despite several meetings with representatives from Rike's, Elder Beerman's, and Shillito's, all large department stores in the area, Stewart had no serious proposals from any of them. Hill was the only local who had said he would come into the mall —and that was contingent on the city buying the old Citizens' National Bank. Even Eichman was rebuilding across the street. Korte and Lyon agreed that no stone should be laid until there were merchants to occupy the space, but when that might be they couldn't say. Stewart knew, from his trips to Richmond and Kalamazoo, that he was going to have to hire a marketing/real estate pro who could put together the kind of package they wanted. Maybe then, something would happen.

Meanwhile he waited. "When I see all the rhetoric combine into something concrete, that's when I'll feel we've accomplished something." But the waiting wasn't easy. When Stewart traveled to other cities, to Washington, Chicago, and San Francisco, to address interested groups on Xenia's handling of its disaster, he was invariably told that he had done more than could have been expected. He was told that the direction he was heading in was just exactly right. "And that's gratifying," he confessed. "What hurts a little, and what I don't quite understand, is that our own people don't seem to feel the same way."

Why not? Had something gone wrong? Could Xenia have come back together more satisfactorily? The answers, of course, were not available and may never be. The city had rebounded in so many ways that one could only admire its vitality. When nearly every other part of the country was in a building slump, Xenia was a boom town. When federal programs were being slashed left and right, Xenia was deciding how to spend what Jack Jordan calculated to be 38 million federal dollars poured into the municipal pocket. When other cities spent a decade or more trying to get a downtown plaza, Xenia was well on its way to one in eight months. So why the malaise?

It was an intangible thing. Partly it was the memory of April 3, and the shock and fear of facing death without warning. Partly too it was the emotional aftermath, the horror of emerging from shelter to see the city gone and to hear the cries of neighbors against a background of sirens. The agony of those first days, and the strain of relocating were like combat experiences, remembered because they could not be forgotten. "Where were you when it hit? Will you ever forget . . . ?" was still cocktail conversation in December. Whenever a door slammed, or the wind blew fiercely, or an ambulance passed, they were reminded. And they anticipated the spring—tornado season—with dread. They tried to steel themselves, and rationalize about the odds, but very few were sure how they would hold up.

The malaise went deeper still. Every day the tornado was with them. It was in Central Junior High, sitting silent and battered, awaiting the decision to tear down or repair. It was in the sickly excuses for trees that still clung to the soil, and the naked expanses of land that stared at the sky. King Street was gone forever; they knew that now. The West End might or might not survive: a few new houses floated in a sea of "FOR SALE" signs. The high school was a cement slab, the "snake pit" a ghost where memories of victory chants echoed from the girders.

"The Plan was a fiction," one man said. "And the mall—if they didn't talk about the mall, what would they talk about?" His voice was plaintive, like the loudspeakers on the Courthouse tower, blaring Christmas music across the vacant land.